Clyde Singer's America

Clyde Singer's America

M. J. Albacete

with an essay by Nannette V. Maciejunes and Christopher S. Duckworth

Published in cooperation with the Canton Museum of Art

The Kent State University Press Kent, Ohio

Published in cooperation with the Canton Museum of Art

Library of Congress Catalog Card Number 2008001488

ISBN 978-0-87338-921-1

Manufactured in China

Designed by Christine Brooks and set in 11/15 Adobe Garamond Pro. Printed on 157 gsm Japanese enamel stock by Everbest Printing Co. Ltd. of Hong Kong.

LIBRARY OF CONGRESS CATALOGING-IN-PUBLICATION DATA

Albacete, M. J.

Clyde Singer's America / M. J. Albacete ; with an essay by Nannette V. Maciejunes and Christopher S. Duckworth

p. cm.

Includes index.

ISBN 978-0-87338-921-1 (hardcover : alk. paper) ∞

1. Singer, Clyde, 1908—Criticism and interpretation. 2. Singer, Clyde, 1908—Catalogues raisonnés. 3. Social realism—United States. I Maciejunes, Nannette V. (Nannette Vicars) II. Duckworth, Christopher S. III. Title.

ND237.S558A43 2008

759.13—dc22 2008001488

British Library Cataloging-in-Publication data are available.

12 11 10 09 08 5 4 3 2 1

To Marilyn Kauff Sheridan and Mike and Nancy Siddall,
whose support and encouragement made this book possible

The Canton Museum of Art, The Butler Institute of American Art, and The Kent State University Press gratefully acknowledge the following individuals, organizations, and foundations for their generous support of *Clyde Singer's America,* with exhibitions at Canton Museum of Art and The Butler Institute of American Art, September 7, 2008–January 7, 2009, and a book by M. J. Albacete, with an essay by Nanette V. Maciejunes and Christopher S. Duckworth.

Major Sponsors:
- Marilyn Kauff Sheridan
- Mike and Nancy Siddall
- The Hoover Foundation
- The Stark Community Foundation
- The Butler Trustees Circle Members
- The Ohio Arts Council
- Thomas W. Darling
- The William L. Luntz Family Philanthropic Fund
- Evan and Suzanne Morris

Media Sponsors:
- *The Vindicator* (Youngstown, Ohio)
- *The Repository* (Canton, Ohio)

Platinum Sponsors:
- Arts in Stark
- Mr. and Mrs. Theodore Boyd
- Bob and Lesa Schnabel
- Lazar and Mary Ann Tarzan
- Bill and Sue Wise

Gold Sponsors:
- The Belden Brick Charitable Trust
- Mr. and Mrs. Fred Olivieri

Silver Sponsors:
- Jeanne and Ronald Cullen
- Wanda Miller
- Marty and Susan O'Brien

Contents

Foreword

People always ask me to name my favorite Clyde Singer painting, and my reply is always the same: I do not have a favorite Clyde Singer; I have two, and both are untitled works. Actually, the two works have been on continuous display since the early 1960s and are missed by virtually every visitor to The Butler Institute of American Art. If you examine the marble baseboard in the north and south permanent collection galleries, you will discover that the marble is adhered to the base of two closed doors that are covered with wall material so as not to interrupt the exhibition design. Look closely at the marble on those doors and you'll discover that what you are actually looking at are original Clyde Singers. Years back, in an attempt to save the museum money, Clyde created faux marble sections that look exactly like the actual marble base. These are trompe l'oeil works that surely rival the Butler's William Harnett painting.

I tell you that these are my favorite works by Clyde since they reveal so much about Singer, the man. Never the elitist, Clyde lived his life not as the most famous artist in Ohio but as a "working stiff" (to use a favorite phrase of his) who did his job and did it well. As assistant director of The Butler Institute of American Art, Clyde was not above taking out the museum trash, sweeping the floor, salting the walks, and even painting a sign or creating the illusion of marble on gallery doors. While he took the greatest pride in his painting, I don't believe he felt his art would ever be valuable. He didn't paint for money or fame. In fact, his lack of any kind of ego was displayed annually at the Butler staff Christmas party where the gift exchange required that no one exceed a gift value of two dollars. Every year Clyde's gift would be one of his paintings with a large tag attached to it that read "$1.98." Naturally we all hoped that Clyde had pulled our name from Santa's hat.

Clyde cherished Mondays, when the Butler was closed, as his day to paint. What he produced in his studio basement were among the greatest works of art ever done by an Ohio artist. But never would he brag about his accomplishments or attempt to promote his own works. He did, however, feel a need to place his Monday's output in frames that he bought from a five-and-ten store, yard sale, or furniture store markdown. Even if he believed that what he had created was a masterpiece, you would never hear it from him, and it was guaranteed to be framed in a genuine Salvation Army special. In fact, we at the Butler still use the term "a Clyde frame" to describe cheap framing. But we also recognize that Clyde Singer's work was elegant regardless of the frame.

I miss talking baseball with Clyde, whose wife, Bernice, converted him to a Cincinnati Reds fan. He would listen to every Reds game no matter how poor the radio reception was. He and Bernice had also been avid fans of the minor league Youngstown Gremlins, who played back in the 1940s at the old Idora Park field. Clyde told me that on some September nights it was only he and his wife in the stands rooting the team on. He recalled how the dew would settle on the stands except, of course, where he and Bernice had been sitting. He loved baseball and would often say, "I don't know if I'm catching or pitching," as a way of describing a particularly hectic day. On such occasions he might also exclaim, "details, too many details," or "oh gollies."

Clyde Singer was always a gentleman, and never do I remember him being angry or unkind. He spoke to everyone and tried always to be encouraging. People would often come to the museum with a family "treasure" for Clyde to assess. On those occasions when Clyde could find nothing positive to say about the object, he would simply respond with, "There's nothing wrong with that . . . nothing at all." To this day I wonder what he thought about much of what he was asked to evaluate. He and I juried a number of exhibitions together. I remember him sitting in the dark looking at slide entries and never making a negative comment about the works that he chose not to include. He simply said nothing and awaited the next slide. He was respectful of fellow artists no matter the level of skill or knowledge. This, to me, was class.

When I first began my work at The Butler Institute of American Art, I shared a tiny office with Clyde and the museum's director, Joseph Butler III. The intimacy of that work environment was a wonderful educational opportunity for me, as I witnessed the interaction between these two men whose lives were devoted to the art of this country. It was then that I came to realize the remarkable depth of Clyde Singer's knowledge of art and artists. Long before there were computer databases, there was Clyde Singer's memory. He could share information about the kind of canvas used by some obscure nineteenth-century painter or recall how the most insignificant drawing entered the collection in 1931.

When I became director of the Butler in 1981, Clyde and I walked downtown and had lunch at his favorite lunch counter in the old Strauss department store. He had the very same lunch virtually every day: a bowl of soup and a piece of pie with coffee. I teased him that his nutritional choices were probably the secret to his brilliance and artistic abilities. But it was on one such occasion that he said something to me that jolted me and made me feel so badly. "Lou," he said, "just tell me if you'd like me to resign. I mean this!" My teary response was, "Clyde, you'll never hear those words coming from my lips." I believe he was concerned that I would move the museum away from its traditional mission and would prefer perhaps a younger curator. He soon learned that I valued his abilities as much as Butler had, and never did he hear those words from me.

A few months before his death, Clyde paid me the ultimate compliment: "In all the years we've worked together, you've never disappointed me." Those words sustain me to this very day, and I wish that I could tell him, over a bowl of soup and a piece of apple pie, how much they have meant to me.

Lou Zona

Preface and Acknowledgments

Several years after Clyde Singer's death in 1999, Joseph R. Hertzi, former executive director of the Canton Museum of Art (CMA), suggested that the museum might honor this beloved Ohio artist by presenting a comprehensive exhibition of his work. We were well aware of Singer's popularity within our community, since we had drawn on regional collections on at least three occasions for modest exhibitions over the last few decades. Surely it would require no major effort to bring together a representative selection of Singer's work in a relatively short time and within a nominal budget. As the idea germinated over the next few months, we decided to go exploring farther afield, perhaps throughout Ohio and even into the contiguous states. After all, Singer boasted of having produced well over three thousand paintings across a span of more than sixty-five years; we knew perhaps of only 10 percent of his paintings.

We began the search by inquiring with known collectors and regional museums and by disseminating press releases to the media. Almost magically, the word spread in an ever-widening circle across the nation. Within a short time, CMA staff members were overwhelmed by the response, not only from many collectors within Ohio but also from far beyond: Kentucky, Oklahoma, Florida, Pennsylvania, and California. It soon became apparent that the galleries of the Canton Museum of Art, large as they were, could not contain all the items that we felt were essential to our survey. Early on we obtained the enthusiastic cooperation of Louis Zona, director of The Butler Institute of American Art in Youngstown, Ohio, and the staff at the Butler, where Singer had worked most of his adult life. The museum owned a number of his finest paintings and was willing to loan them all to us. Now we approached the Butler staff with a different request: would they enter into a unique collaboration with the CMA in order to present a simultaneous two-museum exhibition? Once again the response was positive, and together we set to work. Appropriately, the working title of our project was "Clyde Singer's America," a title that has endured to the project's completion.

When we decided to publish a book—something more than just an exhibition catalog—I was able to fall back on a short biographical article I had written for a Singer exhibition at the CMA in 1988. This article was based on several interviews I had recorded with Singer during visits to the artist's studio in the basement of his home in Boardman, Ohio. However, the CMA staff felt that a more extensive biography would be in order, requiring additional research. Fortunately, the tapes had been preserved, so I reviewed them for further details. I also referred to several articles and publications, which are listed in the bibliography. The editorial decision was made not to clutter the article with footnotes, as there were only a few original sources. I also had the good fortune of encountering a number of individuals who knew Singer personally and who shared their memories and recollections of him with me. Some of their stories have found their way into my essay, adding touches of warmth, color, and humor.

With the new biographical article in hand, I felt that we still needed an informative artistic analysis of Singer's work, which would describe his techniques and style and place him in the context of the American Scene painters. For this purpose, we turned to a respected authority on twentieth-century American art, Nannette Maciejunes, executive director of the Columbus Museum of Art, Columbus, Ohio. Most ably assisting her in this task was Christopher S. Duckworth, executive editor at the Columbus Museum and former editor of *Timeline,* the magazine of the Ohio Historical Society. Melissa Wolfe, associate curator of American Art at the Columbus Museum, proved enormously helpful by sharing many personal recollections of working with Singer during her tenure at the Butler. Michael D. Hall, an independent scholar who has written extensively on the American Scene, was also an excellent research resource for the two authors. Their informative and scholarly essay along with the biography provide the most definitive commentary on Singer's life and work to date.

Such an undertaking—a two-part exhibition and an illustrated book—would not have been possible without the assistance of many individuals and institutions, beginning with the board of trustees and staff of the Canton Museum of Art. "Clyde Singer's America," launched during the presidency of Nancy Stewart Matin, has come to fruition under the term of Paula Mastroianni. To both presidents we extend our sincere gratitude for their support.

The prime mover behind "Clyde Singer's America" was Lynnda Arrasmith, the CMA's curator, with the aid of Kathy Fleeher, curatorial assistant. In addition to the awesome task of searching out the many Singer paintings across the nation, Lynnda cataloged the collection, obtained file photos of each piece, prepared loan agreements, designed the budget, supervised the collaboration with the Butler, readied all materials for publication, and, ultimately, installed the Canton portion of the exhibition. Kathy provided additional help in all these areas and also collated excerpts from Singer's letters and prepared a chronology.

Marketing manager Robb Hyde was responsible for an expanded program of marketing and publicity, and our education coordinator, Lauren Kuntzman, implemented various educational programs. Business manager Kay McAllister kept us apprised of budgetary concerns and offered many practical suggestions regarding fund-raising and cost-cutting. Administrative secretary Lynn Daverio participated in every important meeting, taking detailed and copious notes of each step along the way. Other staff members who merit recognition include our two invaluable maintenance workers, George Samay and Rick Richardson, who perform multiple functions.

Dr. Lou Zona, executive director of The Butler Institute of American Art, supported our project from the beginning, even though its structure and size seemed to change week to week. Each time I called or sent him an e-mail, something new had been added to the concept, several important paintings had been "rediscovered," and of course the budget had been adjusted upward. We had agreed on a fifty-fifty split of total expenses, so each contact usually meant an increase in dollars. But Dr. Zona remained calm and even tempered, quietly agreeing to everything. Our visits to the Butler were always a delight, and I found his staff to be cooperative, personable, and happy to answer questions. Staff members also were enormously helpful with their memories and anecdotes about Clyde. In particular I am grateful to Jean Shreffler, librarian and archivist; Ken Platt, manager of the Butler's Beecher Center; Pat McCormick, curator; Rebecca Davis, registrar; Ray George, custodian; Ray Johnson, preparator; and artist James Pernotto, former curator of prints.

We regularly networked with the Malvern (Ohio) Historical Society and are grateful to its president, Linda Byrd, for responding to numerous inquiries that only she could answer, being based in Singer's hometown. Sonia Stock and Frances Montella assisted her. Linda, I might add, visited the home of Clyde Singer's sister, Clara Reed, to obtain information for us. As far as we can tell, Clara alone survives of the six Singer children.

We are profoundly indebted to all the individuals who lent us their Singer paintings and other memorabilia for the two-part exhibition. When we made a plea for financial support to offset the escalating expenses of our project, we were deeply touched by the generosity of many of these same people. Michael Lawlor and Kathleen Wieschaus helped us locate a number of important Singer paintings, as did gallery owner Lazar Tarzan. Close to the publishing deadline, Joseph Milan Vutuk brought to our attention several items of Singer's military gear, a wartime sketch pad, and a collection of letters.

One individual deserves special recognition. Marilyn Kauff Sheridan, who served as the executrix of Clyde's estate, was closest to Clyde and Beatrice Singer in their autumnal years. On first hearing of our plans, Mrs. Sheridan committed herself unconditionally to the "Clyde Singer's America" project, determined to see both the book and the exhibition through to completion. A former trustee at the Butler for many years and a chairperson of the Woman's League fund-raising affiliate, Marilyn volunteered at once to meet the subvention costs of the publication either through her own means or through contacts known to her. She shares this honor with Mike and Nancy Siddall, who responded enthusiastically to her appeal. Through all the difficult days of laboring over contracts, budgets, negotiations, and manuscript writing and revisions, Marilyn was a constant source of inspiration, a prime motivational force. Her e-mails recorded a wide range of emotions, from exhilaration to frustration corresponding with the ups and downs of the work in progress.

Early in our fund-raising campaign, William L. Luntz volunteered to sponsor a luncheon for a number of community leaders—some of whom owned Singer paintings—thus providing me with an opportunity to acquaint them with the Singer project. In this way, several generous individual contributions and foundation grants came forward, primed by Mr. Luntz's own commitment.

We are ever indebted to our regional foundations and arts organizations for supporting so many Canton Museum of Art projects over the years. Once again, the following groups were generous in the present instance: the Hoover Foundation, the Stark Community Foundation, Arts in Stark, and the Ohio Arts Council. Canton Fine Arts Associates and the Museum Guild of the Canton Museum of Art continue to support all museum projects as they have done for many years now. The two collaborating museums in both cities received the endorsement of their local newspapers, *The Vindicator* (Youngstown) and *The Repository* (Canton).

We are particularly proud of our association with The Kent State University Press and its director, Will Underwood, who felt our effort was worthy of publication under its esteemed logo. Having collaborated successfully with Will and the Press on a previous book/exhibition project, we were honored when they accepted our manuscript for publication. Will's calm temperament and infinite patience were an inspiration, and his advice was always on the mark.

Throughout the lengthy process of creating our book and assembling our exhibition, many people, too numerous to mention, came forward to provide services in modest but important ways, and to them we extend a sincere expression of appreciation.

M. J. Albacete
Executive Director
The Canton Museum of Art
August 2007

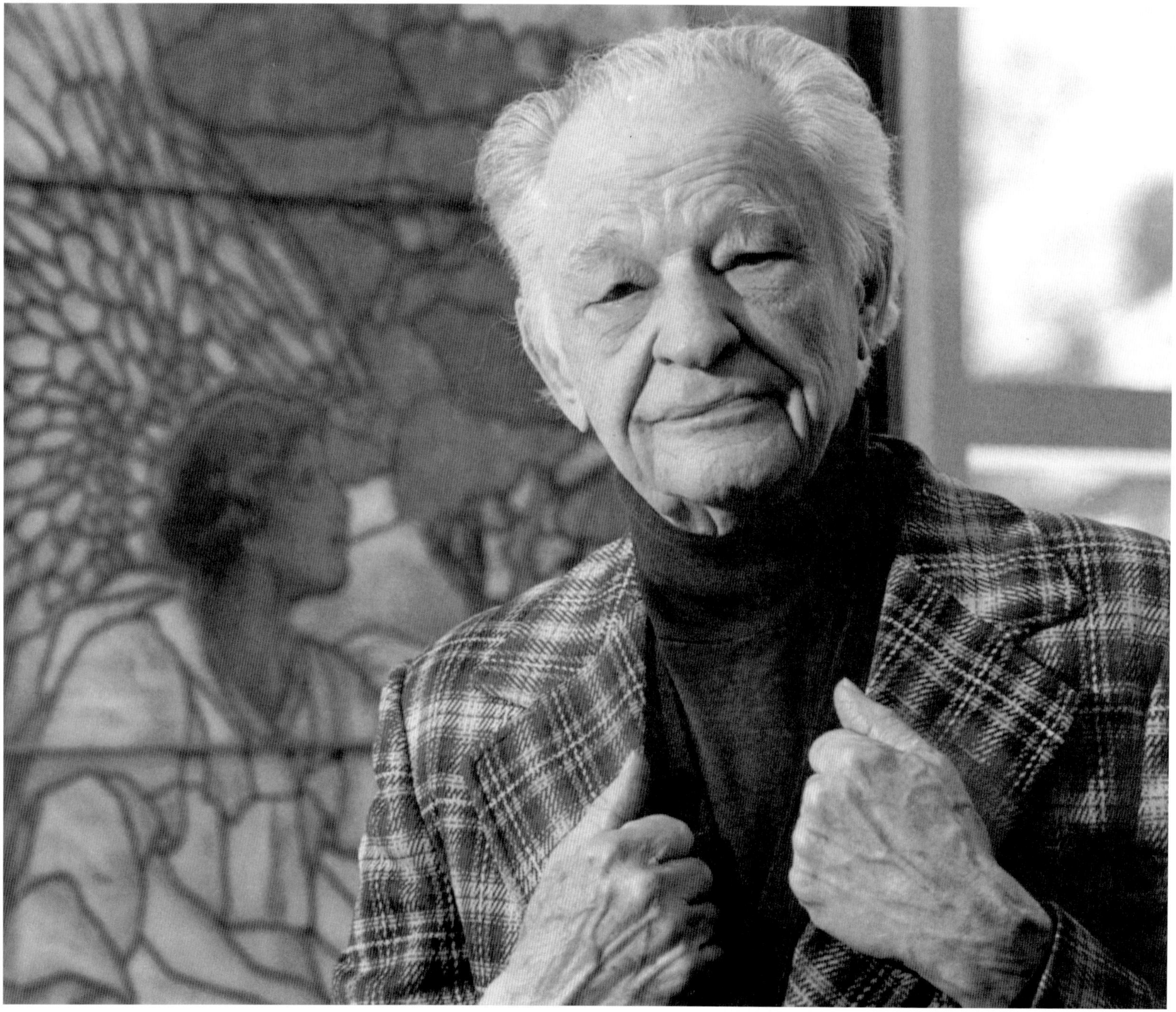

Clyde Singer: Painter of the American Scene

M. J. ALBACETE

Back in the early years of the Depression, daily life for the citizens in the small midwestern community of Malvern, Ohio, followed a rather mundane and predictable work routine—for those few fortunate enough to have jobs. The news on the street most often revolved around world issues the folks heard on the radio, much of it dismal and ominous, tempered with abundant political promises for a rosy future. Local events as reported in the *Malvern News* focused on births, deaths, marriages, mounting farm prices, escalating unemployment, and countless other tidbits of gossip and general interest.

Perhaps it was a Malvern businessman who had ventured into Canton or Akron one April day in 1933, bought a copy of the *New York Herald-Tribune,* and, while rifling through its pages, came across a story about "Exhibits in the Art Students League Contest." This in itself would not have meant much to the reader, but what would have caught his eye were the two photographs that accompanied the article, both pictures of paintings he probably recognized at once: *Medicine Man* and *Adolescence.* The first was inspired by a tent show that had taken place in the nearby town of Minerva and that many of the locals had attended; the second was a portrait of Clara Singer, one of the six children of Malvern's Singer family. Both of the paintings—along with many others—had been admired in Malvern not long before they were sent to New York City. They were the creations of a local boy named Clyde Singer, well known to everybody in town as the kid who was obsessed with painting and drawing. Here at last was living proof that the young man was making good on his promise to become a famous artist.

Imagine the pride of the folks in Malvern when they saw Clyde's paintings reproduced in this big New York City newspaper and their amazement when they read that the prestigious Art Students League had awarded only ten scholarships out of almost a thousand candidates from all over the country. One of them was their own hometown boy, Clyde Singer, who had won the scholarship based on "creative talent" and "artistic ability." In the lengthy article, the highly respected American artist Reginald Marsh, vice president of the League, drew specific attention to the young artist from Malvern, Ohio. According to the newspaper, Marsh said, "The judges had been particularly impressed with the portraits and scenes of Clyde Singer. . . . The twenty-four-year-old Ohio boy had shown remarkable color sense and feeling of form, especially in his *Medicine Man.*" The *Canton Repository* picked up the story by wire the same day, adding a photo of the ruggedly handsome, bright-eyed artist with his crop of dense, curly hair.

Although he attended several art schools and was exposed to numerous artistic influences, Clyde established his painting style in his early hometown days, and it never changed dramatically across the span of almost nine

Facing page: Clyde Singer, 1993. Bob DeMay, *Youngstown Vindicator.*

decades of activity. His masters were few, including such respected notables as John Sloan and George Bellows, and he considered himself a direct descendant, perhaps the last, of a select body of American artists collectively referred to as the Ashcan School. Despite childhood ambitions, he never seriously aspired to become a famous artist later in life, nor did he ever consider himself one, even when his name appeared regularly in the *New York Times, New York Herald-Tribune,* and *American Artist* magazine.

No matter how busy he became with various responsibilities in later years, most important to Singer was his free time, the precious time he dedicated to his painting and which he regarded as sacred. When our paths crossed for the first time in the late 1970s, Clyde and his wife, Bernice, were already settled into their small home in Boardman, Ohio. For Clyde, this was as close as he could come to heaven on earth. Once a day, every day if possible, he would descend the stairs to his crowded basement studio where he would paint, sometimes for two or three hours or more at a time. And when he was away from his studio, he longed to get back; he dreamed of painting all day long. Humble by nature, Singer viewed himself simply as a man who loved more than anything to paint and draw, and if some people liked his work and cared to buy it, that was fine with him. That he sold so many pictures was an incredible feat, considering he never had a professional agent in any of the big cities and was never represented by a major gallery. There is some evidence that for a short time a dealer in Youngstown handled his work, and he had a relationship of almost twenty-five years with a gallery in Canton. But that was all. When he died in 1999 at the age of ninety-one, he left behind an enormous legacy of almost four thousand paintings and drawings, many of which are in both private and corporate collections and in museums all over the United States.

Clyde's long association with the Canton Museum of Art dated back to its beginning in 1935, when it was known as The Little Civic Art Gallery, a one-room operation on the second floor of the old Canton Public Library. In fact, the first exhibition ever presented at the gallery was a showing of Clyde's work. He must have been acquainted with every director in the museum's history, because over the passing decades he was honored with solo shows at eight- or ten-year intervals, and there are a number of his paintings in the museum's permanent collection. I came to know Clyde Singer professionally when I worked on collaborations with The Butler Institute of American Art and when Clyde attended his exhibition receptions in Canton.

It was in anticipation of one such exhibition that I decided to conduct my own interview with the artist, and we arranged a time to meet and talk on location in his basement studio in Boardman, Ohio. What a striking individual he was. Quiet, modest, and soft-spoken with a peaceful demeanor, Clyde sported a thick mane of hair. When I met him, there were still traces of the original red streaked through the white, wavy locks, with the characteristic part just right of center. At the time of our first meeting he was already well into his seventies, but he carried his years with an easy, relaxed grace and talked about contemporary art with enthusiasm and gentle authority. He thoughtfully chose his words and responded concisely, and yet he never tried to dominate the conversation.

When I questioned Clyde about the "good old days" of American art, his soft dark eyes glowed with introspection and a smile of fond recollection played across his face. Then the old memories and anecdotes crowded one upon the other in an enthralling stream-of-consciousness soliloquy, addressed more to himself than to me. As he spoke, he illustrated his stories with photographs and an assortment of memorabilia, some from his earliest days as a young, hopeful artist in Malvern.

Clyde Jacob Singer was born in Malvern, Ohio, on October 20, 1908, taking his first and middle names from his maternal and paternal grandfathers, respectively. Today, if you walk down the streets and alleys of Singer's hometown, it is easy to feel the presence of the late artist, as little has changed in this tiny community since he was born. Malvern was once surrounded by five prosperous brickyards, their kilns spewing smoke around the clock

Facing page: Singer's work on display in The Little Civic Art Gallery, 1934. Seated is gallery director Gordon Pryce. Canton Museum of Art

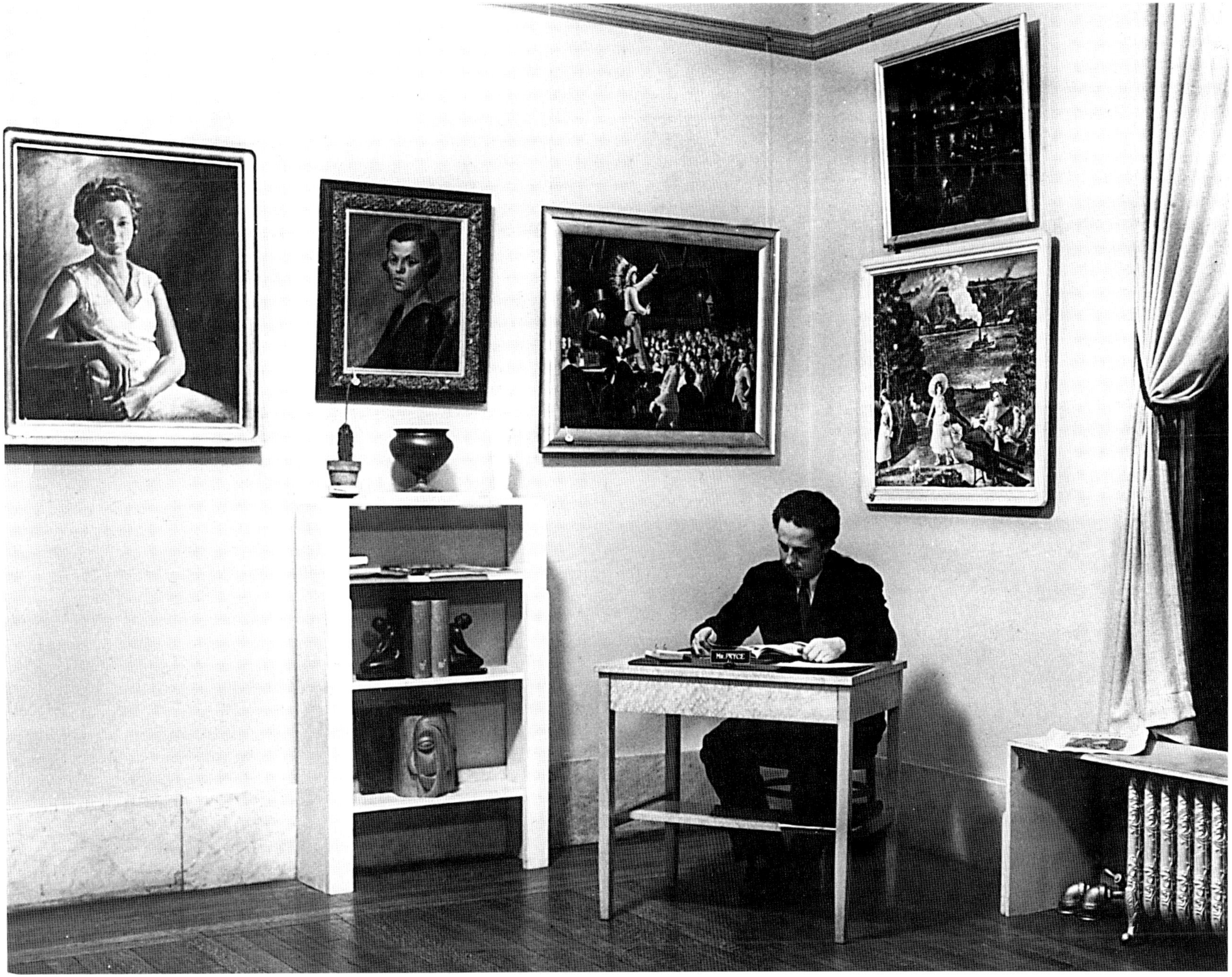

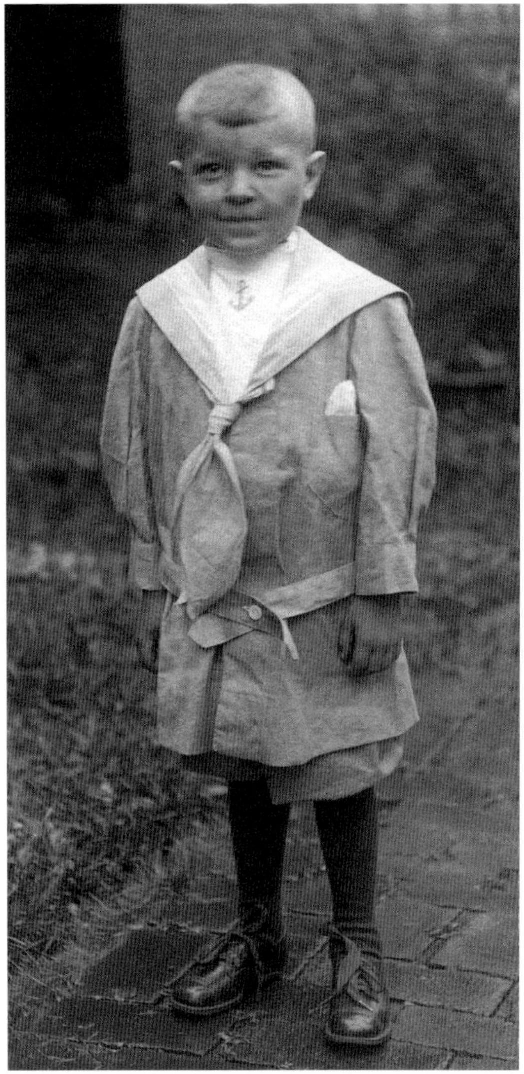

Clyde Singer, age six. Malvern Historical Society

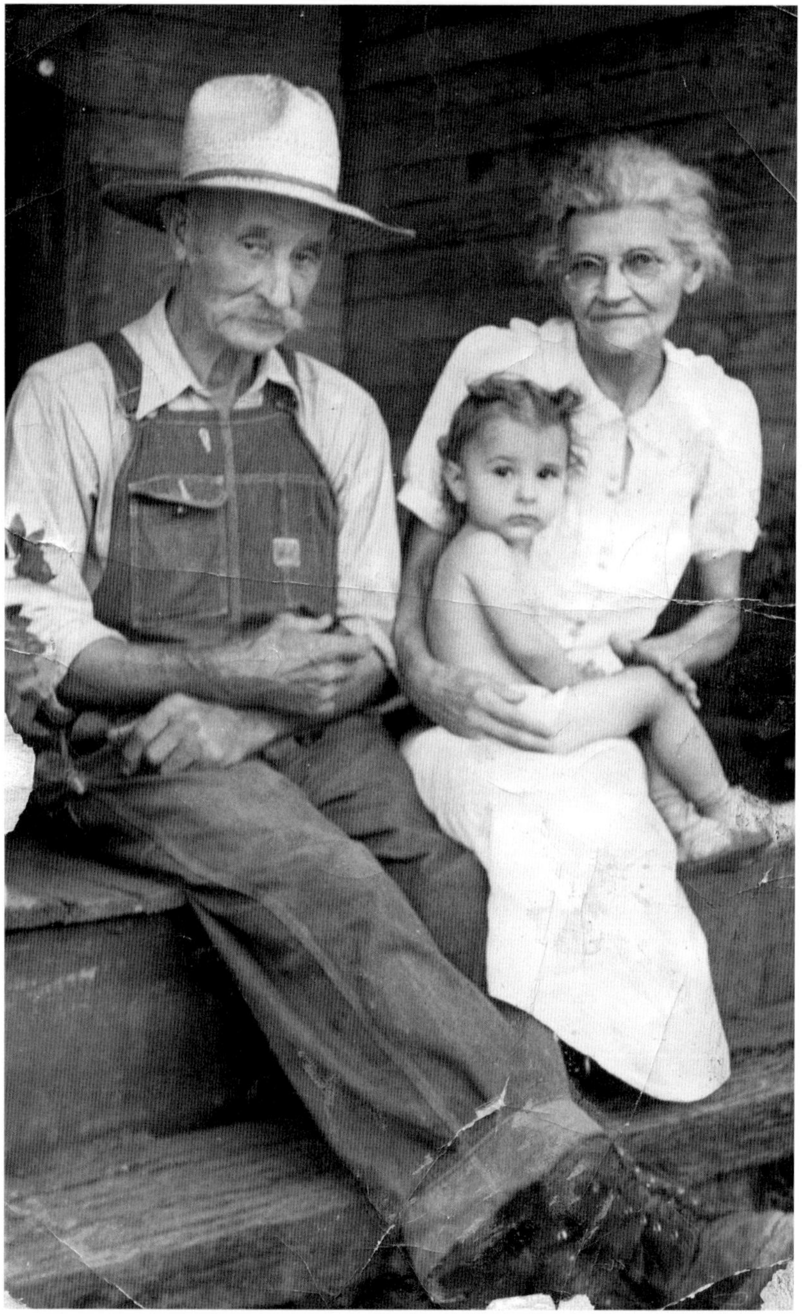

Far right: Andrew and Margaret Singer, ca. 1940, here with granddaughter Marcella. Singer Family Collection

as hundreds of employees labored to meet orders from all over the country. Only one small clay company survives today, and most residents now work out of town. The astute observer may recognize some scenes much as Clyde had painted them, while others hide underneath a thin veneer of modernization. An unpaved roadway curves up a steep hill on the edge of town that leads to the original homestead, and one would think from its size and hilltop placement that his parents, Andrew and Margaret Sorg Singer, were well-to-do. But in those days the large brick house was divided into two apartments, one of which was rented out to the Singers. Andrew worked in the Big Four coal mine nearby, adding to his meager income by tending a little farm on the side.

Not long after their marriage in 1900, the Singers took up residence in Malvern, and over the next few years their family grew to four sons: Harry, Paul, Walter, and, last of all, Clyde. Harry went on to become a farmer; Paul took up a career as an electrician; and Walter left home as soon as he could and was never heard from again. A pair of girls, Clara and Mary, came along in the next few years. Clara remained close to Clyde to the end of his life; like Walter, Mary eventually severed her relations with the family. Of course, just about everybody in and around Malvern knew the Singer family. They were poor as church mice, poorer than just about everybody in town, and unpleasant memories of those early years haunted Singer all his life. He could not easily be induced to talk about his youth, and when he did, it was in the most general terms. And yet the early lessons he learned in the struggle for survival would prove beneficial to him later in life as he pursued his artistic ambitions beyond the confines of Malvern.

As far back as he could remember, Singer was fascinated with pictures. He copied them from the "funny papers," as he called them, and loved illustrated books too. In later years he recalled destroying a whole set of Horatio Alger books "because they had no pictures in them." When at age five he received a box of crayons as a gift, he readily took to drawing with a flourish. His parents were amused with his talent and reacted favorably, though not enthusiastically, when he expressed a desire to become an artist. To his knowledge, he was the first artist of any sort in the family. A mature boy for his years, Clyde boasted that he could "draw anything from cows to Tarzan, but preferred to draw women." Certain tastes, it appears, were fixed in his mind at a very young age.

Once Clyde was enrolled in Malvern School, the family moved to a house in town on Water Street, and that became his home for many years.

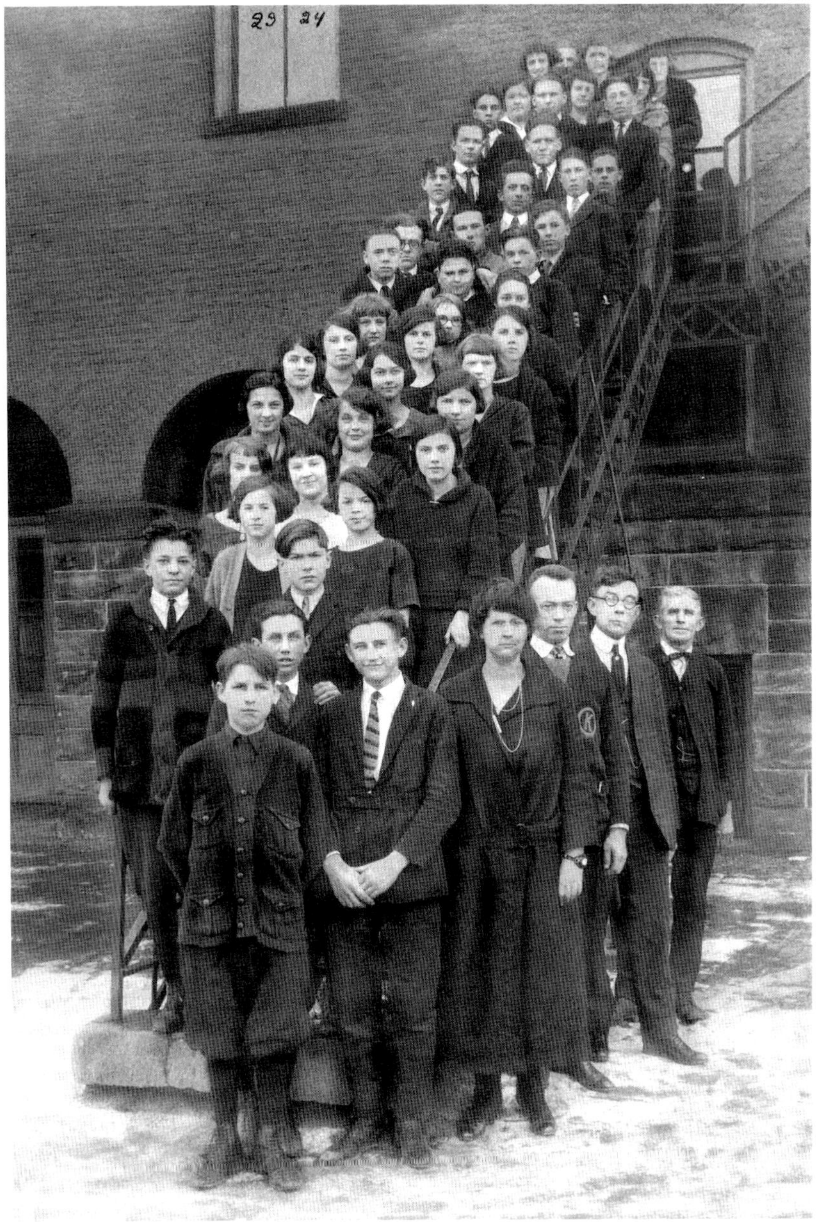

Malvern School, ca. 1924–25. Clyde is on the first step at left. Malvern Historical Society

Although the house has long since been demolished, surviving paintings from this early period represent views from his bedroom window. Clyde's classmates referred to him disparagingly as "Rags" because of the tattered clothes he wore. Still, he seems to have been a popular student who amused his friends and irritated his teachers by drawing incessantly on tablets, in textbooks, on pieces of cardboard, on sheets of wallpaper, and even on sidewalks.

Inspiration for his art came in a curious assortment of experiences. "When I was about ten I'd go to serial movies and come home and draw what I thought would be the ending of the thriller," he said. With the occasional coin or two that came his way, he'd attend Vaudeville performances, where he apparently fine-tuned his life-long penchant for drawing "passionate women." Clyde's first serious work was a painting of a tree on a piece of panel nailed to an outhouse wall. Occasionally, he earned a little pocket money by painting posters and signs for businessmen and farmers in the community.

In 1928, a year after graduating from Malvern School, Singer was hired as an apprentice at the Canton Sign Company doing an assortment of odd jobs and serving as "fill-in guy"; the older, more experienced painters would outline words and letters, and Singer would fill in the colors. During the cold winter months, when jobs were few, he would accompany the men in the unpleasant task of washing neon signs. His employers discovered his natural talent to draw and assigned him the task of painting a twelve-foot Santa for a Christmas display outside the Stark County Courthouse. This was his first big success, and he now boasted a take-home pay of nineteen dollars a week. The old Alhambra Theater on North Market Avenue in Canton commissioned Clyde to prepare a lobby advertisement in the form of a cut-out, life-size figure of a woman, a promotion for a 1929 Warner Brothers Vitaphone film called *The Sacred Flame.* Singer's voluptuous interpretation (representing the film's sexy star Lila Lee) left little to the imagination. When he returned later to admire his work in the theater lobby, he discovered to his profound disappointment that the management had censored his work by placing a Coming Attraction sign over the sensually delineated breasts.

Despite the hard times that had fallen on the country after the Crash of 1929, Singer managed to keep his job until 1931, saving as much of his pay as possible. And his savings came in handy. While working at the Canton Sign Company, Singer was assigned the simple task of painting a few lines of text on a sign. Unable to suppress his artistic instinct, he added decorative flourishes of holly leaves. When his boss, Homer Unkefer, saw what he had done, he told Clyde that he would never work out as a sign painter and showed him the door. In later years, Clyde often said that his entire career in art began with that dismissal.

With the tidy sum of $300, Singer left the Canton Sign Company and signed up for classes at the Columbus Art School (now the Columbus College of Art and Design), mainly because he had an uncle in Columbus who could put him up at no cost. Eager to learn about art, he enrolled for both day and evening classes in the spring of 1931. His determination was rewarded with a scholarship for a second year. At the end of the 1932 school year, despite the offer of yet another scholarship, Singer felt that the Columbus Art School had given him all that he needed to explore larger ambitions.

Returning home to Malvern, he painted extensively and produced several hundred drawings, watercolors, and canvases. Elizabeth McClelland records (*Timeline,* Nov.–Dec. 1996) that among these was a Malvern scene painted in December 1932 called *Christmas Rainbow* (Fig. 14), which was exhibited a few years later at The Little Civic Art Gallery in Canton (first home of the Canton Museum of Art). Albert Hise was the longtime curator and director of the Massillon Museum. According to McClelland, Hise "saw the painting and bought it for five dollars. Over the years, Hise purchased nearly fifty works by Singer and also acted for a time as an agent for the young artist's work." Hise never took a commission on any sale. Singer boxed up *Christmas Rainbow,* along with others, filled out the appropriate application forms, and shipped it all off to the Art Students League in New York, with little hope of acceptance. Interestingly, the two paintings that appealed most to the League judges, *Medicine Man* (Fig. 15) and *Adolescence,* were painted on common burlap that Singer found in the barn, since he didn't have sufficient funds to purchase canvas.

The Art Students League scholarship award, announced in the April 17, 1933, edition of the *New York Herald-Tribune,* changed everything for Clyde Singer. It meant, among other things, that Clyde would receive free tuition for a year at the school. But more significantly, it meant that Clyde could live on his own in the art capital of the nation: New York City.

With his scholarship in hand and his life savings of a few hundred dollars in his pocket, Singer departed by bus for New York in October 1933. For only $2.50 a week, he took up residence in a dismal, windowless room at 241 East 35th Street by the East River close to the Second Avenue L-train and within earshot of the nocturnal boat whistles. But he didn't mind. In fact, some of his best watercolors were done here, sitting on the edge of the bed working under a bare filament lightbulb. Thanks to some invaluable advice from new friends and his tendency to economize, Singer became street smart, quickly learning where to find such bargains as day-old bread and overripe fruits and vegetables. Clyde's first great adventure in New York involved rushing to Rockefeller Center in hopes of observing Mexican artist Diego Rivera at work on his controversial mural, *Man, Controller of the Universe,* only to discover that it had already been covered up and scheduled for demolition.

Within a few months Clyde had become a seasoned New Yorker, and like his fellow students, he used the city and its residents as topical matter for his art. This is evident in a 1933 *New York Times* photo showing the scholarship winners gathered on the seventieth-story observation deck of the RCA Building. The caption describes them as observing the work of League instructor Bernard H. Bernstein, when in actuality their eyes stare out into the vast expanse of space between them and the city below. Bernstein sits precariously on the balustrade, feet dangling over the side, sketchpad spread on his lap. One can only speculate on where the *Times* photographer was standing in order to take this picture. But one's eyes are immediately drawn to Clyde Singer, who, easily identified by his head of curly hair, stands silent and austere toward the back of the group. The image suggests much about the artist he was to become, a vigilant but altogether invisible observer of the American Scene who would capture candid vignettes of people going about their daily routines unaware of his presence.

The depictions of city life and country landscape comprise another splendid body of work, from the crowded streets of his beloved New York to the small-town quaintness of Youngstown and Canton and the pastoral settings around his hometown of Malvern. However popular he was to become, Singer remained throughout his life a humble, shy, and withdrawn individual, gently self-deprecating when lavished with praise, which he accepted with a gentle smile.

For the better part of two hard but happy years, Singer studied at the League, signing up for as many different teachers as possible in order to learn about different techniques and methods. Among his teachers were such notable American artists as Thomas Hart Benton, Kenneth Hayes Miller, Alexander Brook, George Bridgman, Ivan Olinsky, and John Steuart Curry. It was a Curry painting that may have had the greatest initial impact on the young artist. Walking along 57th Street one day, Singer saw a huge painting by Curry in the window of the Ferargil Gallery. *Tornado in Kansas* had just been returned from the Carnegie International exhibition in Pittsburgh, where it had taken second prize. Thrilled over Curry's dramatic interpretation of the stormy scene, Singer determined to study under this artist. Teacher and student took to each other at once, and Curry so admired Singer's work that he frequently chose one of his paintings as "best of the week" over all his classmates, much to Singer's embarrassment. To the end of his life, Singer kept a reproduction of *Tornado in Kansas* in his studio, claiming that its effect on him never diminished over the years.

Of all his teachers it was Kenneth Hayes Miller who not only made the greatest impression on Singer but also proved to be his severest critic. Methodical and precise, Miller believed that every square inch of a picture should be planned. When Miller chose to display one of Singer's works as "best of the week," Singer was profoundly moved. He described Miller as "such a sophisticated person," someone who talked about things not found in books.

A favorite pastime of Singer's was to walk up one side of 57th Street and down the other, taking in all the exhibitions and visiting every gallery. In this way he saw hundreds of paintings and drawings and kept himself fully abreast of the arts in New York. Grant Wood, Benton, and Curry were the chief exponents of the popular American Scene movement. But other movements were afoot as well. For example, the majority of artists in the Art Students League were interested in Socialist themes, which were in vogue at the time. "But the Socialist paintings were mostly bad; just bad painting," Singer said. "Still, some abstract artists were working, like Stuart Davis, and others were doing geometric abstractions, even Alfred Maurer, all affected by the Armory Show. Walt Kuhn was still around, and Georgia O'Keeffe." He recalled seeing the first show of Alexander Calder's mobiles at the Pierre Matisse Gallery. "But the Moderns weren't making much impact, not like the American Scene painters."

Singer's years at the Art Students League began a lifelong love affair with New York. While not exactly a starving artist, Singer was constantly struggling financially, and so he spent most of his time in New York on foot. He walked everywhere and at all hours of the day and night. He walked every day from his 35th Street room to the Art Students League, exploring side streets, alleys, tunnels, and other amusements along the way. Frequently, he skipped classes at the League in his enthusiasm to see more of the city. As he later observed about his love for New York, "I find that every place I go is a painting."

Notable painters John Sloan and George Bellows were Singer's heroes, and one of his first personal projects in New York was to find scenes that these artists had painted in order to see how they interpreted them. Whenever he found such a spot, he sometimes painted his own version of the scene. Sloan had painted the interior of McSorley's Old Ale House, a popular watering hole on East 7th Street near Greenwich Village. It was one of Singer's favorite paintings, and that's what attracted him to the place. Opened in 1854, this quaint and picturesque Irish men's tavern, with its floor strewn thick with wood shavings and its two-beers-at-once service policy, had long been a gathering spot for artists like Sloan, Bellows, and Reginald Marsh, who liked to paint and sketch there. McSorley's was a tiny, tangible chunk of New York history, which among other attributes boasted that it had continued to serve homemade brew right through Prohibition without a single raid.

So fascinated was Singer with McSorley's that it was one of the first places he visited on his arrival in New York, and it would prove to be one of his favorite haunts. On one particular occasion, a radiant morning, Singer wandered down to McSorley's. The place was almost empty, and he sat in a chair that gave him the same visual angle as Sloan in one of his paintings. Soon thereafter, Singer produced his first painting of McSorley's, to be followed over the years by more than a hundred other versions.

Living in Depression-era New York on a meager artist's income became increasingly difficult, and so Singer decided to leave the Art Students League at the end of the term in May 1934. Thinking that his teachers might discourage him, he was surprised at John Steuart Curry's reaction: "Oh, you're going home to paint the American Scene! Good!" Singer arrived home with $1.10 in his pocket. Fortunately, his mother had held back a few dollars from his original savings to help him on his return. Several new "cafes" (polite euphemisms for *bars* in post-Prohibition parlance) had sprung up in Malvern, all requiring professionally executed signs, and some local Democrats hired him to make Roosevelt banners. At least there was work.

From 1934 to 1939, Singer painted diligently: the countryside, scenes in town, and the people. From the very start, he entered competitive exhibitions. An honorable mention in 1934 from the Denver Art Museum was an encouraging sign. Aware of the honor of being accepted into the annual Pennsylvania Academy Show in 1935, Singer submitted his first large-scale efforts, *Sandy Valley* (Fig. 19) and *Democratic Rally* (Fig. 82), to this exhibition; to his great joy, the latter was accepted. The following autumn he entered the same two paintings in the 46th Annual Exhibition of Contemporary American Paintings at the Art Institute of Chicago. Not only were both accepted, but he was awarded the Norman Wait Harris Silver Medal for *Sandy Valley* and a prize of $500. Good fortune seemed to bless every effort. Singer noted at the time that he "felt very rich. Deposited $400 in the bank, walked across the street, and bought a five-cent beer. Extent of celebration."

In northeast Ohio, Singer was becoming something of a celebrity, a small-town artist who appeared to be headed for the big-time. The Depression had set in with a harsh reality, and while any kind of a job was a rare privilege,

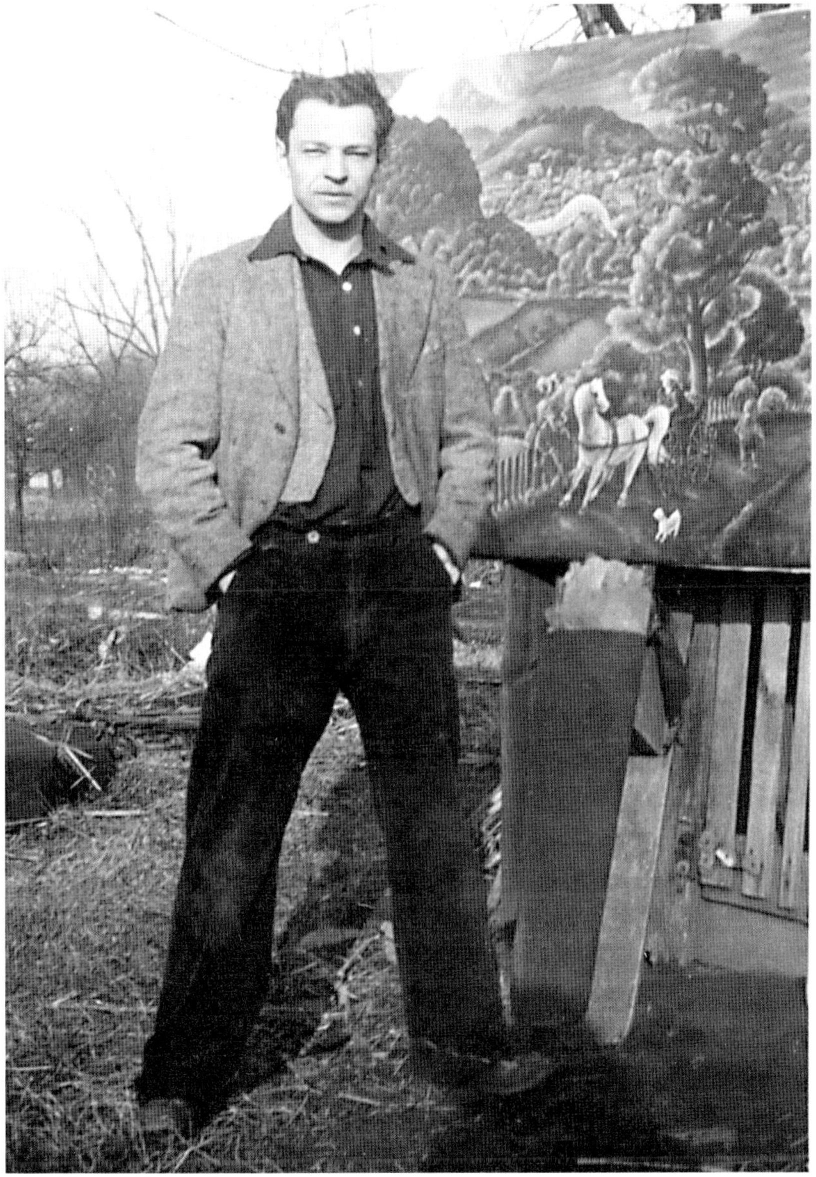

Clyde standing outside in front of his painting *Approach to the Village,* ca. 1935–36. Gifted to the Archives of the Canton Museum of Art by a relative of Clyde Singer

the thought of making a go of a career in art bordered on the absurd. Still, Singer was determined. In 1934, The Little Civic Art Gallery was formed in Canton in a second-story room of the Public Library on Second Street. Its purpose was to provide a showcase for community artists. As soon as Singer learned about it, he arranged to have a body of his work displayed there, a double premiere: his first solo art exhibition and the gallery's first exhibition.

Other important awards and honors followed in rapid succession. In fact, during eighteen months in 1935–36, Singer participated in eighty-two exhibitions in fifty-six cities, an astonishing record for so young an artist. He was obviously marking out his territory. He was awarded the 1936 Lambert Purchase Award of the Pennsylvania Academy of Fine Arts, which acquired his painting *Bill* (Fig. 74) for its permanent collection. The subject for the painting was a neighborhood kid whom Clyde liked to use as a model because he was always punctual. There was also the severely criticized Isochromatic Exhibition sponsored as "a scientific experiment by the research laboratories of M. Grumbacher [a manufacturer of artists' paints and supplies] to show the latest works of artists using new, permanent pigments," apparently authorized and endorsed by the twelve thousand artists of the American Artist Professional League (C. H. Bonte, *Philadelphia Enquirer,* Nov. 10, 1935). The show kicked off at the Grand Central Galleries in New York in 1936 and, after a lukewarm reception there, traveled on to a hundred galleries nationwide, eventually making its way to The Little Civic Art Gallery and Baldwin Museum in Massillon, Ohio.

Singer took first prize in figure painting at the Columbus Art League in 1937. He also won first prizes in landscape and figure at the Columbus Art League and received the Orlando Miller Purchase Award at the Columbus Gallery of Fine Arts that same year. In 1939 he won second prize at the Portland Art Museum and the special Award of Merit at the Columbus Art League. For five consecutive years, Singer's works appeared in the Pennsylvania Academy shows, for four years at the Carnegie International and the Portland Art Museum exhibitions, and for six years at the Cincinnati Art Museum. Invitations came from the Texas Centennial Exhibition in 1936 and the Golden Gate International in San Francisco in 1939, in addition to jury acceptance at the 1939 New York World's Fair. In 1936 alone, Singer's paintings were featured in fourteen major exhibitions across the United States.

Ever searching to perfect or improve his style, Singer accepted an invitation in 1939 to participate in a series of abstract art sessions at the Research Studio in Maitland, Florida, a kind of artists' colony founded a year earlier by American artist and architect Andre Smith and funded by the Bok Foundation of the *Saturday Evening Post.* According to Singer, "You come there to experiment, to do work unlike anything you've done before. I worked on all kinds of materials and papers, did about 150 works, mostly on paper. I did several abstracts. Mostly they're nothing. I did satirical things, highly stylized, comical things." But he concluded, "It wasn't for me." Despite the exposure to a variety of new and unusual styles, the experience left no lasting impressions. Still, a number of these experiments survive and provide an interesting perspective on Singer's work.

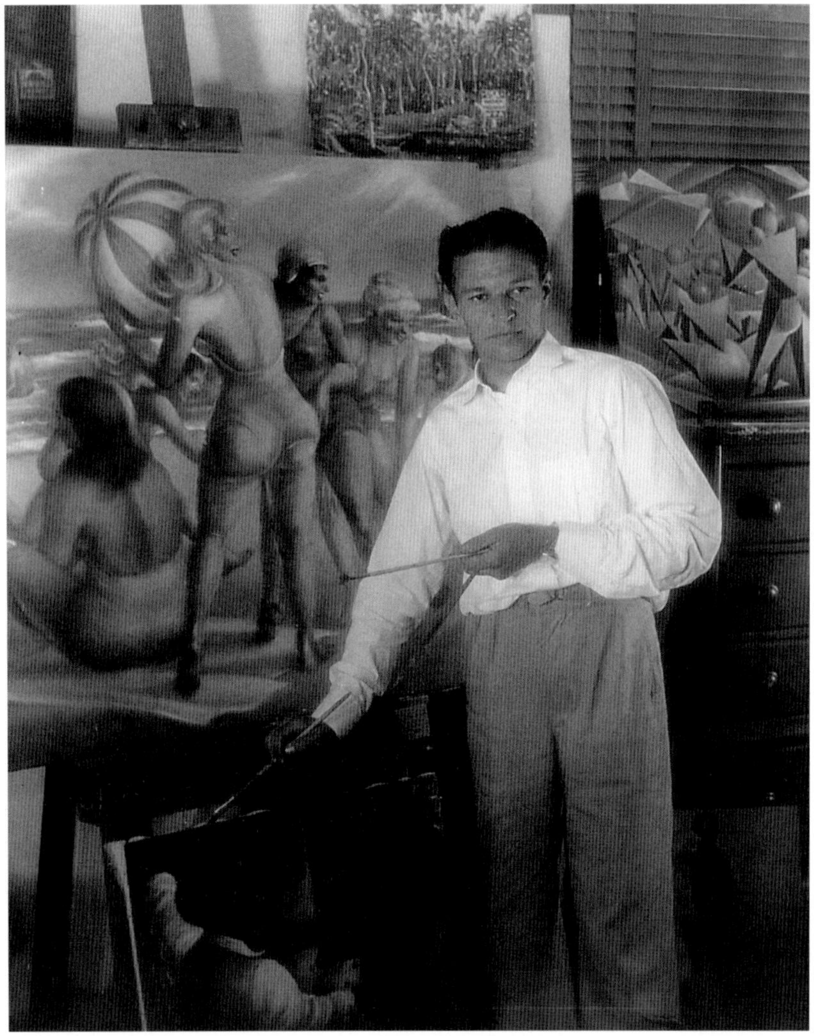

Clyde standing before a painting of women in bathing suits, 1939, Maitland, Florida. Gifted to the Archives of the Canton Museum of Art by a relative of Clyde Singer

For a time during the summers of 1939 and 1940, Singer teamed up with Akron artist Harry H. Shaw to teach art classes at the Ohio River School of Painting in Marietta, Ohio. According to its 1940 brochure, the school had just been organized the year before in order to provide low-cost, intensive ten-week summer sessions in painting landscapes and still lifes and drawing for beginners as well as advanced students. Singer described Marietta as the "best town in Ohio." As he wrote to Louise Lehmiller, being in Marietta was "a releif after seeing doity old Yunkstown and doity old Canton all these past months." Situated on the busy Ohio River, Marietta inspired several superior paintings, including *Down by the Ohio* (Fig. 48) and *Steamboat on the Ohio* (Fig. 49).

A student in one of Singer's Marietta classes was a pretty young lady named Bernice Elizabeth Shimp, who seemed to take quite an interest in her teacher—and eventually he in her. But for the time, Clyde corresponded with girlfriend Louise Lehmiller in North Industry, Ohio. The couple seemed to work much better apart than together, and despite a lengthy exchange of letters, the relationship never blossomed. A kind of alter ego emerged in Singer's letters, a comedic, almost Vaudevillian character who played with words, jargon, dialect, misspellings, and ribald humor, and when words failed him, he resorted to an occasional cartoon. Yet at times he managed to reach depths of emotional expression and an eloquence approaching poetry, all addressed to Louise, who found her long-distance boyfriend amusing. But for the most part, her relationship with Clyde revolved around providing him with transportation, even driving him between Malvern and Marietta.

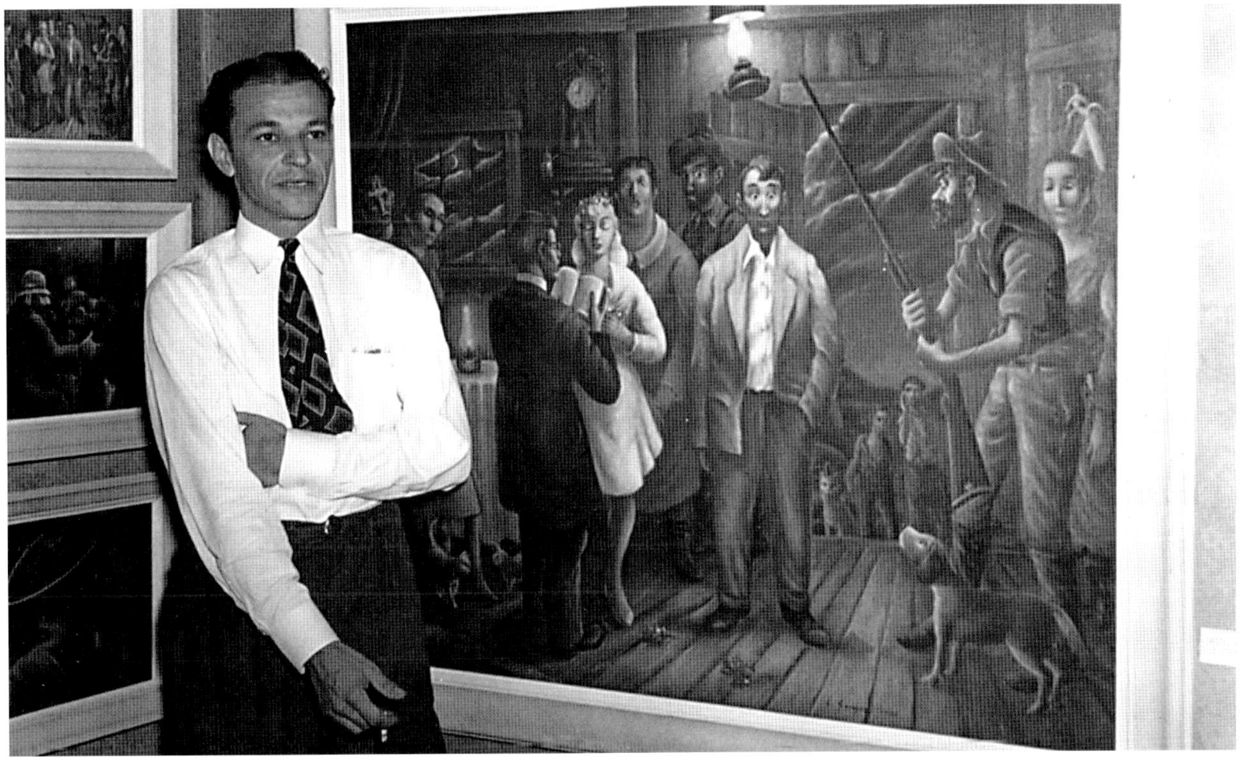

Clyde in front of *Shotgun Wedding,* ca. 1939–40. Gifted to the Archives of the Canton Museum of Art by a relative of Clyde Singer

Clyde did not drive—and never learned to drive—so he was dependent on others for transportation. Or, the distance not being too great, he walked or took a bus.

Singer's artistic talents caught the attention of Joseph Butler III, the new director of the family-owned Butler Institute of American Art in Youngstown, Ohio, and the grandson of the founder. Impressed with Singer's academic credentials and artistic track record, Joe Butler realized his potential as an asset to the museum and offered him the position of assistant director. Already the recipient of several important awards, Singer had only a few months earlier carried off the first prize in the Butler Institute's 1938 New Year Show and had just received the First Halgarten Prize at the National Academy of Design in New York for a large painting called *Barn Dance* (Fig. 32).

Although Singer considered the job offer a great honor and a guarantee of financial security, he was at first reluctant to accept a full-time position, fearing it would compromise the time he dedicated to his painting (at this point in his life, he still hoped to make a living as an artist), so he declined the position. When Butler extended the offer again in December 1939, Singer accepted with two conditions. First, he insisted that he be given plenty of time off to paint and, second, that he be allowed to make occasional artistic junkets to New York City. Butler agreed, even honoring him with the title of artist-in-residence, and Singer assumed his position in 1940. Clyde moved into a vacant Butler family property just across the street from the museum at 525 Wick Avenue. Referring to this opulent Victorian mansion as "the spook chamber," Singer occupied "two dinky rooms" on the second floor, although he was "permitted to move into the big long room with the fireplace" (undated letter to Louise Lehmiller). A photograph of this room—its walls crowded with paintings in massive frames—justifies Singer's description of it as forbidding at night, especially when he was alone and when the wind howled and the dry leaves brushed across the windows. Sometime thereafter the house was damaged by fire and eventually torn down. (The site is now occupied by Bliss Hall, Youngstown State University's Performance and Fine Arts Center.)

Sensing an ideal collaborative opportunity with Youngstown College next door, Joe Butler invited Margaret Evans, head of the fledgling art department, to make use of the museum "as a classroom and laboratory." It was an offer she could not refuse, since it gave the college full access to Clyde's remarkable artistic talents as a member of the faculty at a time when student enrollment was climbing. In December 1939, Joe Butler and college president Howard W. Jones simultaneously announced to the press Singer's two new jobs: he began at once as the assistant director at the Butler and on February 1, 1940, taught his first classes at Youngstown College.

Considering his various duties at the Butler, Clyde assumed a rather heavy teaching load. According to the museum's "Catalogue of the Permanent Collection," dated September 1940, Clyde taught "figure painting and the figure in motion two nights a week, and still life and landscape on Saturdays, both mornings and afternoons. . . . In addition to his college classes, Singer gives two hours a week to exceptional students of junior and high school ages, teaching figure drawing and painting and still life at very nominal expense to the student." Fortunately for Clyde, he never had to leave the building—all of his students came to the Butler for their classes.

As if these responsibilities were not enough, Joe Butler approached him again that same year, this time with a request that he write an art column for the *Youngstown Vindicator.* In an October 10, 1940, letter to Louise Lehmiller, Singer wrote, "Right now I'm trying out for the job as art critic on the *Vindicator.* I'm doing this almost under pressure. I'm to submit 3 stories to the editor as a trial. . . . Don't know if I can make this grade or not, but in any case I'll have to prepare newsy items for the paper." Admitting that he was not a good writer and an even less-qualified critic, he agreed to give it a try.

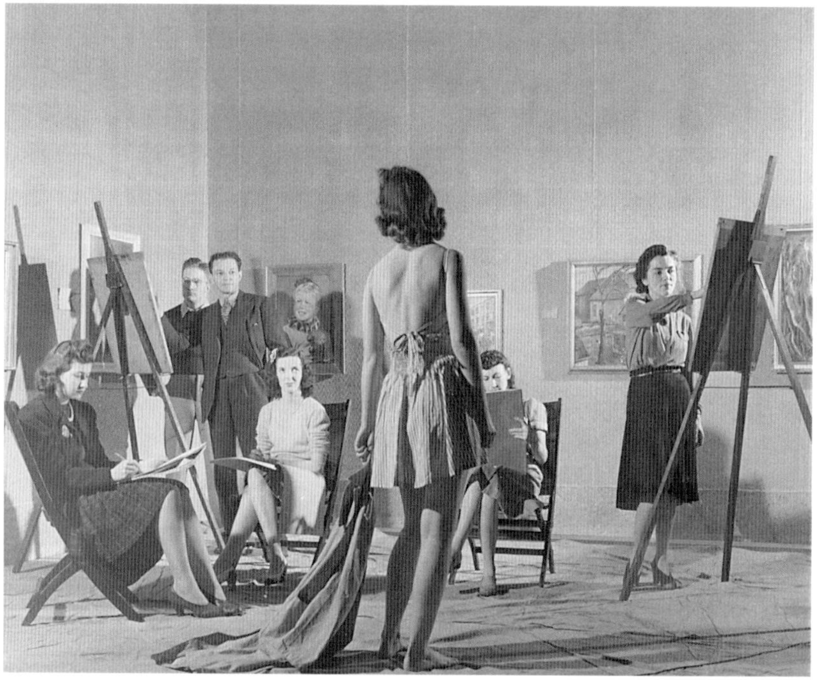

Clyde teaching a class at the Butler, 1940. Gifted to the Archives of the Canton Museum of Art by a relative of Clyde Singer

Singer's first published review of watercolors on loan from the Art Institute of Chicago turned out to be a caustic evaluation of a current exhibition *at his very own museum.* The newspaper editor loved it, published it verbatim, and then asked him to submit an article every week for the Sunday edition. Singer reluctantly accepted, and yet thereafter he faithfully contributed articles on a rigorous weekly schedule almost until the end of his life.

Although some of his preliminary reviews were noted for their harshness, he mellowed considerably with the passage of time. "I can always find something of interest, and I learned how to be positive rather than negative," he said. He rationalized that if he could find no redeeming virtues in an exhibition or an artist's work, he would say nothing at all. His readers came to recognize that Clyde's silence was condemnation enough.

Across more than five decades, Singer faithfully met his weekly deadline for the *Youngstown Vindicator*, each article tediously handwritten on a makeshift desk atop a radiator in the small first-floor office he shared with Butler and a secretary. (Many years later, when the Butler Institute was enlarged, Singer was finally given his own office in a downstairs room close to the permanent collection storage areas. His former "office" was converted into a closet.) Except for the three years he spent in the Army during World War II and the occasional vacation when a small number of ghostwriters covered for him, Singer logged more than two thousand articles and reviews in his long career. He was paid a meager sum per article (between $12 and $20), a fee that remained the same throughout his lifetime. At one point the editor of the *Vindicator* wanted to syndicate his column, but Singer politely refused.

In those early days at the Butler, Singer did everything from curating and installing exhibitions to performing such odd jobs as building a float (presumably for a Youngstown State University homecoming parade). Over the years he developed an encyclopedic knowledge of American art and artists; he collected a vast archive of catalogs, brochures, magazines, and other published materials, all meticulously filed, dated, and labeled by hand, noting the artist's name, genre, and other relevant information. In an age before computers, this was a prodigious undertaking. Each winter, Joe Butler vacationed in Antigua for three months, leaving Clyde fully in charge of the management of the Butler Institute. According to senior employees, he was an excellent administrator. Singer carefully documented all transactions, kept accurate records, and interacted with every member of the staff on a daily basis.

Singer accepted just about any challenge that came his way at the Butler. One of his most unusual duties was recorded years later by Butler director Lou Zona in a memorial tribute to Singer, a story he recalls in his Foreword. Zona revealed that some of Clyde's "cleverest masterpieces" reside in the north and south galleries where "Clyde's skill as an artist is forever on display on the baseboards of gallery doors made to look like the marble trim at the base of each wall." Zona considered these fine examples of trompe l'oeil painting that truly fool the eye.

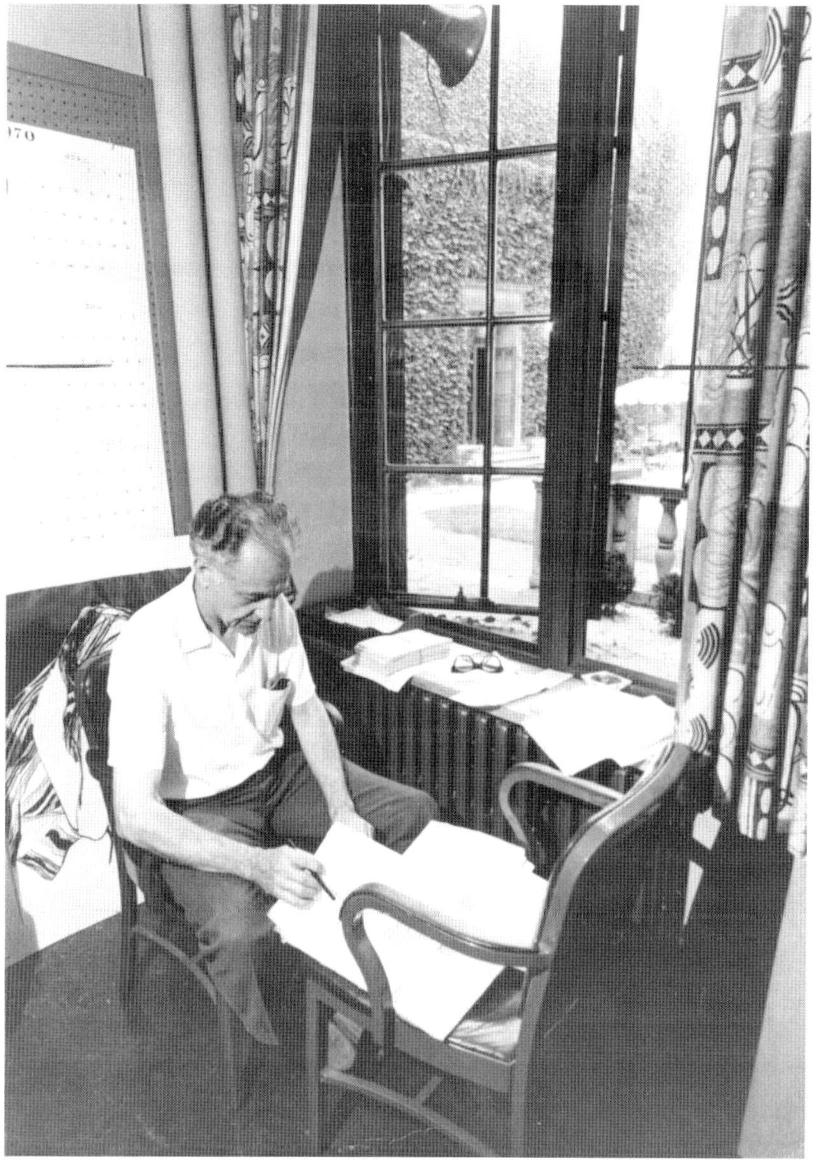

Clyde and Joe Butler shared an office. Clyde (shown here in 1969) worked on a card table and Joe had a desk. There was room for little else, but they did have shelves on the walls. Lloyd S. Jones, *Youngstown Vindicator*.

Only once did Singer have an opportunity to produce a mural, a WPA project awarded by the Public Buildings Branch of the U.S. Treasury Department. Much of the work on this mural was done in the bowels of the Butler Institute, which provided him with an adequate studio. Finished in September 1941, the twelve-by-five-foot painting on fabric was installed on a wall panel in the lobby of the small post office in New Concord, Ohio. *Skaters* (Fig. 39) represents students enjoying this winter activity on the pond in front of Muskingum College. Singer received considerable publicity as this mural progressed, and the $700 check he received was "icing on the cake," as he himself would have put it.

Now that he was over the peacetime draft age and financially secure, Singer thought conditions were ideal for marriage. On November 3, 1941, Clyde Singer married Bernice Elizabeth Shimp, his former student, in the rectory of St. Francis Catholic Church in Malvern, with Rev. John H. Diegelman presiding. Witnesses to the ceremony were his sister Clara and her husband, Harold Reed. The newlyweds then departed by bus for a short honeymoon in Pittsburgh before taking up residence in a second-floor apartment above the Shriver-Allison Funeral Home at 292 W. Madison Avenue. Only a month later, the Japanese attacked Pearl Harbor, drawing the United States into World War II. Much to his surprise, Singer, now thirty-four years old and married, was drafted into the U.S. Army on June 18, 1942.

While stationed at Camp Rucker in Alabama and on maneuvers in Tennessee, Singer executed a number of watercolors, three of which appeared in *Art in the Armed Forces,* edited by Aimee Crane (New York: Hyperion Press, 1944): *Tennessee Maneuvers, Sailors in New Orleans,* and a romantic vignette called *Week-end Pass.* Singer was eventually shipped overseas with the Eighth Army, serving first in New Guinea and then in the Philippines. Rising to the rank of technical corporal with a tank unit, he took part in several major battles on Luzon and was awarded the Asiatic Pacific Theater Medal with three bronze stars. He also received a Philippines Liberation Medal with one bronze star, an American Theater Ribbon, and a Good Conduct Medal. Of his twenty-six months of active duty, fourteen were served overseas.

On September 26, 1945, Singer left the Philippines to return home and was honorably discharged one month later at Camp Atterbury, Indiana. Singer's exemplary participation in combat may be surprising, considering he was a pacifist by nature. But he rarely spoke about his military experiences thereafter and never claimed his awards, even though he was notified of them. As a result, very little is known or recorded about the actual nature of his duties, although he left a large and curious catalog of drawings, paintings, caricatures, handmade postcards, and even one or two grim representations of war.

Fresh out of the Army, Clyde returned to Malvern with Bernice for a brief visit with his parents when tragedy struck. Monday, January 7, 1946, was a particularly foggy day, and Clyde's seventy-five-year-old father, Andrew, was walking home along Route 43 in Malvern when he was hit by a passing vehicle. Rushed to the hospital, Andrew died from his injuries later that same evening. (Clyde's mother outlived him by almost a quarter-century. She died on July 18, 1970, at the age of ninety-one.)

With the Armistice, both Singer and Butler (who had also served in the Pacific Theater) resumed their former duties at the Butler Institute. Among other things, Singer taught art classes, conducted children's tours, and acted as curator of the museum's collection. As assistant director, Clyde worked closely with Joe Butler and resumed most of his prewar duties, including writing reviews for the *Youngstown Vindicator.* Ever faithful to his art, Clyde also managed to dedicate one or two personal hours to his painting.

For at least two years after the war, Clyde and Bernice continued to live in their small apartment on the second floor above the Shriver Funeral Home. Eventually, they bought a house in Boardman and began a contented life there. For whatever reason, Clyde adamantly refused to learn how to drive, and so he typically used public transportation to commute to his job at the Butler Institute. After work, Bernice usually drove to the bus stop to pick him up. Occasionally she made the full journey into town. She was an attractive woman, and the two were socially active, though neither cared much for the public spotlight. Bernice took little pleasure in cooking, and so meals in the Singer household were simple affairs, prepared mostly with a can opener and a pot. Their basement was well stocked with a variety of canned goods. Periodically, when Bernice was visiting family, Clyde took advantage of her absence and stopped at a market on the way home to pick up his two favorite items: a spit-roasted chicken and a tin of smoked oysters. He looked forward to such banquets, describing his solo dinner plans to staff members with a big smile of delight and anticipation. Bernice gradually became a recluse, seeking comfort and solitude in their humble home. Bernice had several miscarriages, but their marriage produced no children.

After his homecoming from the war, Singer found a dramatic change in American art, which he attributed in part to the influx of foreign art teachers and professors such as Hans Hoffman and Joseph Albers seeking refuge in this country. These artists brought with them what they considered more "advanced" concepts of art, thus provoking a rebellion among the younger, more impressionable American artists. Then came along the "Irascible 18," the abstract expressionists. Singer was not impressed with their modern methods, which involved dripping paint onto canvas and or misrepresenting the true colors of nature.

Singer was often accused of clinging to the same style, and to this he readily admitted. Still, he made efforts from time to time to develop his talents in a more modern vein, or to kick off in a new direction. But in the end, he always remained faithful to his 1930s style. And it paid off. In 1972 Singer won an award from the Ohio Library Association in Columbus for "preserving the contemporary scene." He was proud of that award, perhaps because it seemed to justify his preference for the American Scene over the more modern style.

Life for Clyde Singer settled into a pleasant routine from 1946 on. He worked days at the Butler and painted at home during the evenings and weekends in a year-round cycle interrupted only by occasional artistic junkets to New York City. For more than four decades, Singer made his solo pilgrimages, sometimes two or three times per year, to the city of his greatest inspiration. He found in New York artistic freedom, cherished solitude, and liberation from his Youngstown routine. Upon his arrival by bus, he would drop off his luggage at a low-budget hotel in the heart of Manhattan and then begin to wander the streets in search of the right scene to fire his imagination and set his mind to work. On foot for hours at a time, picking up an occasional bite of food along the way, Singer would explore the big boulevards, the long diagonal stretch of Broadway, the congested alleys of Soho and the Bowery, "Central Park, 57th Street, Fifth Avenue, the automat, Times Square, the subway, the Village—and always McSorley's Old Ale House," Richard Bonham recorded.

By the time Bonham composed his article on Clyde Singer for *American Artist* magazine in 1969, Singer was no longer entering many of the major exhibitions. "He feels his reputation is assured; he has a good following in his own little corner of the world, and besides, he's having fun doing what he likes to do best," Bonham wrote. In fact, with the death of Joe Butler in 1981, the museum trustees offered Clyde the full directorship, but he declined, saying it was too much responsibility.

Shortly thereafter Lou Zona assumed the helm of the Butler Institute of American Art. Acutely aware of the dichotomy between his own deeply entrenched traditionalist views and the new director's fascination with contemporary art, Singer expressed his concern that perhaps he was no longer needed and offered to resign. Zona, however, assured him that was not the case. The two quickly became fast friends, and true to his word, Lou Zona not only advanced Singer to the position of associate director but retained Clyde to the end of his life.

Singer enjoyed a comfortable life as an artist. He had a fairly lucrative second-tier administrative position in a prominent art museum, was regarded with considerable prestige in the Ohio arts community, had a weekly column in the local newspaper, and had plenty of time to paint. Over the years, he evolved into something of an institution, often perceived as eccentric in his dress and mannerisms. Hardly more than five-and-a-half feet tall and youthfully thin, Singer still seemed larger than life. His wardrobe consisted of one or two suits, a few tweed sports jackets, and his most distinctive trademark: garish plaid pants.

While generally quite focused on his work, Clyde enjoyed taking long leisurely walks through the museum. He was especially fond of visiting the vast basement areas, particularly his beloved permanent collection storage spaces. Lunch hour found Clyde walking a short distance down Wick Avenue to the center of town, where he frequented one or two of his favorite restaurants. His order was always the same: a bowl of soup and a piece of pie. His snack of choice was Fig Newton cookies, and he always carried a supply in his pocket, which he offered to all takers.

But if Clyde's daily life at the Butler Institute was fairly routine, his artistic life was a different matter. Liberated from his chores and cut loose on his own timetable to wander the streets of Youngstown, Canton, Malvern, and his beloved New York, Singer assumed another personality as an artist. Roger Bonham described Singer's modus operandi in his *American Artist* article of February 1969: "He enjoys nothing more than tracking down the native American in his habitat, particularly the often appealing and amusing female of the species. These subjects . . . he puts down with consummate skill learned from the masters of the Ashcan and Benton-Curry-Wood schools of art."

Singer was unobtrusive, keeping his presence hidden so that his subjects were never aware of him. He never attempted to set up the composition and simply regarded himself as an observer and commentator on the passing scene. Singer relied on his knowledge, memory, and imagination when painting. His own paintings were often motivated by an individual who happened upon the scene and grabbed his attention—maybe it was a girl in a bright dress, an old man seated at a bar, or a portly woman wandering through a museum gallery. Some little thing about the person spoke to him and fired his creativity.

Singer always carried in his pocket a notepad, about four-by-six inches, in which he jotted down ballpoint pen sketches in a minute or two. He often made dozens of these sketches a day as he wondered around city streets looking for striking scenes, sometimes taking notes on color. At night he made more complete, but still rudimentary, drawings in his sketchbook. He estimated that for every forty sketches he jotted down in his notebook, ten to fifteen scenes were worth painting.

Back in his studio, Singer would lay out a charcoal sketch on canvas, over which he applied a wash of turpentine, followed by black or brown pigment for a ground. Then he was ready to paint. If the drawing was complex, he drew a grid on the canvas and transferred the image freehand from the sketch. Sometimes too, he skipped all these preliminary steps and began right in with the direct application of colors, like a fresco. His ambition in later years was to turn out at least one painting a week, many of them little vignettes or colorful character studies no larger than eight-by-ten inches. He called these his bread-and-butter paintings, because they provided a bit of cash from time to time.

Most often his paintings sold by word of mouth, at regional exhibitions or when art collectors sought him out, turning up at his small home in Boardman where Clyde always had a few items on view. Lazar Tarzan's gallery in Canton and George Ockerman's in Youngstown did a profitable exchange with Singer paintings, the latter actually dedicating a room to the artist's work. Singer was never represented by a major gallery, but that seems to be how he wanted it. Some of his old letters reveal that people in New York City were interested in handling his work, but evidently Singer never accepted their invitations. As one old friend of Clyde's put it, he "was too laid back to deal with big-time operators."

For a long time Youngstown also provided a plentiful supply of scenes and subjects, but "when they tore down the old buildings [in the 1970s] . . . there was nothing left for my type of painting. The old, interesting buildings were all gone, the old international section with the Greek coffee houses, the bagel places . . . disappeared, and there's nothing left. That's why I rely on New York." And he continued to rely on New York as long as his health held out. He made his last trip there in 1985.

Despite the overall diversity of his subject matter, Singer had a limited catalog of favorite topics, including street scenes, parks, McSorley's Old Ale House, sports events, and theater crowds. By far his favorite subjects to paint, however, were New York City and women. Another popular subject for Clyde was sports. He enjoyed just about any type of manly competition,

Facing page: Clyde in his studio in the basement of his Boardman home, 1983. M. J. Albacete

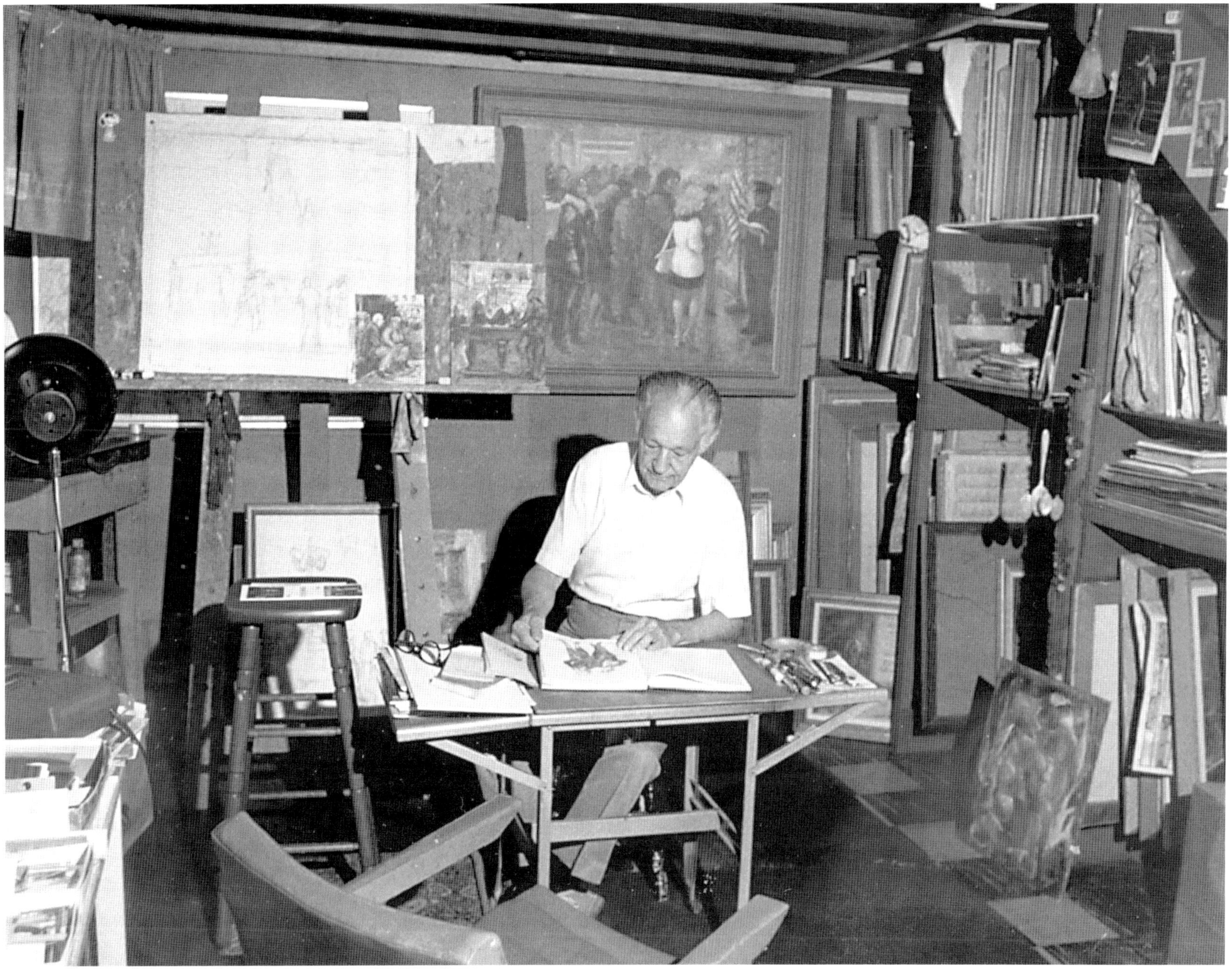

with particular emphasis on football, baseball, boxing, and wrestling, and he took every opportunity to catch any kind of match or game. People also amused him, particularly ordinary people performing their everyday activities. Of special interest to Singer were the down-and-outers, street vendors, bag ladies, and other unconventional types. Paintings of subjects from Malvern are abundantly represented, as are other small-town pictures.

Over the years Singer used all kinds of palettes, from the intense to the subdued. But in later years his choices became more limited. Singer felt that colors clashed, saying that "they just don't please my eye somehow." He preferred browns and grays with red accents and noted on more than one occasion that he was "no colorist."

Journalist Elizabeth McClelland made an interesting observation in *Timeline* about how Singer was different from the other American Scene painters. "American scene painters were usually divided into two camps, the urban realists, who painted the city, and the regionalists, who depicted the American heartland," she wrote. "Singer, living in Ohio and making regular visits to New York, depicted both locales without missing a beat."

In a rather unusual way, Singer took shots at some of his prominent contemporaries who had established reputations dabbling in abstraction, the realm that always eluded him despite several attempts. While poring over photographs of Clyde's works in preparation for our exhibition, Canton Museum of Art curator Lynnda Arrasmith noted that many paintings depicted individuals walking through museums. Clyde took the liberty of "repainting" some of the modern art works hanging on gallery walls into his own depiction, perhaps his subtle way of saying, "I could do that too, if I really wanted to!"

Looking back on his long and prolific painting career, Singer was never melancholy that major recognition had sidestepped him. In a very real sense, and now more than ever, it has not. He has a faithful following of friends and strangers alike who enjoy his work in communities all over the country. In the 1990s, when friends pointed out that his early paintings were selling for thousands of dollars, Clyde expressed amazement, and I once heard him exclaim, "Oh, that's way too much."

Despite his advancing years, Clyde Singer remained astute and content with a comfortable daily routine of writing, painting, and performing a few light duties at work. No one ever asked him in his old age to relinquish his position at the Butler or his column at the *Vindicator.* By the time he reached his eighties, evidence began emerging of his physical and mental deterioration, such as his growing problem with cataracts. A physician (who happened to be the Butler Institute's chairman of the board at the time) convinced Clyde to undergo surgery, and he finally accepted but with great reluctance. Clyde rarely visited doctors or dentists, but he did undergo the procedure on one eye and was impressed with the clarity and richness of his regained vision. He was surprised at how garish his paintings had become. When it came time to do the other eye, he declined, saying that at his age, one good eye was enough.

The numerous awards and honors Clyde accrued throughout his artistic career make quite a long list, easily ranking him as one of the most popular Ohio artists of all time. Recognition for this remarkable record of achievement came in 1993 when he was named one of two winners of the Governor's Award for the Arts in Ohio in the Individual Artist category. Singer, profoundly touched by this honor, received the award on March 31 from the Ohio Arts Council in the State Capitol. Hundreds of people representing the Ohio arts community attended the event. A humble man who rarely spoke in public and never enjoyed the limelight, he must have realized the importance of the ceremony as he stood in the auditorium acknowledging the enthusiastic applause. His acceptance speech was reportedly the longest on record for the event. For this occasion, the nearby Columbus Museum of Art gave pride of place to Singer's monumental *The Old Swimming Hole* (Fig. 28). The trustees of the Butler Institute also dedicated a small area of gallery space for an ongoing Clyde Singer exhibition of recent works. He was eventually presented with an award of recognition for his many years of dedication to the Butler and his artistic achievements, and after his death the Butler trustees created a Clyde Singer Award to honor senior regional artists. This award is presented to one recipient each November.

As their health declined, Clyde and Bernice gradually lost the ability to care for themselves, and the last years of their lives were very difficult. Known as a sociable and friendly couple, the two became reclusive, although close friends were still welcome. In her final years Bernice was terrified of leaving the house; she lived in almost constant fear of burglars, and so the curtains and blinds were always drawn. Clyde became very weak. He and Bernice ate most of their meals at local fast-food restaurants, and sympathetic customers would often pay their bills. Bernice always accepted their generosity, commenting that "God and people are so good to me." On several occasions Clyde lost consciousness at the restaurant and was taken by ambulance to an area hospital. His determination was such, however, that he promptly returned to work after each dismissal from the hospital.

One day as he was leaving the Butler, Clyde became confused and, instead of taking the bus, started to walk home, a distance of six or seven miles. As he crossed over Youngstown's Market Street Bridge, he tripped and fell, suffering an injury that sent him to the hospital. Soon thereafter, in December 1997, Clyde Singer left a telephone message with a Butler employee saying he was resigning. He was then eighty-eight years old. Despite Singer's advanced years, Lou Zona accepted his resignation with regret. In a touching personal note written to Clyde shortly thereafter, Zona invited him to continue using his office whenever he felt up to it, stating that "it's hard for me to even imagine the Butler without Clyde Singer in his office." Although both body and mind continued to deteriorate, Clyde had periods of incredible lucidity, and occasionally he took Zona up on his offer by appearing at the Butler.

Painting and drawing, which gave singular purpose, meaning, and direction to Singer's life, continued to motivate him until the end. If there was one place in his increasingly limited world where he could find consolation and peace of mind, it was in his basement studio. Clyde Singer died in his sleep on January 5, 1999, at the age of ninety and was buried in Forest Lawn Cemetery in Youngstown, Ohio. (Bernice survived Clyde for another six years. After Clyde's death, she lived in a nursing home in Marietta, Ohio, where she died at the age of eighty-seven on May 28, 2005. She was buried next to her husband.) After his death, the few family members and close friends who had access to the little house in Boardman found the studio just as the artist had left it, as if he had merely gone out for a few minutes, soon to return. He left an unfinished eight-by-ten-inch painting mounted on the easel, and brushes, paints, and other materials were close at hand, ready for the artist to take them up again.

In exploring the vast collection of Clyde Singer's work—as we have done in preparation for the 2008 "Clyde Singer's America" exhibition—one can observe that Singer has literally captured moments in time or "little bits of history," as he put it. Each work rivets our attention, stops the clock and carries the spectator back to another era and place. Each painting, with its respective fragment of life, is like a single piece of a larger puzzle that collectively depicts in magnificent detail the rich pageantry of the everyday world: people, objects, street scenes, facades of old buildings, and midwestern landscapes. Except for the central episode or some other "giveaway" detail—a lovely girl in a bright dress or a sign that betrays the time period—all of his paintings convey an almost palpable sense of the era in which they were painted.

Singer was an artist in search of the past, largely indifferent to the present, and perhaps a bit fearful and suspicious of the future. He keenly felt the deterioration and disappearance of the prewar world he loved, a decline that not only affected art but literature, music, and society in general. Artists, Singer once said, are detached from the mainstream of life, engrossed in creating art for art's sake. By contrast, he would argue, today's collectors and art dealers are not so much interested in quality and creativity as in market value. "It's all personality worship now," he lamented. But the emphasis on "market value" did not affect him. As long as Clyde kept painting, people kept buying, and Singer was pleased to think that his paintings sold on their own artistic merits. Although he lived and painted practically to the end of the twentieth century, the decades of the thirties, forties, and fifties were the periods of his greatest inspiration. When the definitive book is written on the artists of the American Scene movement, Clyde Singer, truly the last artist of this school, will take his rightful place in the final chapter.

The Last Ashcan Artist: Clyde Singer and the American Scene

NANNETTE V. MACIEJUNES AND CHRISTOPHER S. DUCKWORTH

> Far more important than his surprisingly fresh technique, is Mr. Singer's accomplishment of the highest Junction of the artist, that of expressing his native environment vividly and truthfully. He has depicted the life of a Midwestern community with a flavor that is not only decidedly American in tone but distinctly local in atmosphere. His appreciative insight into the ways of small town, not without a touch of satire at times a trifle cutting, gives his work the impress of truth. His portraits are warm studies of the sort of persons one sees frequently and knows well; his landscapes and figure pieces reflect an appreciation of values which are an essential and enduring part of a community's tradition.
>
> —Tipton M. Westfall, Princeton University, 1936

Clyde Singer was born in the wrong year. That is not to say that 1908 was an unpropitious or uneventful year. To begin, 1908 was a leap year, and a number of notable events took place during the 366 days. Henry Ford introduced his Model-T, which was to change the American lifestyle. Mother's Day was celebrated for the first time, and the Chicago Cubs won the World Series for the last time, at least to date. William Howard Taft of Cincinnati was elected president handily, and women for the first time competed in the Olympic Games. Physicist and father of the hydrogen bomb Edward Teller, Western author Louis L'Amour, actress Bette Davis, journalist Edward R. Murrow, and artists Balthus, Henri Carder-Bresson, and Roger Tory Peterson were born that year. And, at the Macbeth Gallery at 450 Fifth Avenue in New York City, an exhibition of art opened, the first and only show of a group of rebel artists that became known as The Eight: Arthur B. Davies, William J. Glackens, Robert Henri, Ernest Lawson, George Luks, Maurice Prendergast, Everett Shinn, and John Sloan. Several of them also became identified with the Ashcan School. Had Clyde Singer been born, say, twenty-five or thirty years earlier, he might very well have been included in this groundbreaking show. As it was, Singer became both an heir and a guardian relic of the Ashcan School and its American Scene offspring—and he remained forever true to the fundamental tenets of its creed to depict this nation as it truly is, showing everything, realistically and narratively, from the glories of the harvest to the despair of the slums.

The Ashcan School sprang from Robert Henri, who was born Robert Henry Cozad in Cincinnati in 1865. His father, a sometime riverboat gambler and land speculator, invested in fifty thousand acres of Nebraska and moved the family west. While Robert spent some years on the ranch, he returned to Cincinnati to attend a private academy in preparation for college. Then, in 1883, his father killed a worker in a dispute over wages, and the family fled to Philadelphia where they assumed aliases. Robert simply dropped his last name and changed the spelling of his middle name to the French form—while insisting upon an Anglicized pronunciation. He enrolled in the Pennsylvania Academy of Fine Arts where he was exposed to the realism of Thomas Eakins, even though the famous painter had left the school shortly before Henri's arrival. In addition to his classes, Henri visited the operating rooms and morgue of the Jefferson Medical College, where his brother was a student. This furthered his study of human anatomy and perhaps also enhanced his understanding of the grimmer side of life. Both would figure large in his art.

Henri and a group of fellow students continued their studies with the obligatory trip to Paris in 1888. He found the instruction at the Académie Julian so stiff that he transferred to the École des Beaux-Arts, which was little better. More profitable was a two-year tour of western France, Italy, and Spain. When Henri returned to the United States, he landed a teaching job at the Philadelphia School of Design for Women, beginning a career of distinguished teaching that was marked by his becoming a focus for liberal ideas and new models of representation. In 1895 Henri returned to Paris and gained a place in a Salon show. He married in 1898, and the newlyweds traveled to Paris where Henri now was greeted as a successful artist. With the dawn of the new century, he returned to New York City where he lived for the remainder of his life. Henri's star rose quickly as he joined William Merritt Chase's New York School of Art. He opened his own school in 1909, then taught at the Modern School, and finally began teaching at the Art Students League.

In his teaching and in his art, Henri baulked against the upper-class subject matter chosen by the leaders of academic art. He also rebelled against their style of painting. Henri painted from real life, and he painted of real life. His technique appeared natural and spontaneous. And he found allies. William Glackens, George Luks, Everett Shinn, and John Sloan—four of The Eight—had been artist-illustrator-reporters for the *Philadelphia Press*. A large part of their work, in this age before the press camera, was to make, on the spot, rapid sketches of news events that captured texture and detail. Their more formal art reflected this style, and often the subject matter did as well. To the art establishment, however, their art was vulgar, coarse, and unacceptable. It belonged in an ashcan, a refuse bin.

Henri, who was at the center of this new style, had initiated a revolution. His manifesto to paint real life in a realistic manner—to go beyond the drawing rooms and boardrooms to the barrooms and workplaces—was picked up by his students, including a young baseball-playing painter from Columbus, Ohio, named George Bellows. It also found favor with a growing group of dealers and avant-garde collectors. In 1908, the year of Clyde Singer's birth, the show of The Eight changed American art by rejecting the genteel in favor of the gritty—they had democratized art by depicting life in the city as it really was lived by most people. Like the reporters several of them had been, they walked the streets and haunted the saloons and workplaces searching for stories that they could set on canvas.

A new generation of American artists, some of them students of Henri, furthered the democratization process. Some, like Bellows, painted the city, the new urban environment that sprang from the technologies of streetcars, sweatshops, and tenements. Some also probed the roots of the American political experiment and questioned whether Jeffersonian democracy had been usurped by robber barons and now needed the agent of socialism or communism or anarchism to reassert the prominence of the common man. Their art was not just for ostentatious display. It could, it should, help initiate reform. In 1912, Ashcan artist and member of The Eight John Sloan became art editor of *The Masses*, a revolutionary socialist magazine that addressed working-class issues. Among the notable contributors was George Bellows.

While the Ashcan artists had prowled the streets of New York City in search of subjects, another group of younger artists, also influenced by Henri and The Eight, began to spread the art of realism, of the ashcan, geographically. By broadening the scope of American realism, they further democratized and Americanized it. Painters such as Thomas Hart Benton of Missouri; John Steuart Curry of Kansas; Grant Wood of Iowa; Charles Burchfield of Buffalo, New York; and Edward Hopper, who lived in New York City but traveled extensive throughout the United States, were not content to paint only New York City—they wanted to paint America, its people and its communities. The movement that Henri had initiated had slowed, perhaps even derailed, following the 1913 Armory Show, where the American public was exposed to and became enamored of European Modernism. It gained its second wind with these artists and became the American Scene, a truly apt description of what they strove to accomplish.

We identify the American Scene with the vision of American life created by painters between the two world wars. In the years following the end of World War I in 1918, the United States largely retreated from international involvement and was consumed, as was much of Western Europe, by a new spirit of nationalism. A fervent interest in things American swept the United States, beginning in the 1920s and continuing through the economic upheaval of the Great Depression in the 1930s. This new interest extended to the world of the arts. The American Wing of New York's Metropolitan Museum of Art debuted in 1924, and New York's first museum devoted exclusively to American Art, the Whitney Museum of American Art, opened in 1930. Alfred Stieglitz, who had helped introduce European modernism to the United States prior to the war, in 1925 opened a new gallery committed solely to the advancement of American artists. William Carlos Williams's book of essays, *In the American Grain,* which sought to define the uniqueness of the American character, was published in 1925. Two years later, Charles and Mary Beard's incredibly influential history textbook, *The Rise of an American Civilization,* was published. It, too, presented American culture as unique. So did a rising generation of novelists, poets, and dramatists: Sinclair Lewis, William Faulkner, John O'Hara, F. Scott Fitzgerald, Edith Wharton, Robert Frost, and Eugene O'Neill among them. Americans turned inward and became introspective. It was a time to shed European pretension and look around this vast country, so full of potential.

Through the early 1920s, American Scene painting emerged as *the* American style, and, to artists, dealers, critics, and collectors alike, it appeared to be firmly established. It was American, and American was what the nation wanted after the bloodbath of World War I and European social and political upheavals. American Scene artists not only painted the hinterland, they lived there and were members of the community, as much so as the local lawyer or doctor. In their communities, these artists were regarded as recorders of the past and present of a particular place, journalists in paint, as it were. And their works often remained in the community, sometimes conspicuously. In some ways, the Great Depression actually mainstreamed the preeminent status of the American Scene. The various New Deal arts programs implemented when Franklin Delano Roosevelt swept Herbert Hoover out of office in 1932 not only provided employment for artists, the programs also put art out into the community in the form of murals, posters, paintings, and sculpture. Artists also taught classes in neighborhood art centers, a wholly new approach to integrating art into everyday life. The aggregate impact of the various federal programs involving art was enormous. Art had become an officially recognized part of the community, fulfilling an important social function. Moreover, artists, for the first time, were treated as professionals who were supported and sustained by the American public through their government.

In 1931, twenty-three-year-old Clyde Singer arrived in Columbus, Ohio, to attend the Columbus Art School, which was part of the Columbus Gallery of Fine Arts, now the Columbus Museum of Art. With the Depression on the upswing, the young man had been doing odd jobs at the Canton Sign Company, earning nineteen dollars a week. But he loved to draw and paint, and he had exhibited artistic talent. What he now needed was instruction and exposure to art. The choice of Columbus was perhaps more dictated by economic realities than academic stature: he received a scholarship to the school, and he could live with an uncle to cut living expenses.

Singer undoubtedly learned much in the classrooms and studios of the Columbus Art School. The institution had some solid instructors, including Impressionist Alice Schille. It would seem, however, that Singer gained more when he exited the school building, crossed a narrow street, and walked north a few hundred yards to the Columbus Gallery of Fine Arts. The new building, which had opened that year, featured exhibitions from the recently donated Ferdinand Howald Collection, loans from the Frederick W. Schumacher Collection, and a selection of paintings by George Bellows, several of them lent by his widow, Emma. In numerous communications about his education and time spent in Columbus, Singer never mentioned the Howald Collection, which even then was recognized as an outstanding assemblage of American and European Modernism with its Demuths and Marins. Nor did he mention Schumacher's Old Masters. He did speak, often, about Bellows and how he was drawn to the Ashcan artist's works, including *Polo at Lakewood* and *The Lone Tenement.* Those paintings made a greater impression on him than anything else during his Columbus sojourn.

In 1932, when Singer returned to his Malvern, Ohio, hometown, he was an artist working to further his career. He wanted to attend the Art Students League in New York City, and he sent off two hundred drawings and sketches along with his application. About one thousand others joined Singer in applying. From among them, the league awarded ten scholarships, and Singer received one of them. He found a cheap room, $2.50 per week, and once again was a student. In New York, he also discovered the world of galleries, museums, and new artists. He saw John Steuart Curry's *Tornado in Kansas,* and it made a deep and lasting impact, so much so that he hung a print of it in his studio for years. The teachers whose classes Singer took were more impressive by far than those in Columbus and included Thomas Hart Benton, Kenneth Hayes Miller, Ivan Olinsky, and Curry. Singer was absorbing the American Scene from some of its most prominent practitioners, and he was making a good impression on them.

Before he ever came to New York, Singer had two special painters whose work he admired beyond others: George Bellows and John Sloan. In his non-classroom hours, Singer searched out the locations the two men had painted. He ventured into McSorley's Ale House, a dark, working-class Irish bar that banned women but welcomed the artists into an eccentric gathering place that author Joseph Mitchell later described in *McSorley's Wonderful Saloon.* Singer found the seat that approximated the same perspective as the one Sloan had chosen for a painting years earlier. In McSorley's and in the streets nearby, Singer connected with the New York of Bellows and The Eight. Singer further connected with the Ashcan School when he established a friendship with John Sloan. Bellows, who had died in 1924, was lost to the young artist, but Sloan was very much alive and a living link to Henri and the Ashcan artists. Sloan told Singer stories about Henri, The Eight, and life as an artist, and the younger man came to feel that he knew those who had preceded him. But his money was running out, and it was time for Singer to return to Ohio. When he told Curry, the older man exclaimed, "Oh, you're going home to paint the American scene! Good!"

Clyde Singer returned to Ohio when American Scene painting was at its zenith, and, before long, he was becoming recognized as a talented up-and-comer. He began entering shows and exhibitions. At such venues, American Scene painters met and talked and argued and dreamed. Unlike artists concentrated in a single locale, such as New York City, American Scene painters were spread throughout the country. Their communications medium was the exhibition, where they saw one another and could exchange ideas. The idea of the lone artist is both appealing and popular, but, in truth, artists need to exchange ideas with their colleagues in order to thrive.

Singer was beginning to sell paintings, and he was gathering attention. He was invited to send works to the Carnegie International, the Whitney Museum of Art Annual, the Corcoran Biennial, and the National Academy of Design Exhibitions. His first one-man show was held in Canton, followed by a second in Massillion. The list grew and grew, and so did the awards. Beginning in 1935, within eighteen months, Singer participated in eighty-two exhibitions in fifty-six cities—an astonishing performance. When Joseph Butler III, director of the Butler Institute of American Art in Youngstown, offered Singer a job, the painter turned him down in order to concentrate on his art. Life for an American Scene painter was good. But it was not to remain so.

Few American Scene painters saw the collision coming. Their style of art was riding high, widely accepted by the American public, selling briskly, and well received by critics. But a competing art force, European Modernism, was forging to the forefront. The Europeans who were fleeing Hitler and who now arrived on the New York art scene had little use for "quaint" American Scene representations. They not only did not understand the uniquely American culture that produced it, they condemned it as provincial, which it was, and as anti-intellectual, which it was not. These European exiles soon began to gather around them a cadre of young American artists. Together, they denigrated the public art, the murals and posters and paintings in public buildings, as fascist, and they compared it unfavorably with the public art of the Nazis. American Scene was still riding high, but a prescient artist could see the coming conflict. When, in 1939, Butler offered the job a second time, Singer accepted.

The years from 1939 to 1945 were busy ones. When Youngstown College, now Youngstown State University, offered a teaching position, Singer accepted. And when the *Youngstown Vindicator* asked him to write a weekly column, Singer agreed and continued in the position for more than half a century. In November 1941, he married Bernice Shimp, a former student. He was not selected in the peacetime draft and appeared, perhaps, to be too old for military service. The massive mobilization of World War II, however, required many men, even thirty-four-year-old artists. In June 1942, Singer was drafted, and he served in the Pacific until discharged in October 1945 at which time he returned to Youngstown and his duties at the Butler, the college, and the *Vindicator.*

In stark contrast to the period following the end of World War I, the United States did not withdraw from the rest of the world and become isolationist, far from it. The nation quickly was involved in the new United Nations, with the Marshall Plan for rebuilding Europe, and with the occupation of Japan. The Soviet Union, a wartime ally, was now an enemy, and the Cold War and nuclear deterrence became ways of life.

The art war was neither cold nor over. New York was fighting for ascendancy as art capital of the world. With Paris in postwar distress, the Big Apple had an edge. At the same time, the art of the American Scene was under fierce attack by the Abstract Expressionists. In the aftermath of the Holocaust and A-bomb, paintings that told narratives were hard for some to even imagine. Art had to be evocative and universal. The notion of real artists being part of some Midwestern community was absurd; art was done in New York and the rest of America was to be told what was good.

The art critics joined in the fray. Clement Greenberg, born in the Bronx to Russian immigrant parents in 1909, attended the Art Students League before graduating from Syracuse University with a degree in literature and languages. In 1939, he made his name as an art critic with his essay "Avant-Garde and Kitsch." To Greenberg, the art of the young American Expressionists probed how we experience and understand the world, a noble goal and one far more important than pictorial representation. The art of the American Scene, he felt, was storytelling propaganda, which he linked to Nazi art. Art historian H. W. Janson was born in 1913 in Russia but was raised in Germany. Although he was a gentile, he distrusted the Nazi government and immigrated to the United States. He was a champion of modernism and held a number of positions at various universities before becoming chair of the fine arts department at Washington Square College, New York University. He was a talented writer with a gift for communication with a lay audience, and his dislike for American Scene art was exacerbated by a personal run-in with Grant Wood. Janson was an influential teacher, and his views on American art held great weight. To these scholars and to their followers and to the Abstract Expressionists themselves, this new age demanded the heroic, lone artist searching for fundamental truths and universal understandings through abstraction. At the same time, in an odd way, Expressionism was "safer" art that did not criticize or comment because it did not depict. At the Art Students League, Yasuo Kuniyoshi told his students that "you don't have to know how to draw" to be an artist. Jackson Pollock and his drip paintings were now the cutting edge, with Pollock even appearing on the cover of *Time.*

American Scene painters had few choices. They were under fierce attack on multiple fronts. They were told that their art, which was certainly American and often extolled American virtues, was linked to the art of Nazi Germany and the Soviet Union and was unpatriotic. Their critics claimed that their work was trivial, even quaint—it lacked intellect and introspection. And it appeared that the modernists were going to win. What to do? Some, such as Burchfield and Hopper, could and did successfully make the transition to the new paradigm. Others, like Clarence Carter, made the attempt but fell short of their prewar achievements. Some, like Singer, continued to carry the banner of the American Scene. But they were no longer part of the great national "conversation" of artists—they no longer found their way into the major shows and were no longer the topic of reviews. They continued to sell paintings, but mostly in local or regional markets. They had become outcasts in the international art scene and were isolated in their own country.

Singer continued to paint in his accustomed manner and to lead his accustomed lifestyle. He returned to New York annually and visited the old haunts and walked the same streets. McSorley's was a must, and he painted the place and its patrons many, many times. These trips provided rejuvenation, a touchstone to the past that stimulated his painting when he returned to Ohio. And paint he did. By some estimates, he completed more than three thousand paintings, a prodigious output. And while he experimented with some modernist influences, until the day he died at age ninety, he steadfastly remained an American Scene painter—the heir of Henri, Bellows, Sloan, and Curry. "The things I've done," he said when accepting an Ohioana Library Association award, "are little bits of history, something I've seen, felt, experienced very deeply. Autobiographical. I've never contributed to the Modern movement. Somehow I got embedded in the 1930s, painting the native scene."

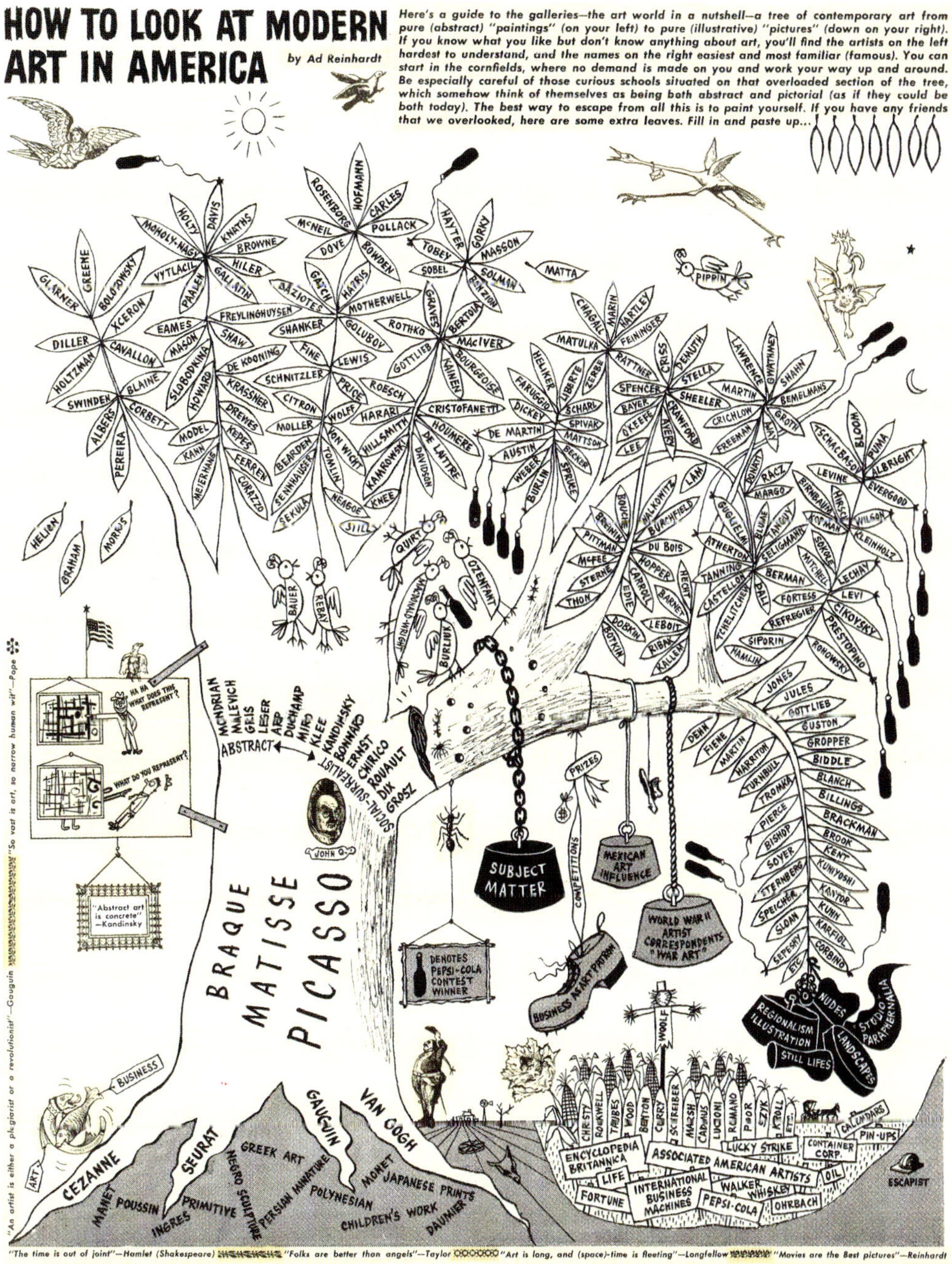

"How to Look at Modern Art in America," by Ad Reinhardt.

The Beginnings—Class Time

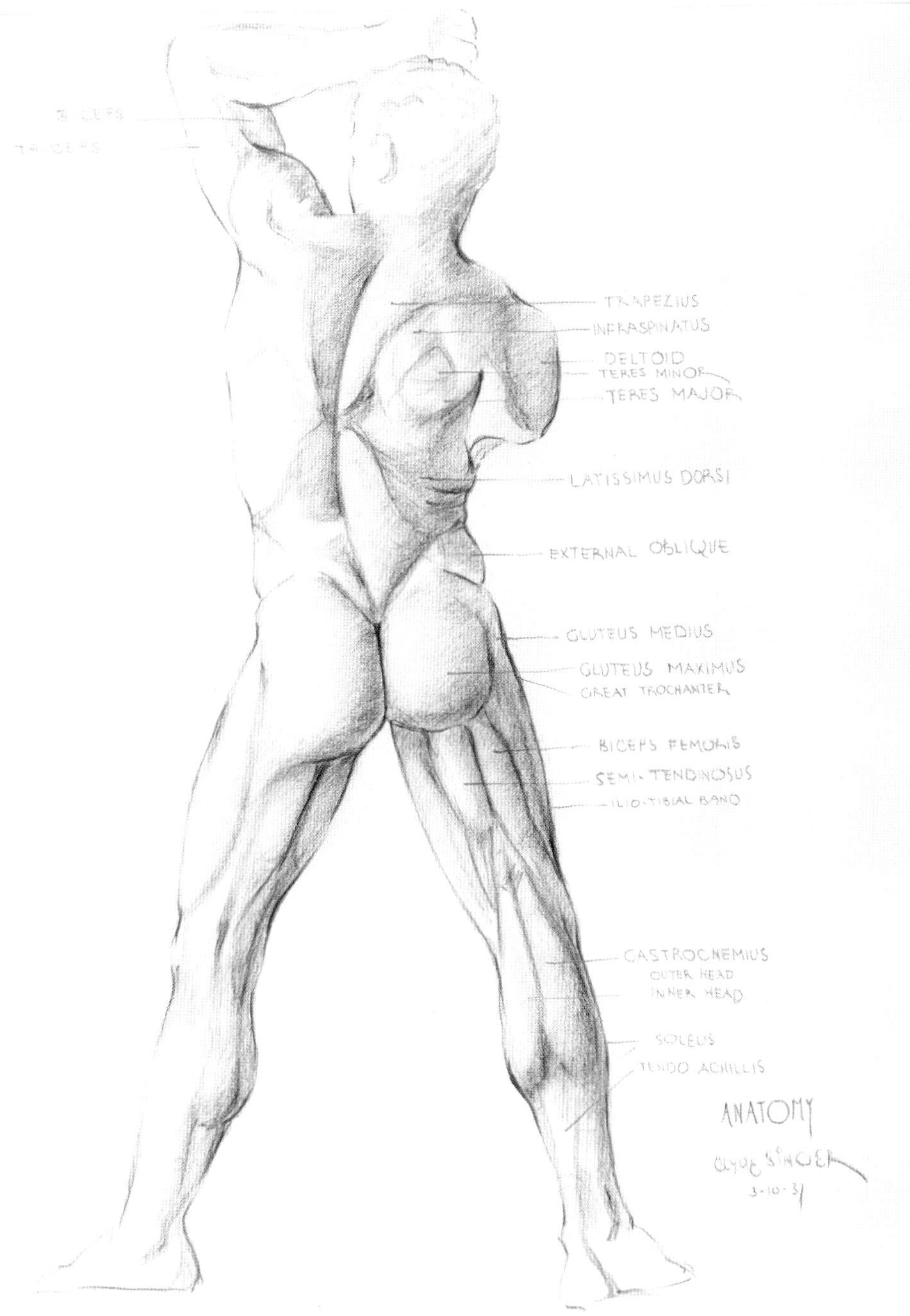

Fig. 1. *Anatomy,* 1931. Graphite, 23 x 17. Courtesy of Lazar's Art Gallery & Creative Framing

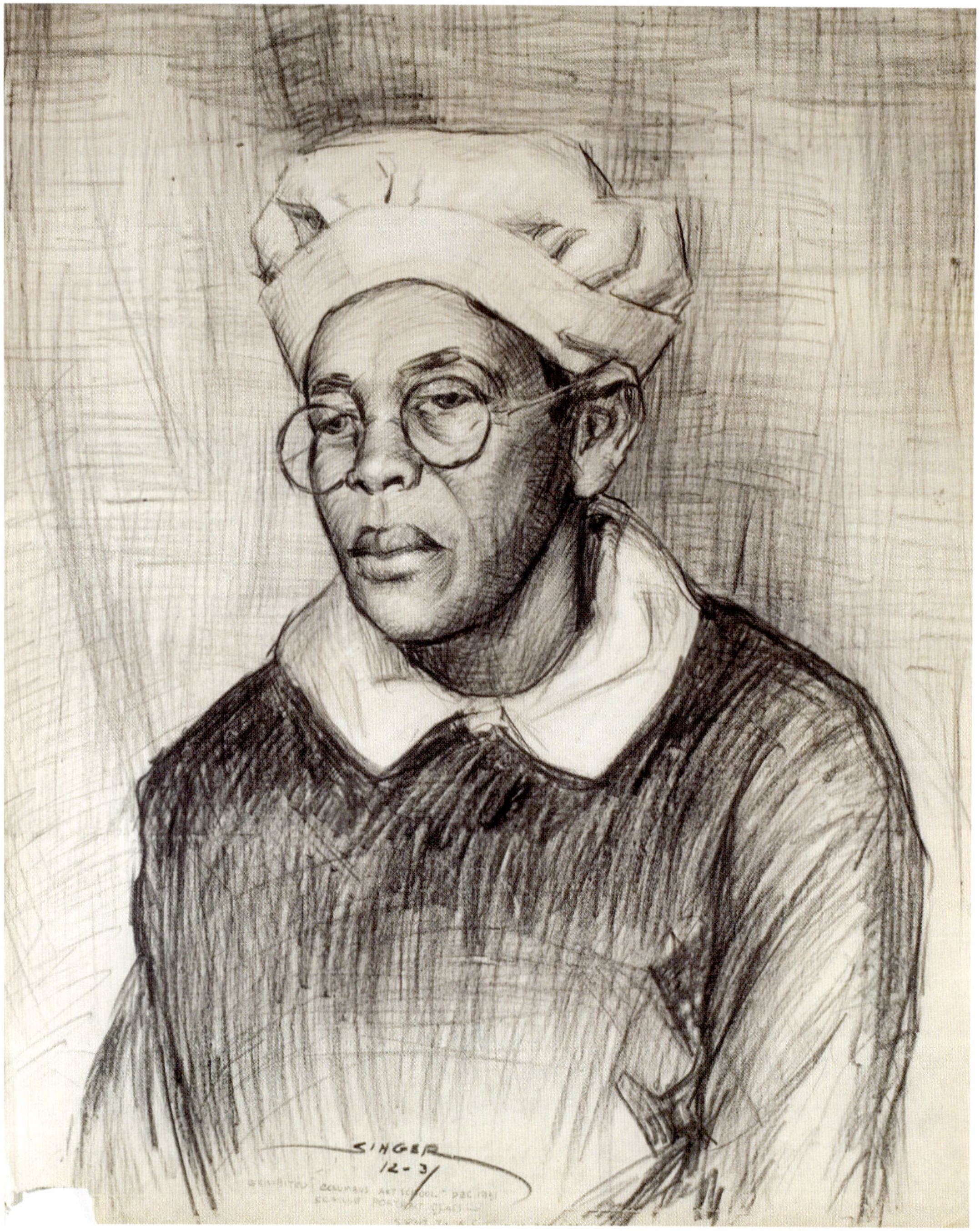

Fig. 2. *Columbus Art School,* 1931. Alice Schille Portrait class. Charcoal, 24 x 18. Courtesy of Robert and Lesa Schnabel

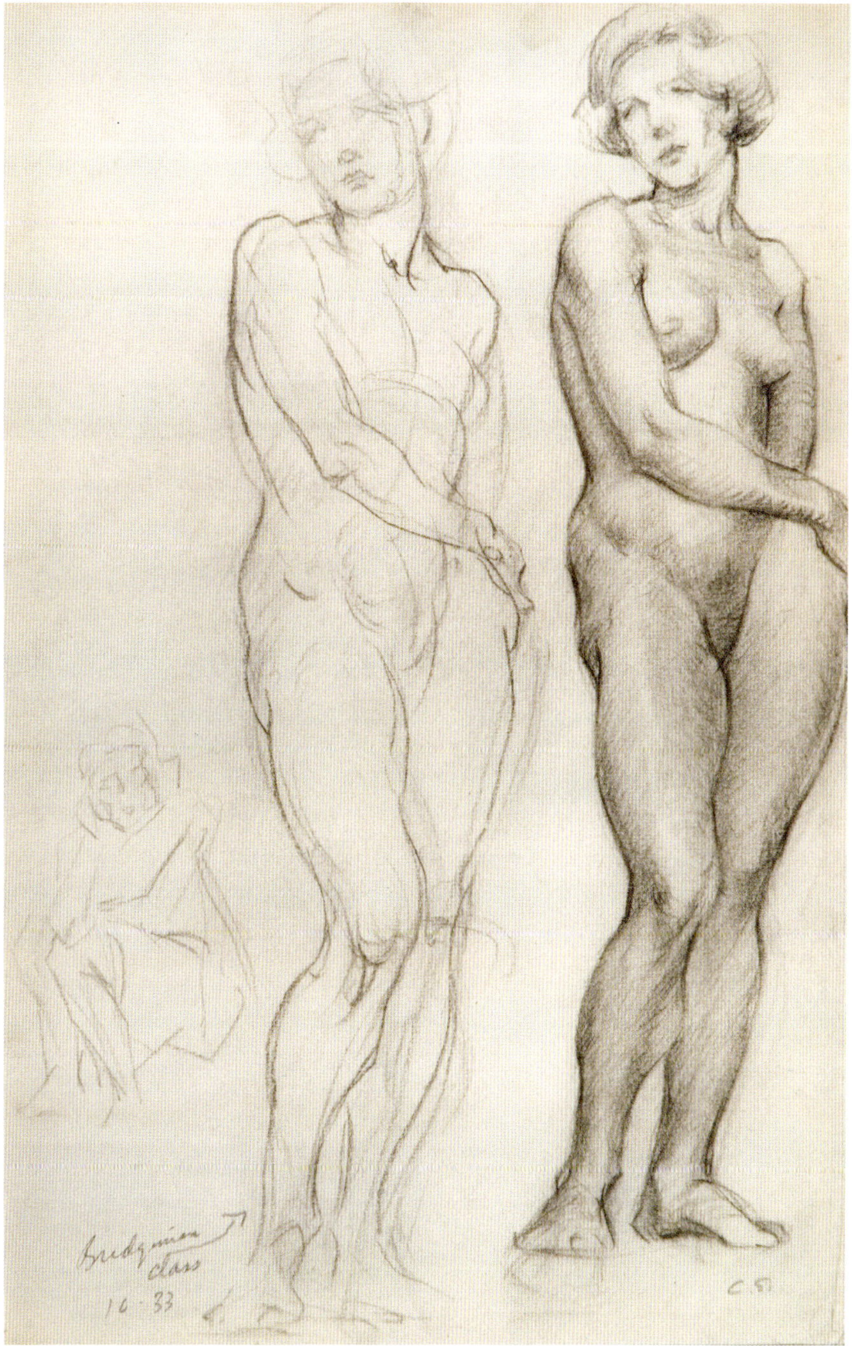

Fig. 3. *George Brandt Bridgeman Class,* 1933. Graphite, 18½ x 12. Courtesy of Lazar's Art Gallery & Creative Framing

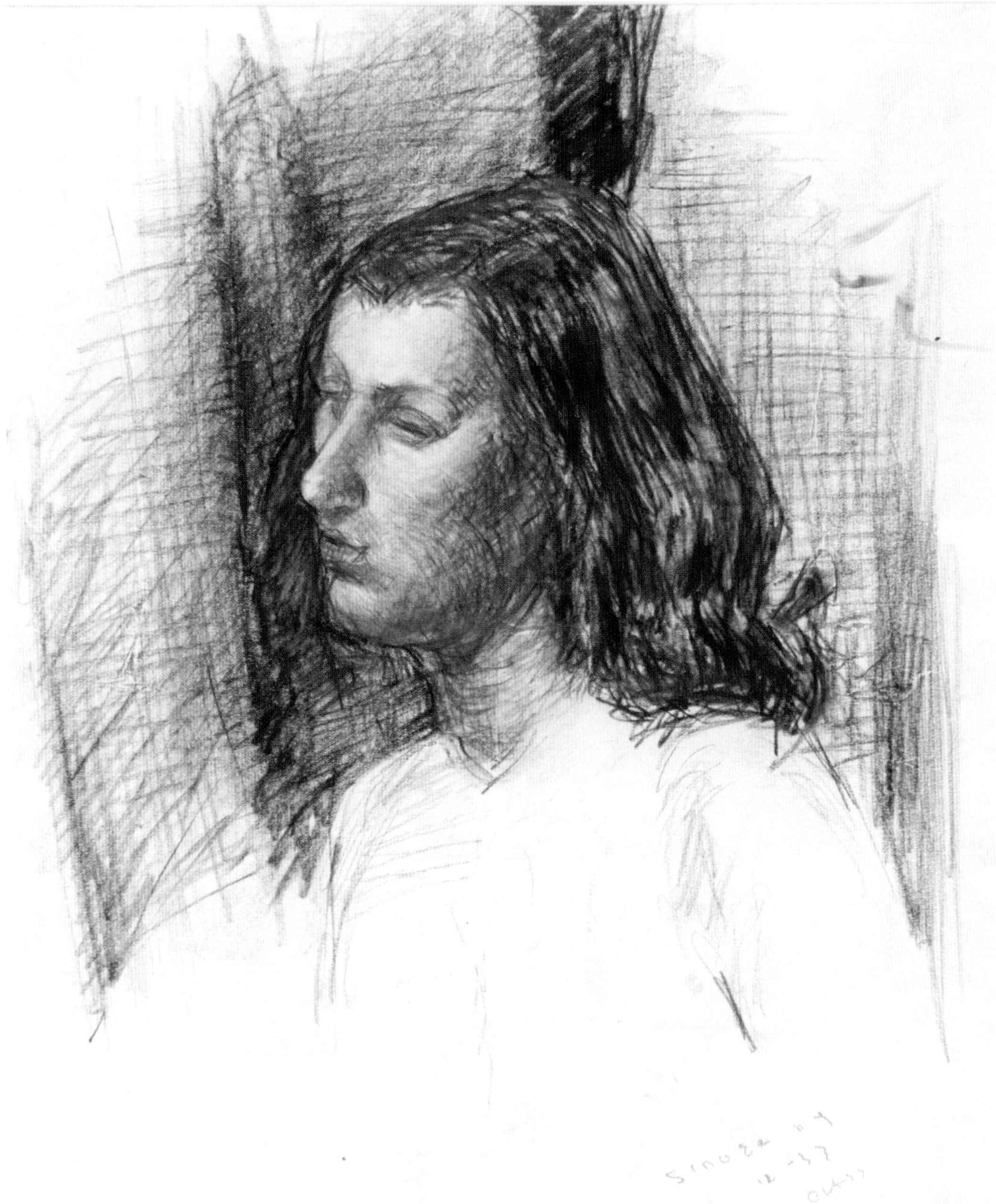

Fig. 4. *Alexander Brook Class,* 1933. Graphite/charcoal, 13 x 10½. Courtesy of Lazar's Art Gallery & Creative Framing

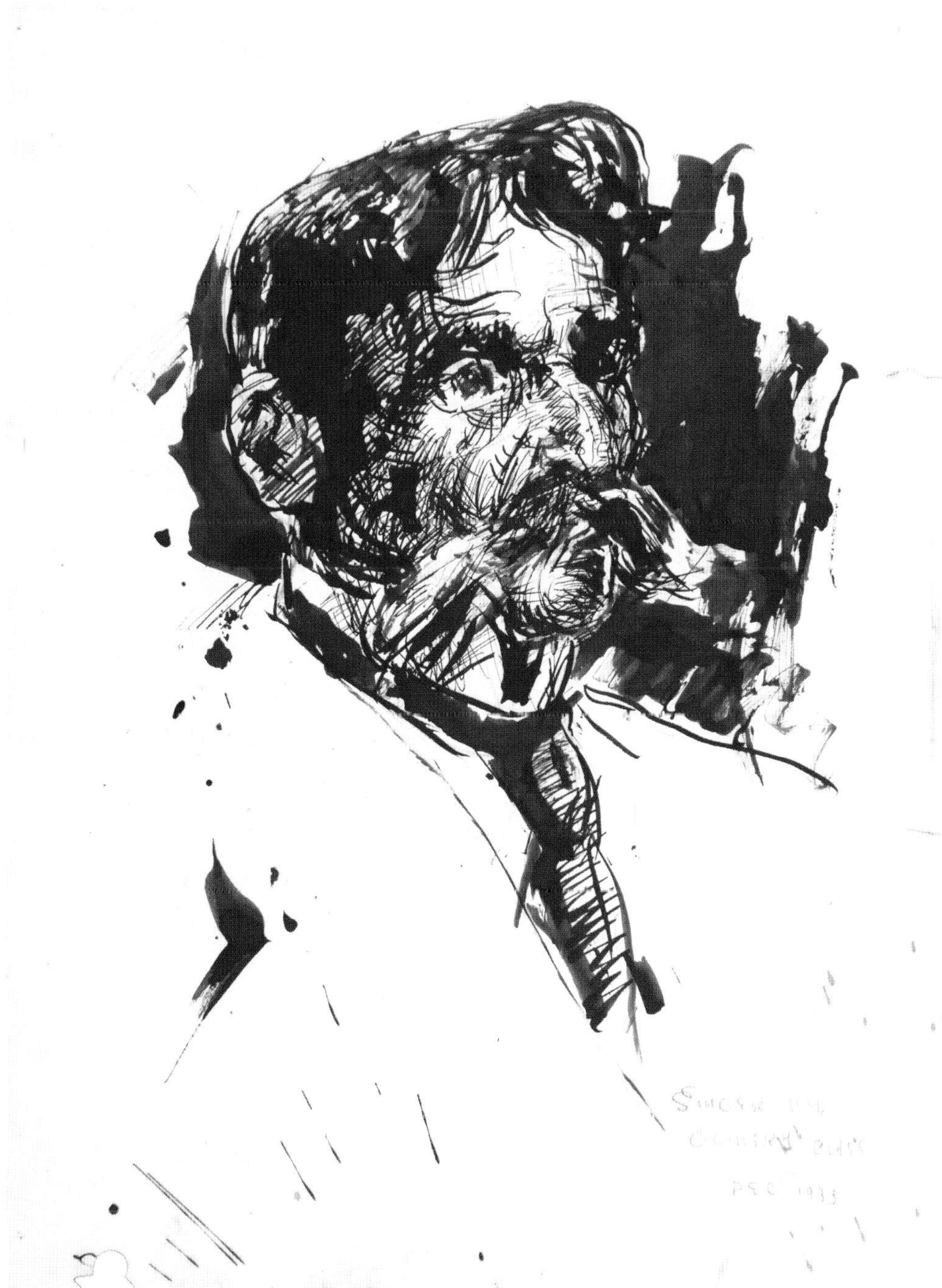

Fig. 5. *Ivan Gregorewitch Olinsky Class,* 1933. Ink, 14 x 10½. Courtesy of Lazar's Art Gallery & Creative Framing

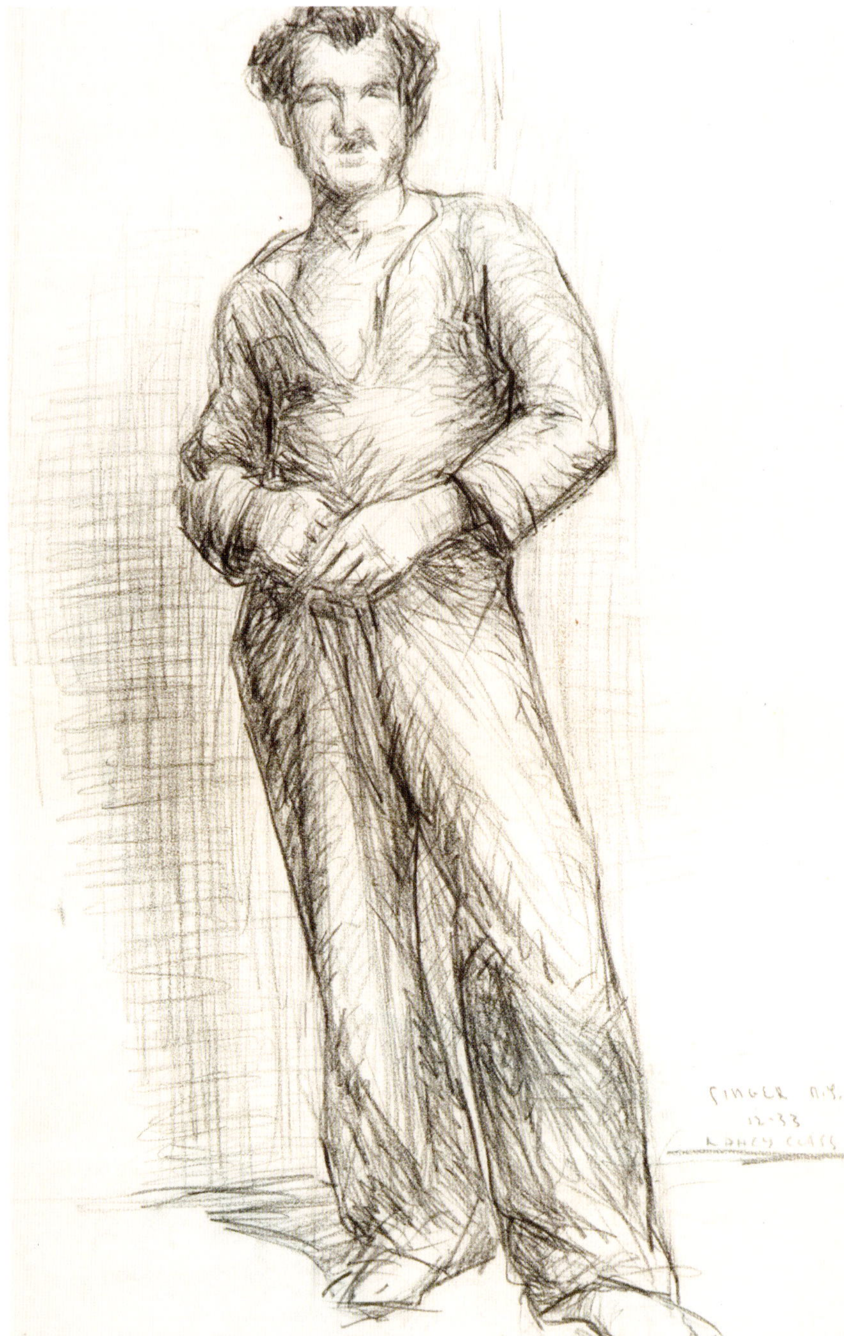

Fig 6. *Richard Lahey Class,* 1933. Charcoal, 18¼ x 12. Courtesy of Lazar's Art Gallery & Creative Framing

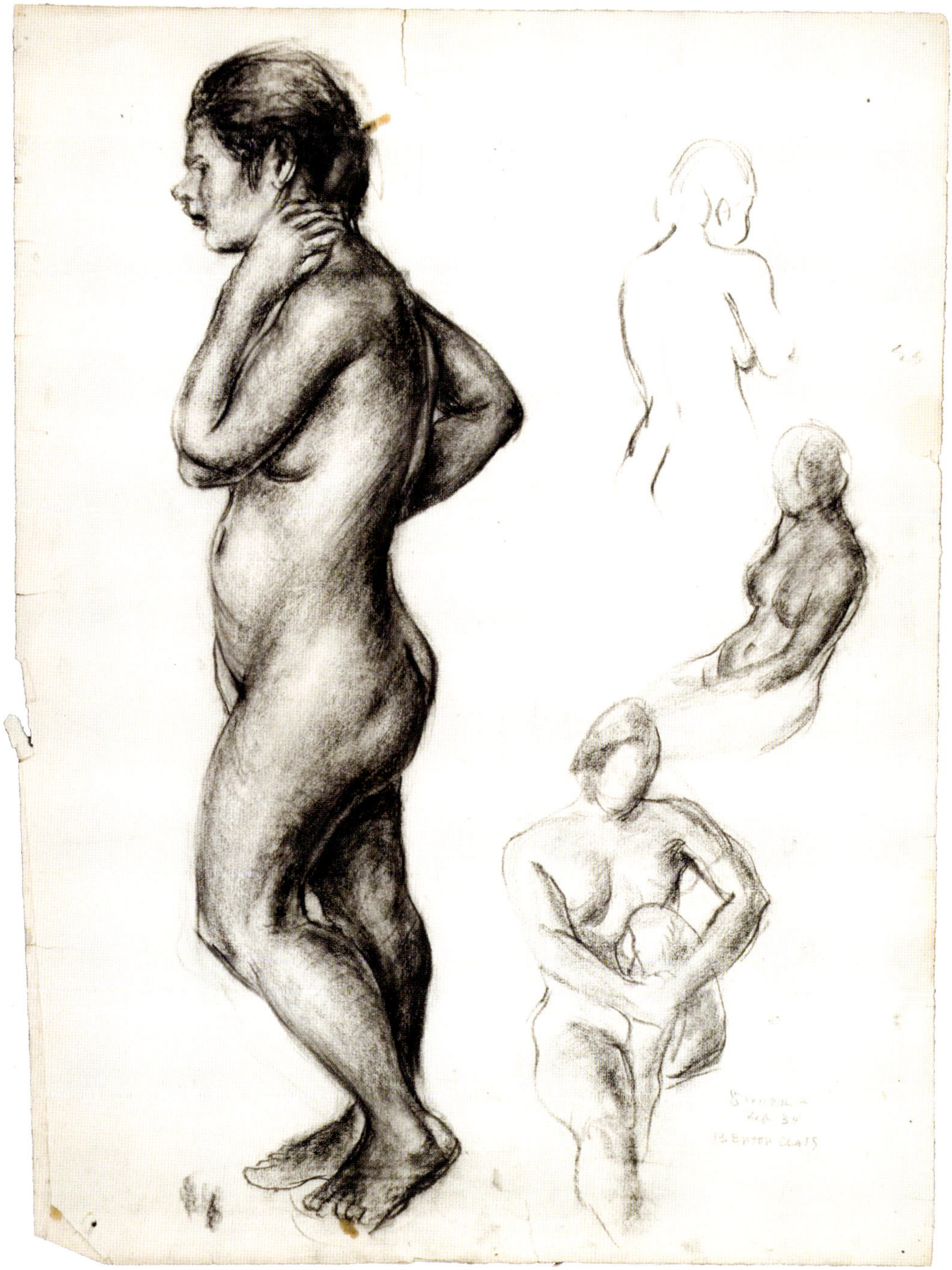

Fig. 7. *Thomas Hart Benton Class,* 1934. Graphite/charcoal, 25 x 19. Courtesy of Lazar's Art Gallery & Creative Framing

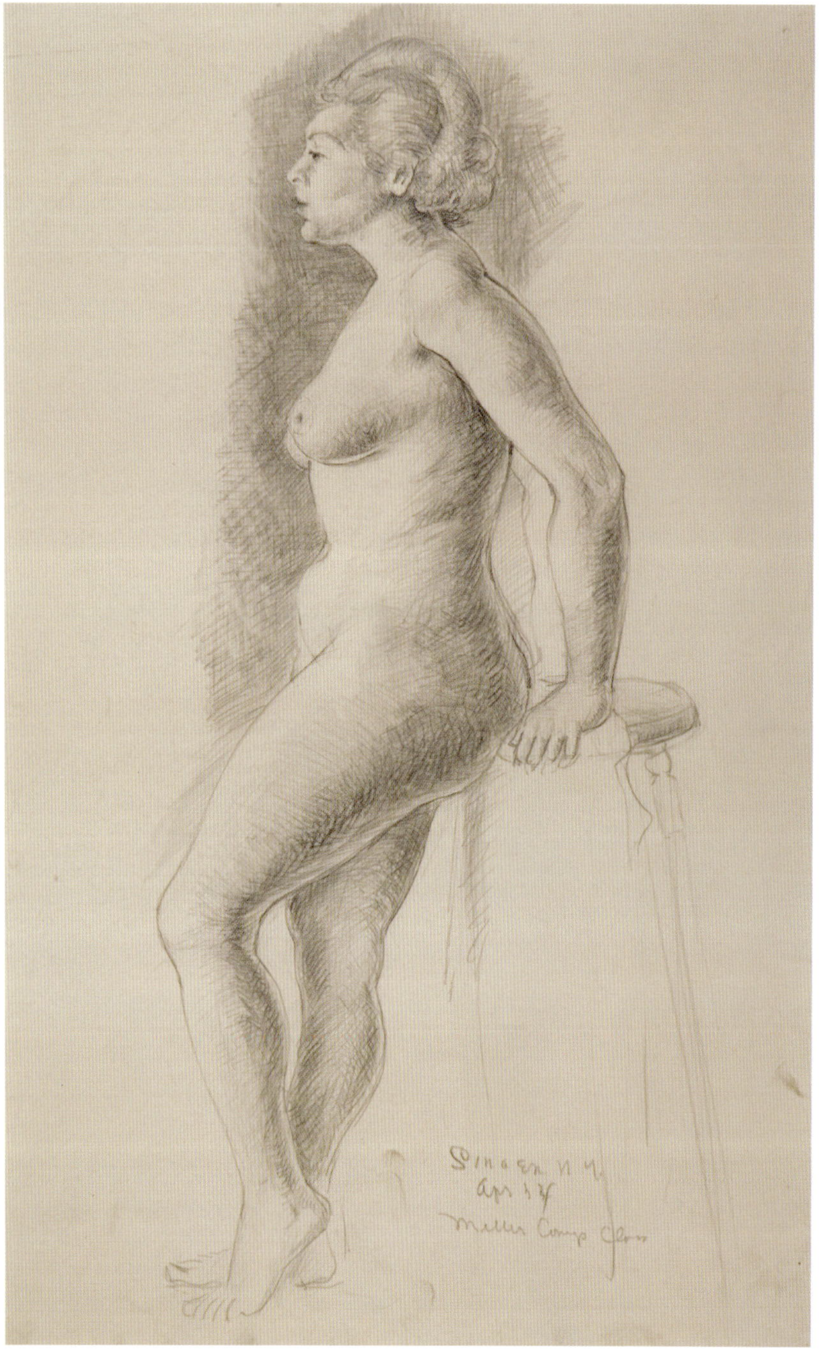

Fig. 8. *Kenneth Hayes Miller Class,* 1934. Graphite, 18½ x 11½. Courtesy of Lazar's Art Gallery & Creative Framing

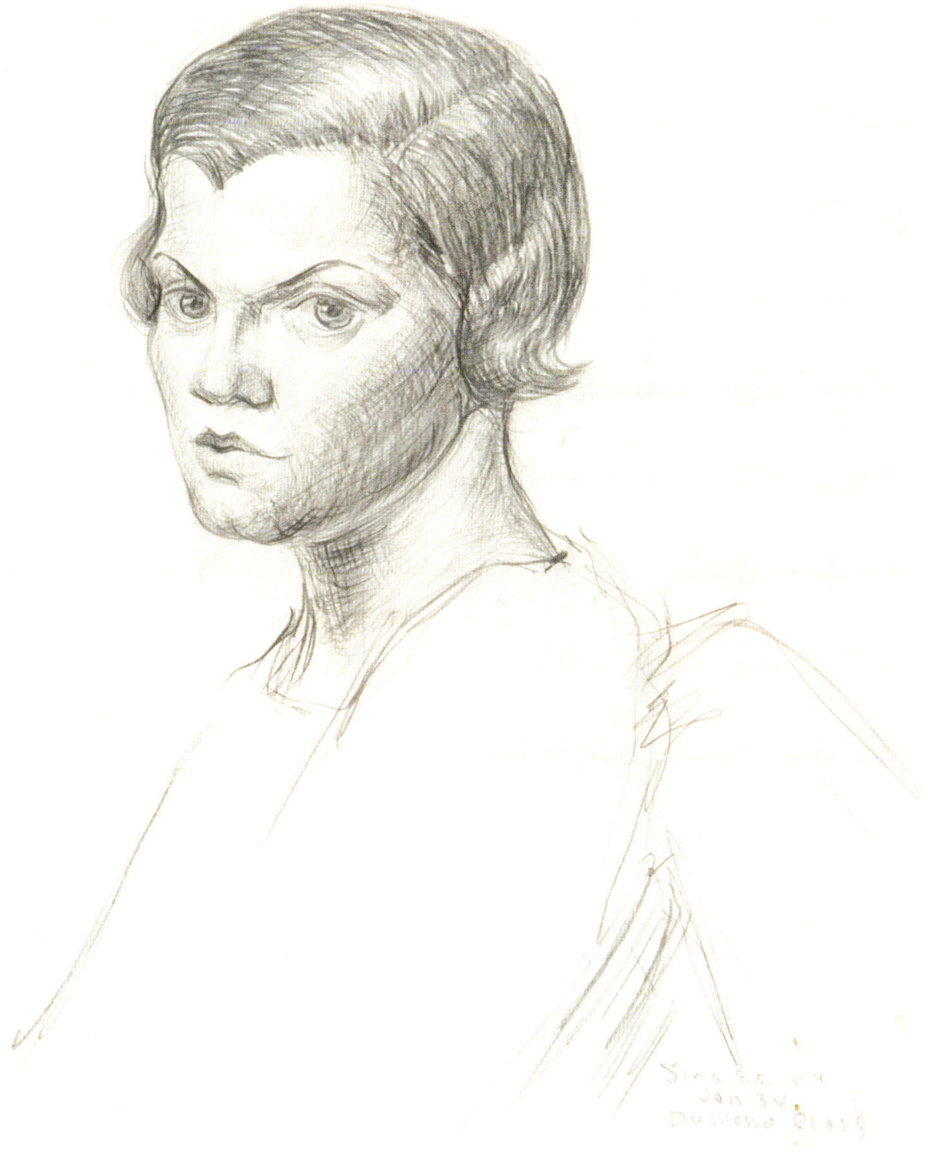

Fig. 9. *Frank Vincent DuMond Class,* 1934. Graphite, 13½ x 11. Courtesy of Lazar's Art Gallery & Creative Framing

Hometown and Down the Road a Piece

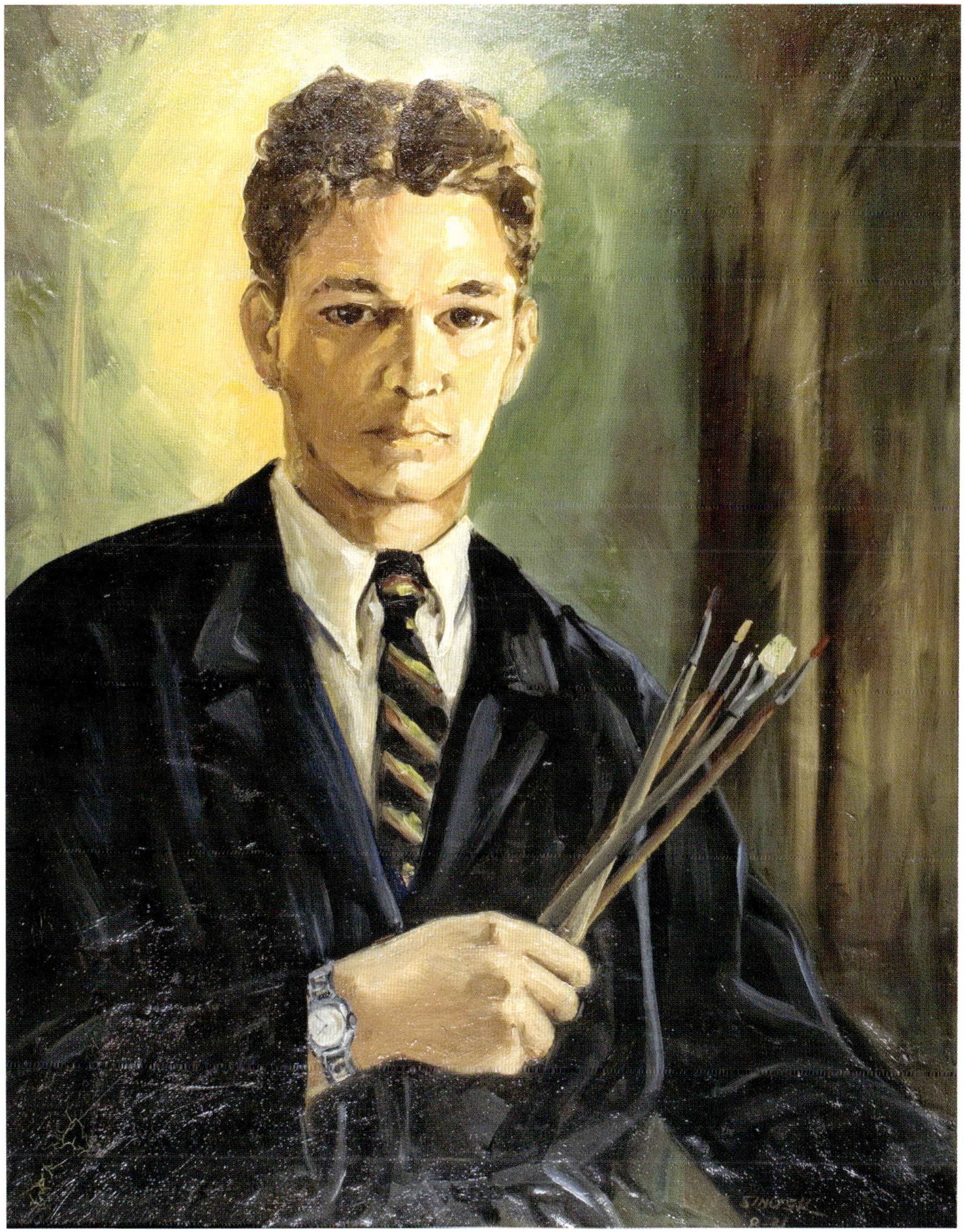

Fig. 10. *Self-Portrait,* 8/1931. Oil, 22¾ x 28¾. Courtesy of a private collector

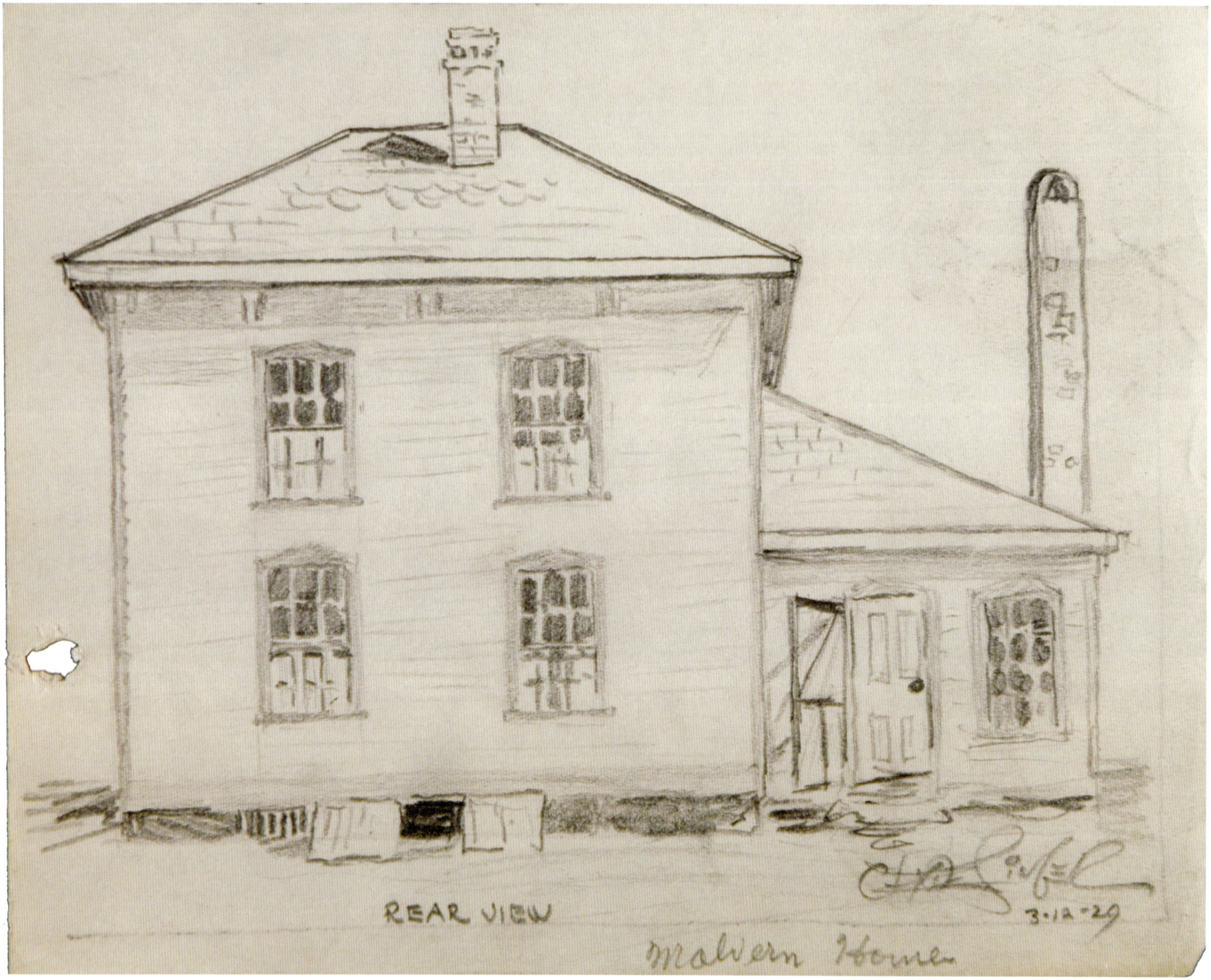

Fig. 11. *Drawing for Malvern Home, Rear View,* 1929. Graphite, 5½ x 7. Courtesy of Lazar's Art Gallery & Creative Framing

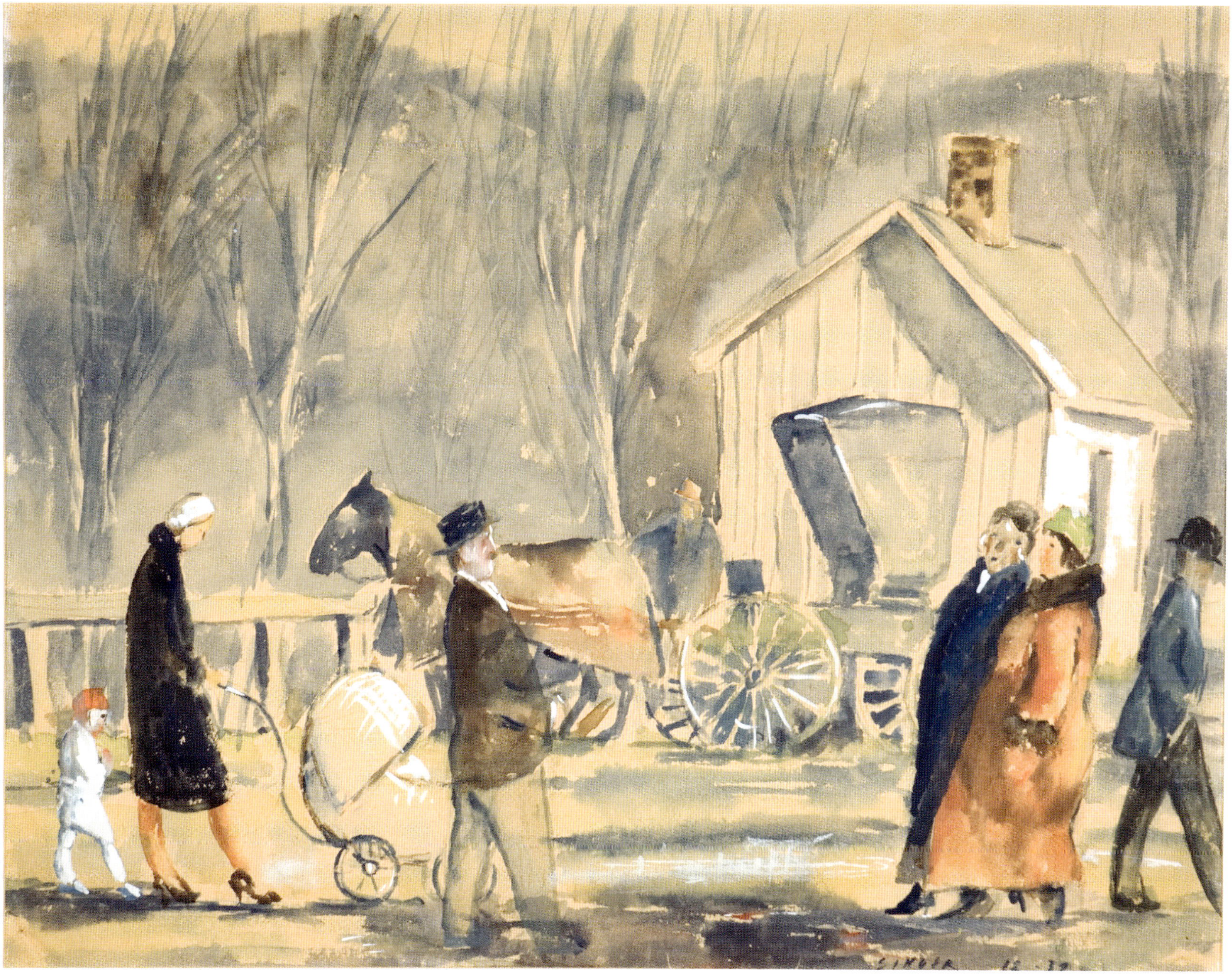

Fig. 12. *Village St. (Old Jail),* 1931. Gouache/Watercolor, 18 x 20. Courtesy of Evan and Suzanne Morris

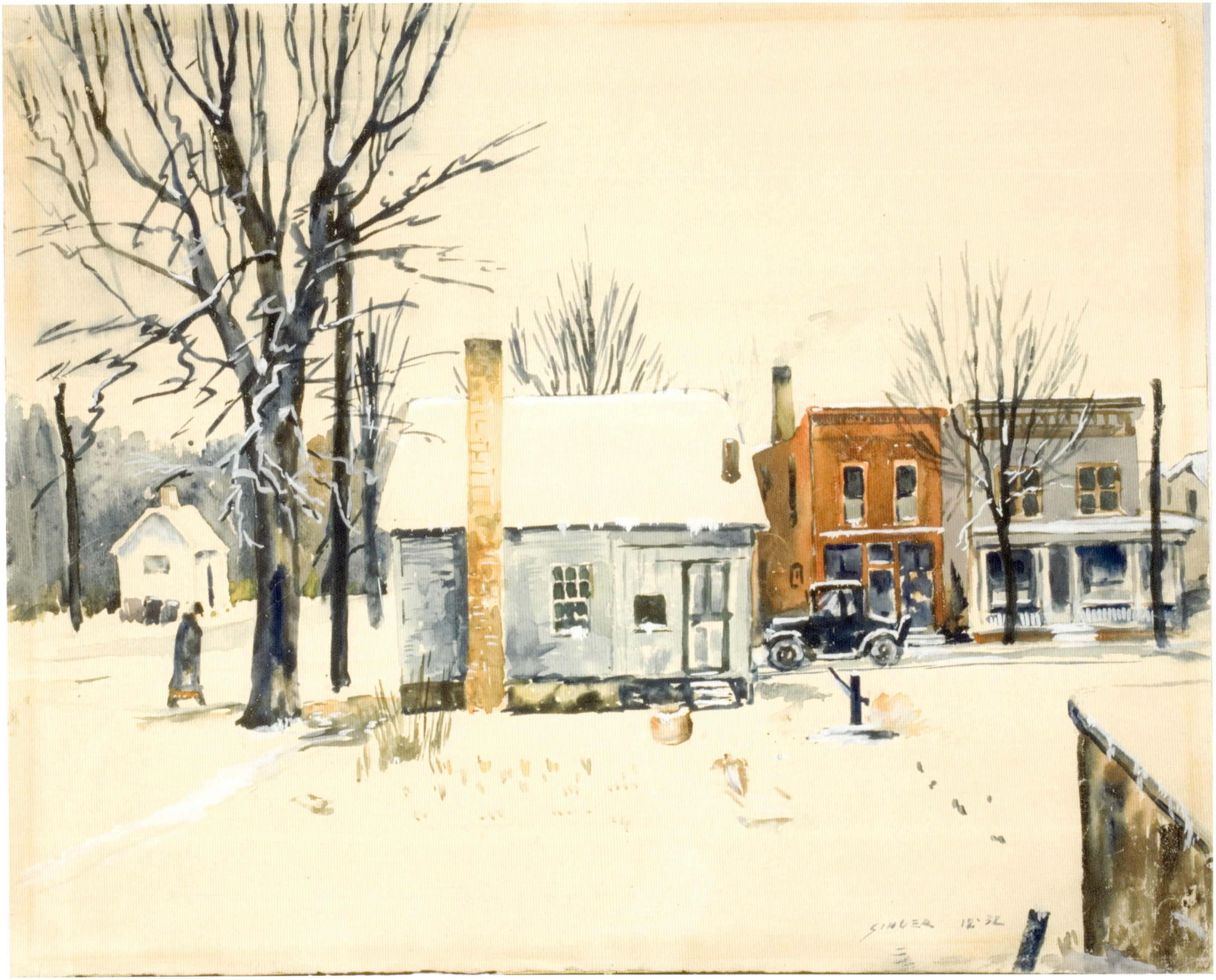

Fig. 13. *Winter, Malvern, Ohio,* 1932. Watercolor, 14 x 18. Courtesy of the Massillon Museum

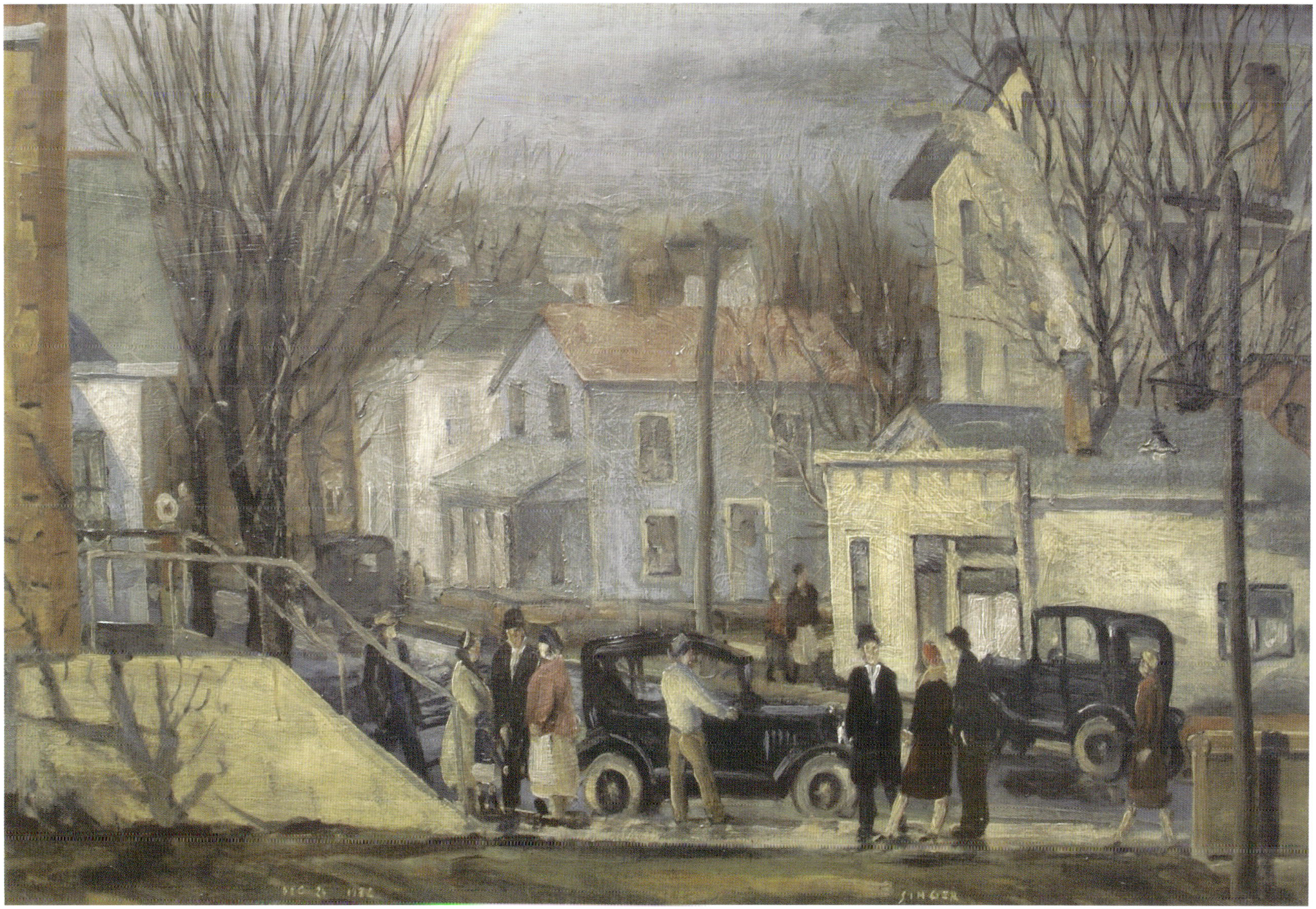

Fig. 14. *Christmas Rainbow,* 1932. Oil, 59 x 41. Courtesy of the Malvern Branch of the Carroll County Library

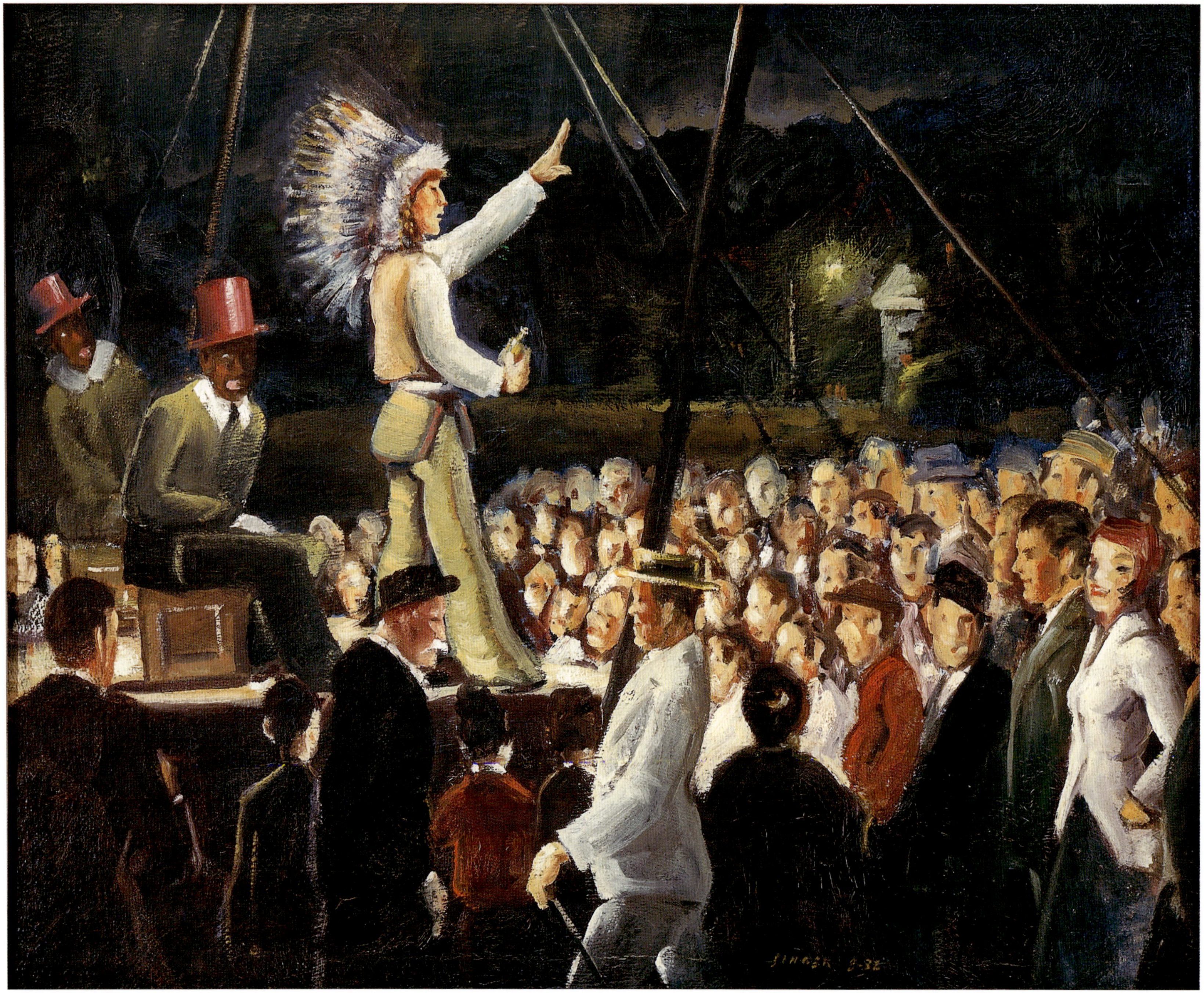

Fig. 15. *The Medicine Man,* 1932. Oil, 34 x 27 (Minerva). Courtesy of the Flint Institute of Arts, the Isabel Foundation

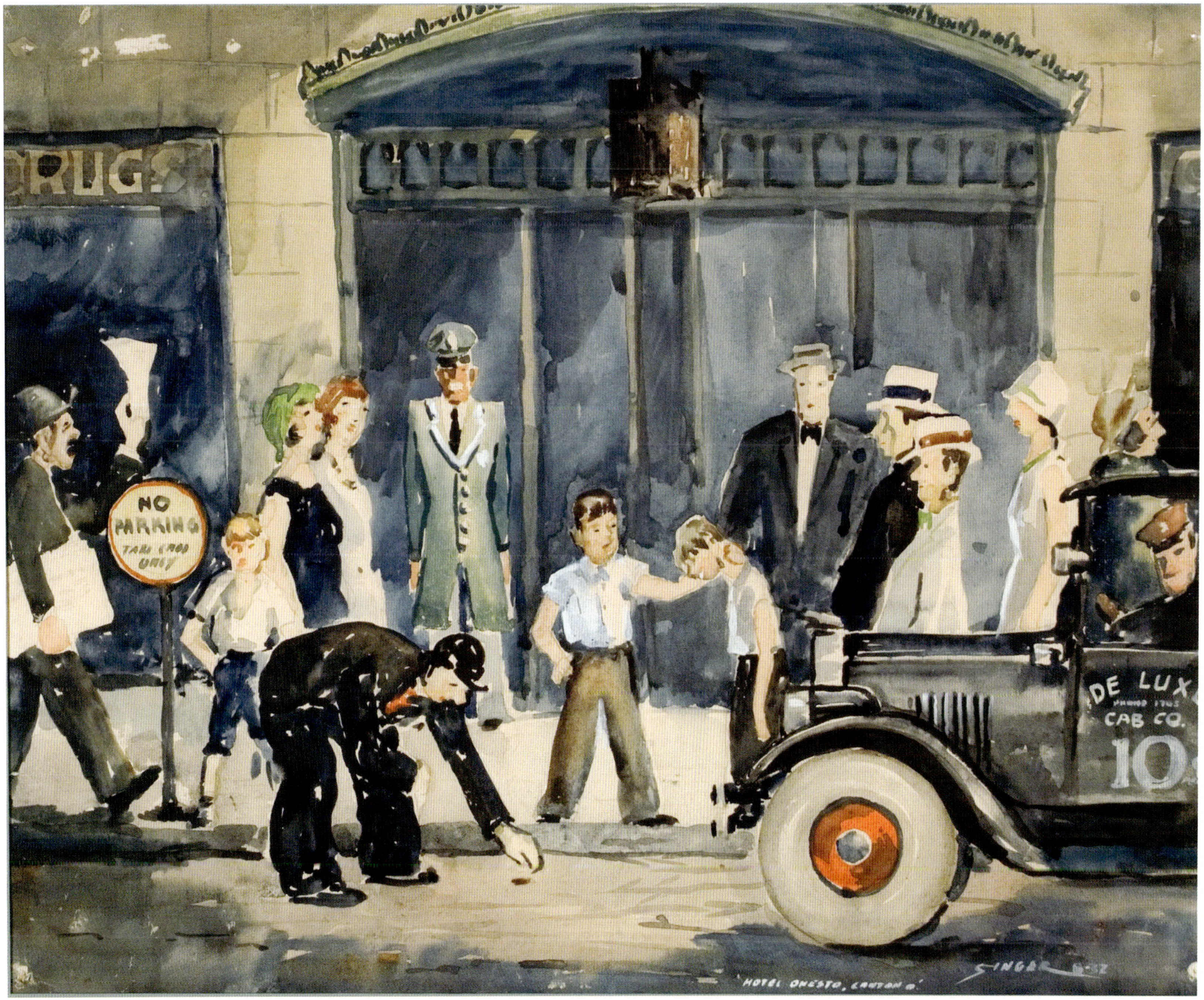

Fig. 16. *Hotel Onesto,* 1932. Watercolor, 20 x 16 (Scholarship Competition). Courtesy of Regina and Byron Bertram

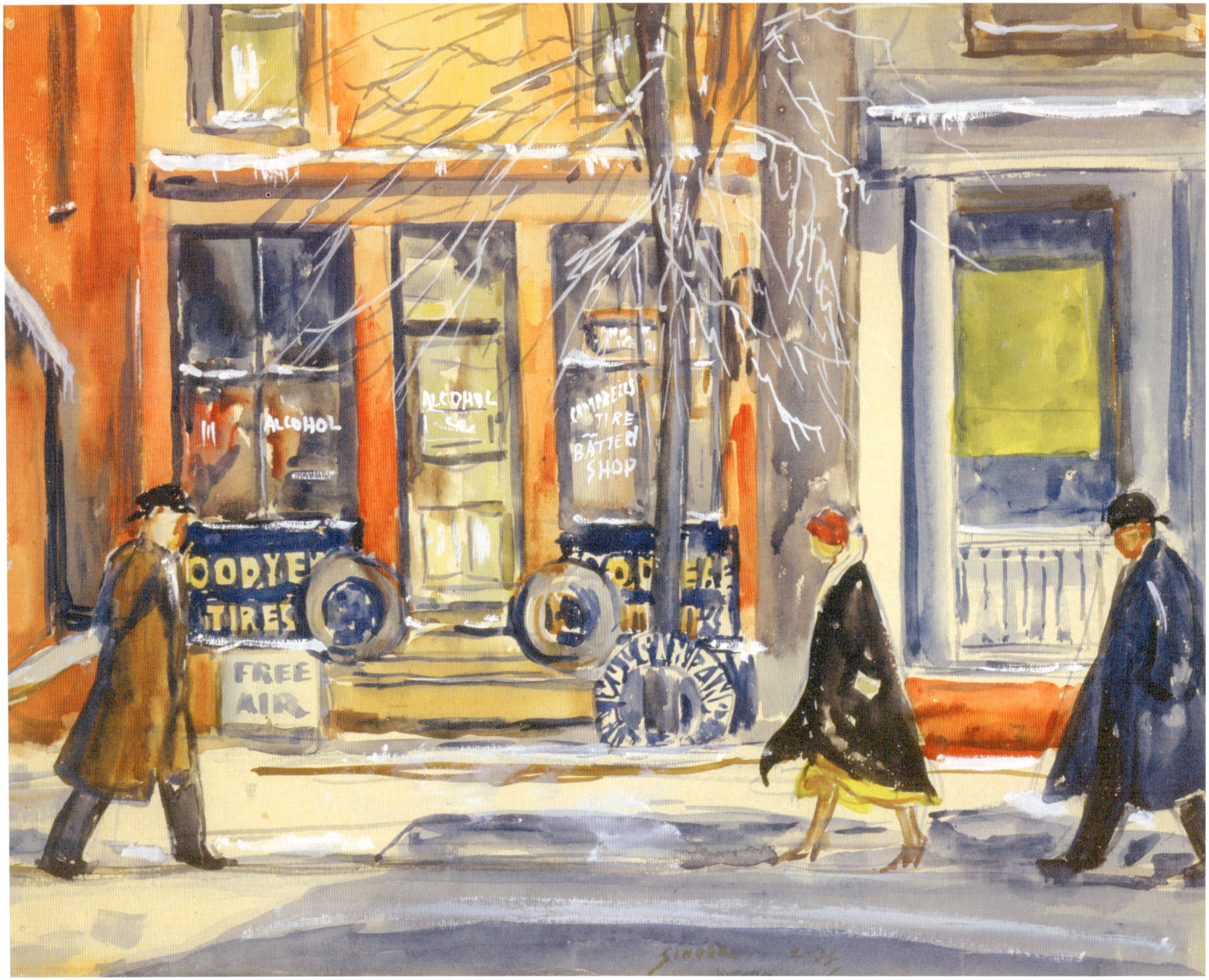

Fig. 17. *The Battery Shop* (*The Tire Shop, Winter Sun*), 1933. Watercolor, 19 x 15. Canton Museum of Art, gift of Dr. Pauline Zinninger

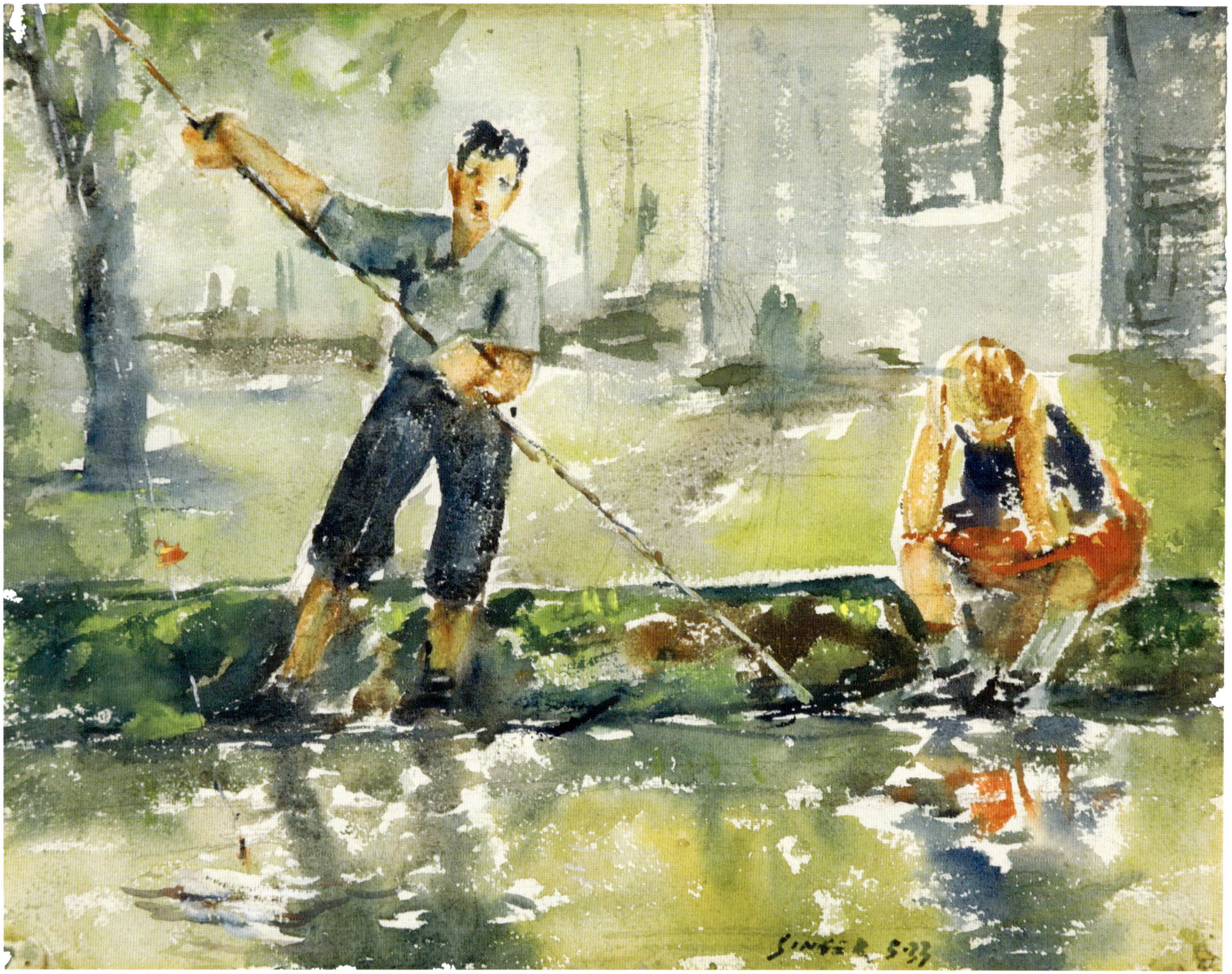

Fig. 18. *Creek and Two Kids,* 1933. Watercolor, 10 x 8. Courtesy of a private collector

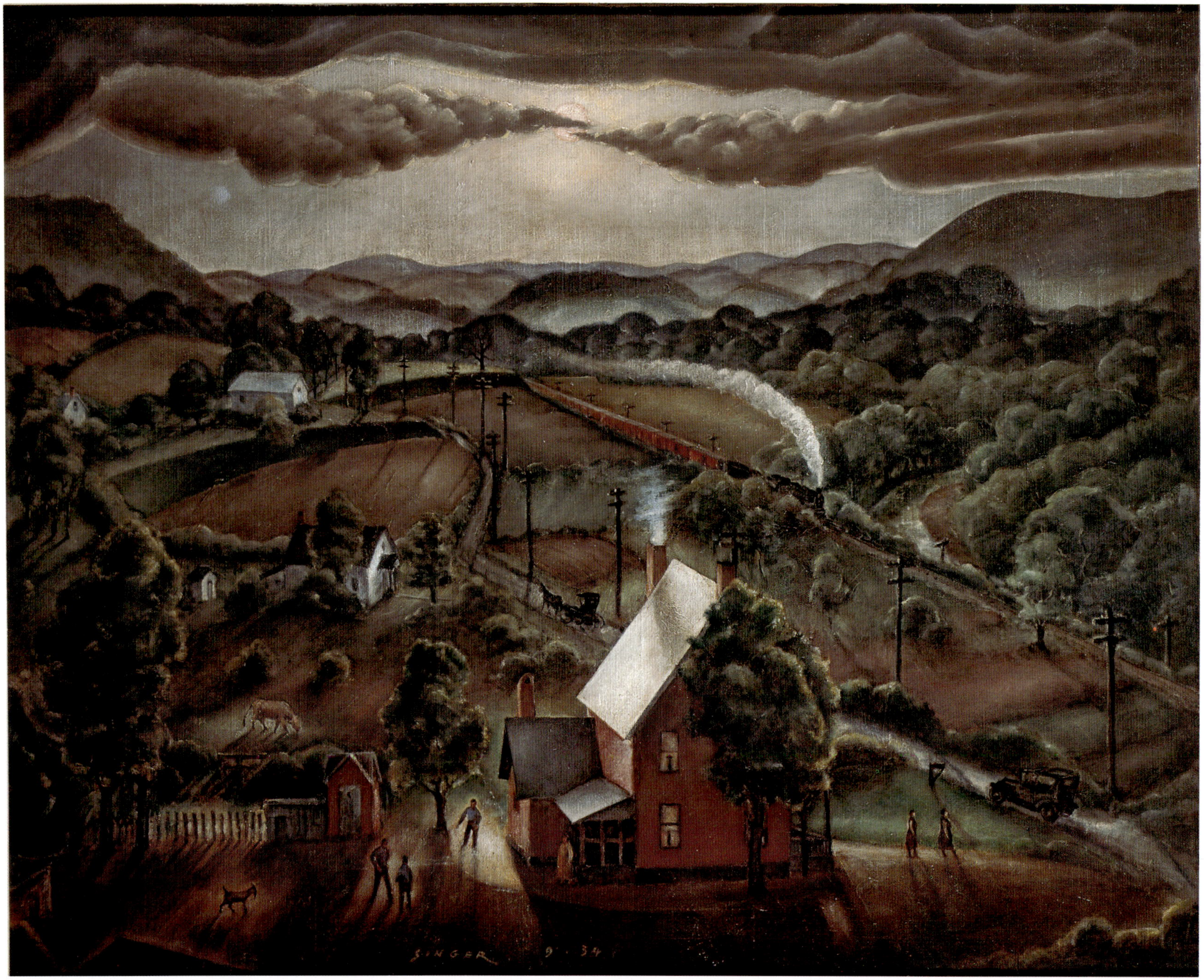

Fig. 19. *Sandy Valley,* 1934. Oil, 38 x 48. Courtesy of Ed and Karen Ogul, Franklin, Michigan

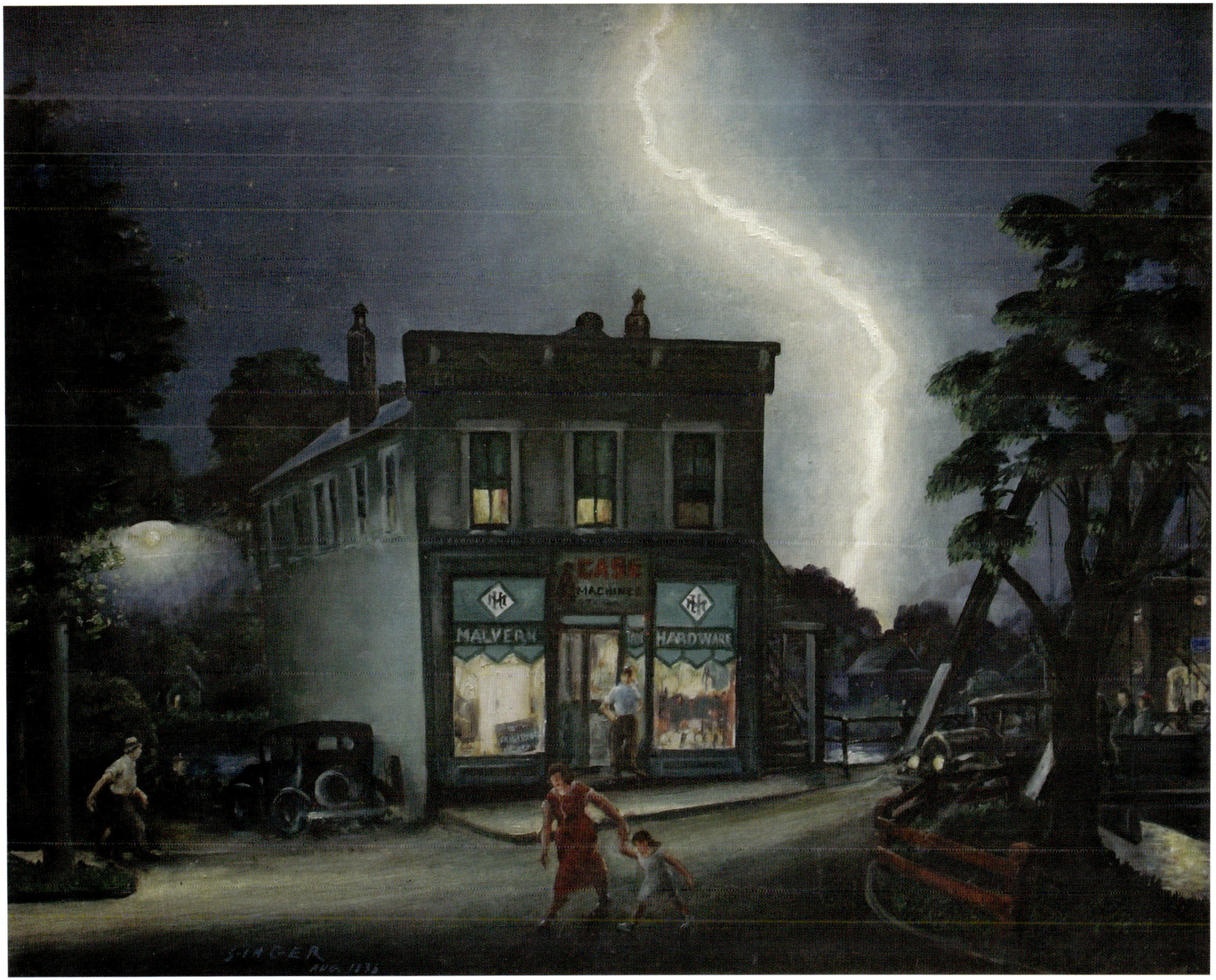

Fig. 20. *Malvern Hardware,* 1935. Oil, 40 x 60. Courtesy of Mr. and Mrs. James M. Conley

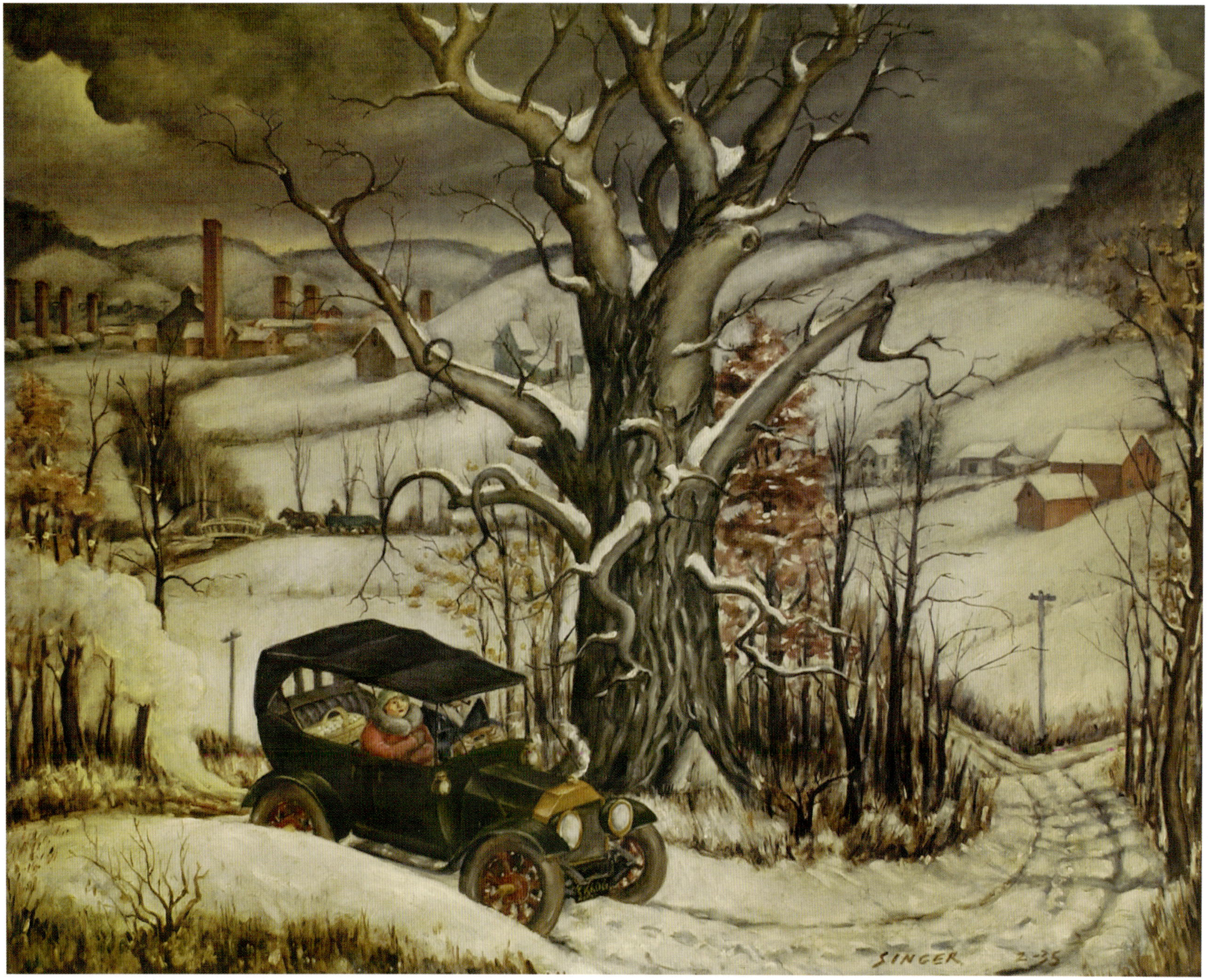

Fig. 21. *Coming 'Round the Bend,* 1935. Oil, 39½ x 49½. Courtesy of the Massillon Museum

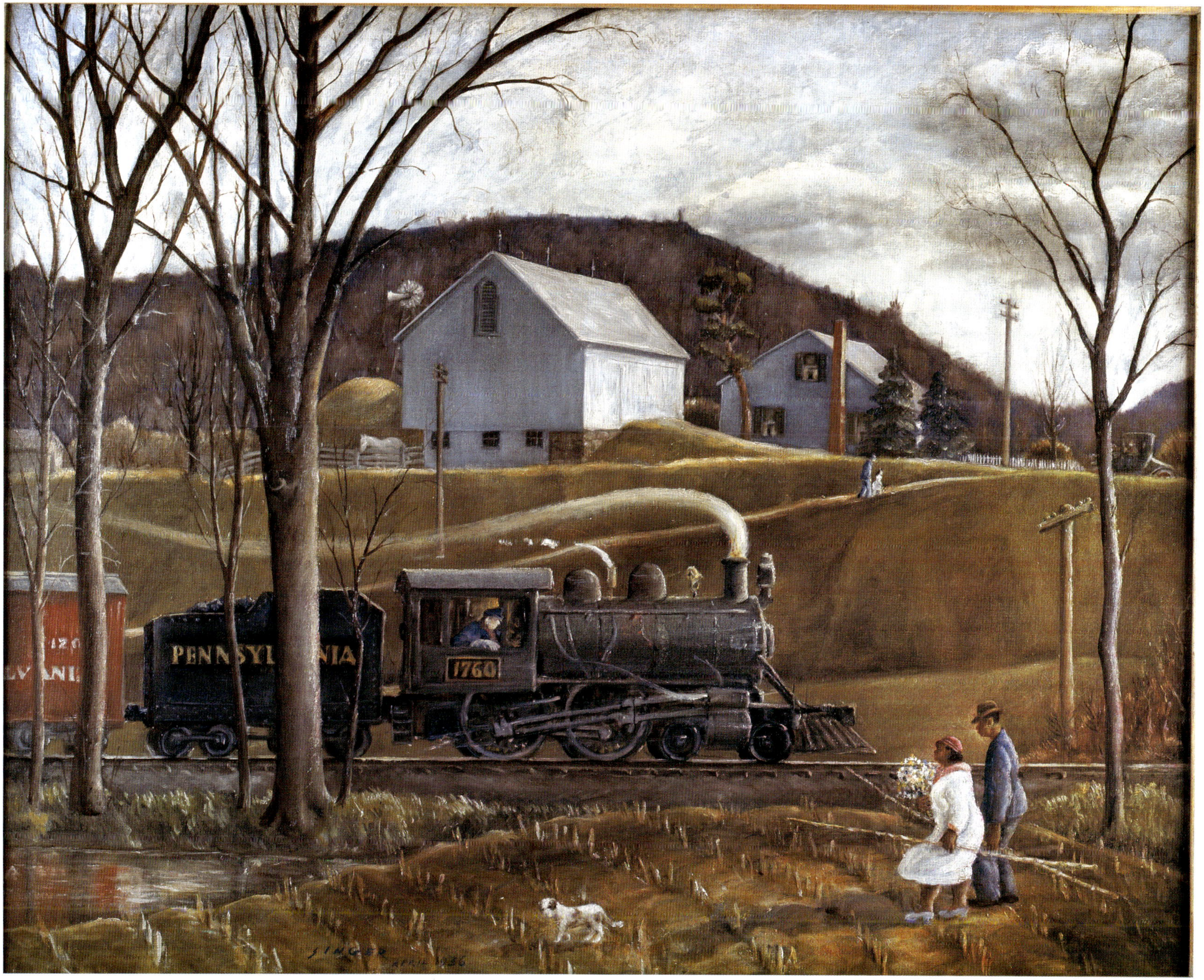

Fig. 22. *Springtime in the Valley,* 1936. Oil, 32 x 40. Courtesy of the Marty and Susan O'Brien Collection of American Art, Sewickley, Pennsylvania

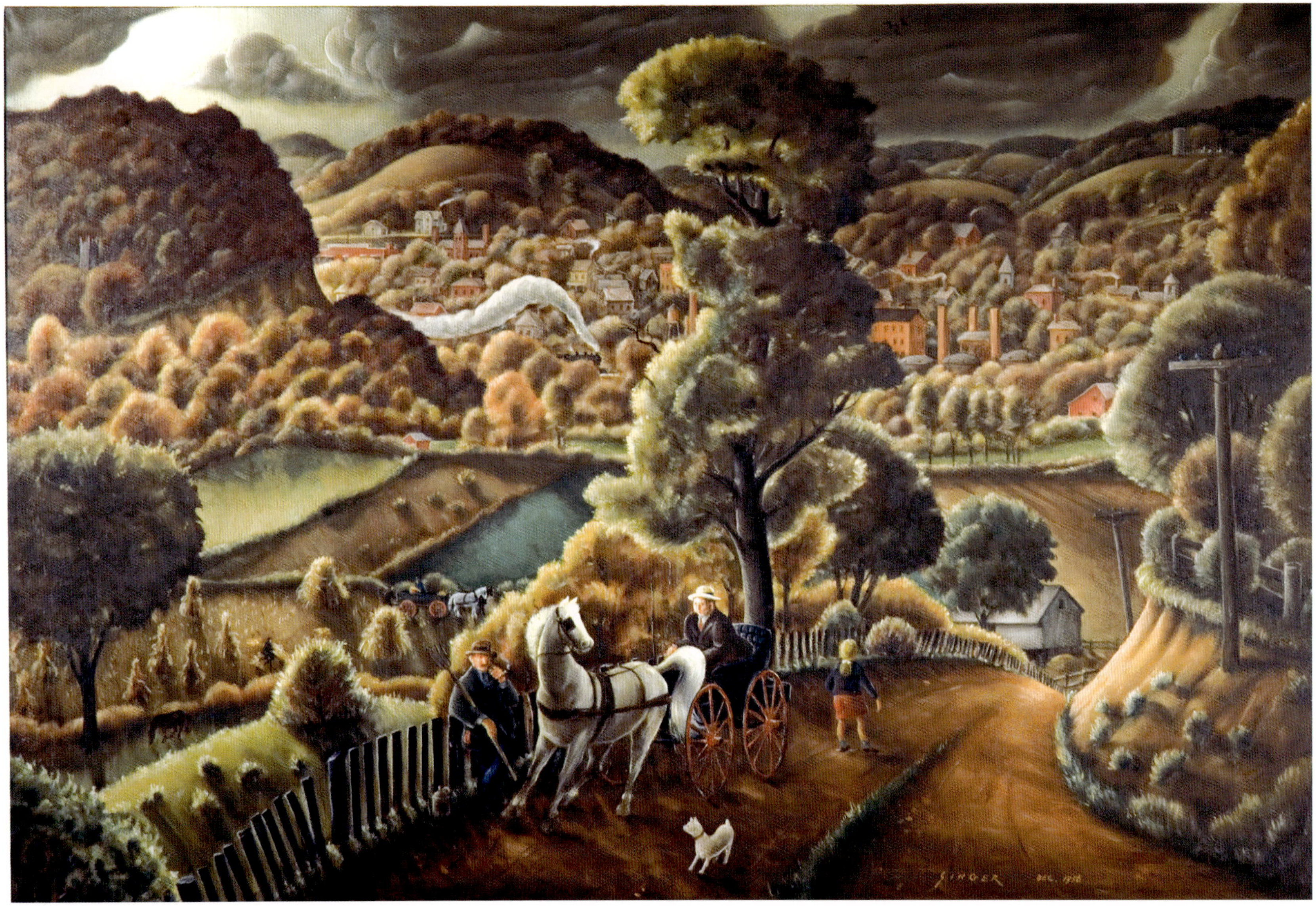

Fig. 23. *Approach to the Village,* 1936. Oil, 40 x 60. Courtesy of a private collector

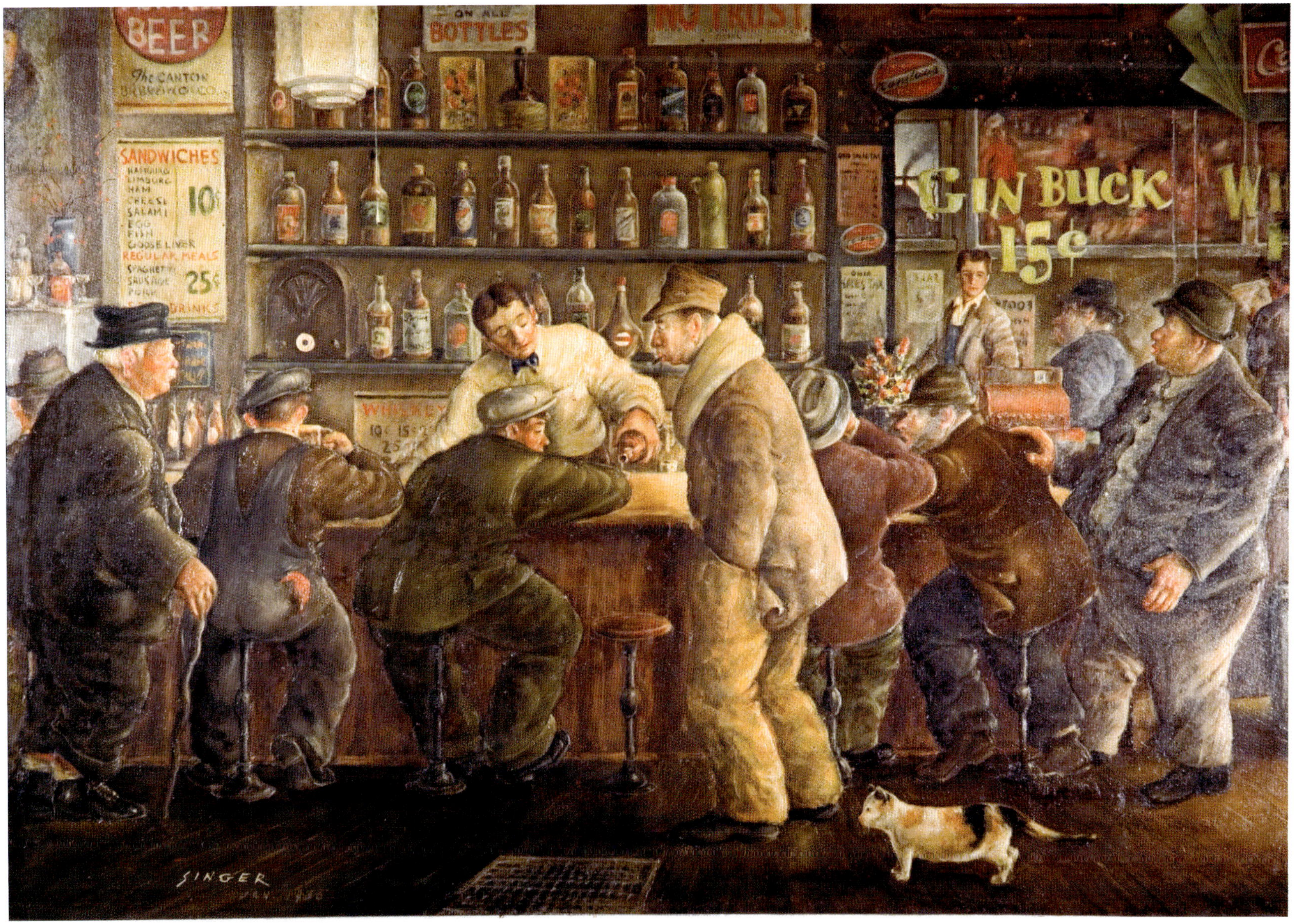

Fig. 24. *Charlie's Place,* 1936. Oil, 44½ x 65. Courtesy of a private collector

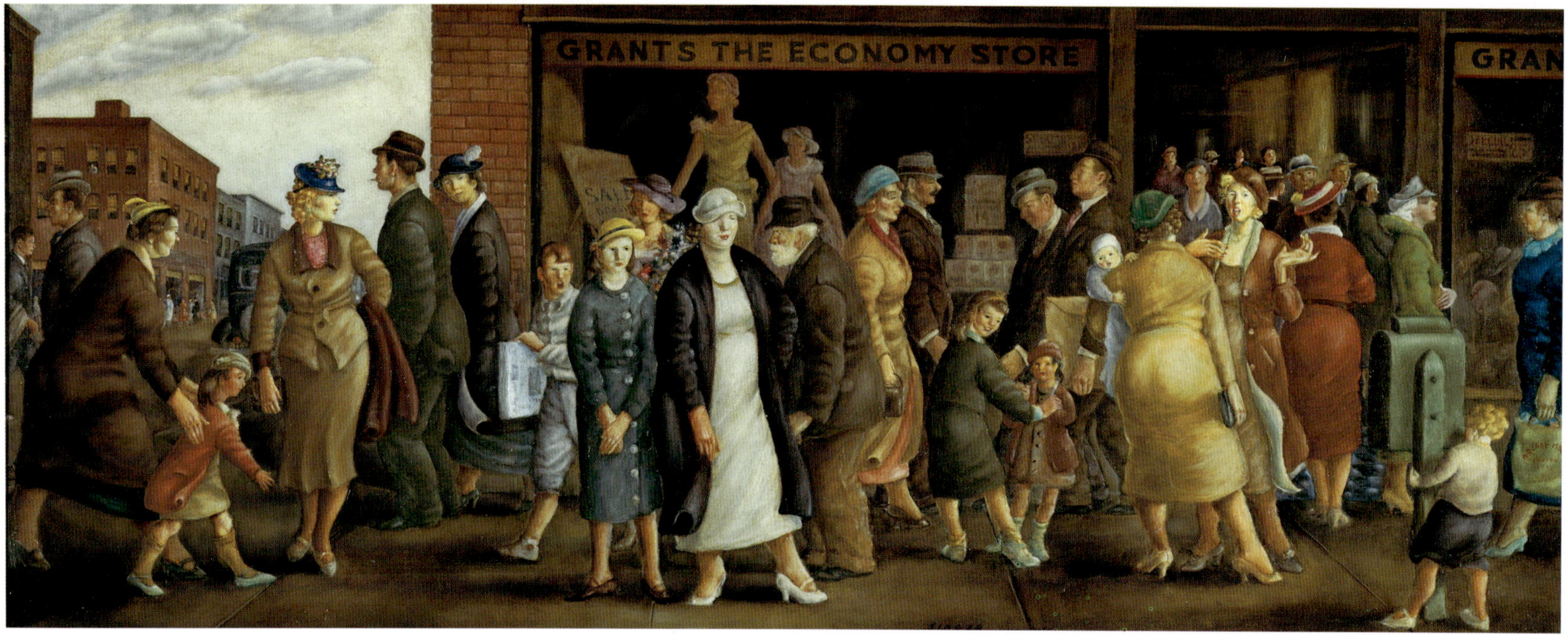

Fig. 25. *Street People,* 1936. Oil, 30 x 75. Canton Museum of Art, given in loving memory of Anne Genshaft by David Genshaft and Family

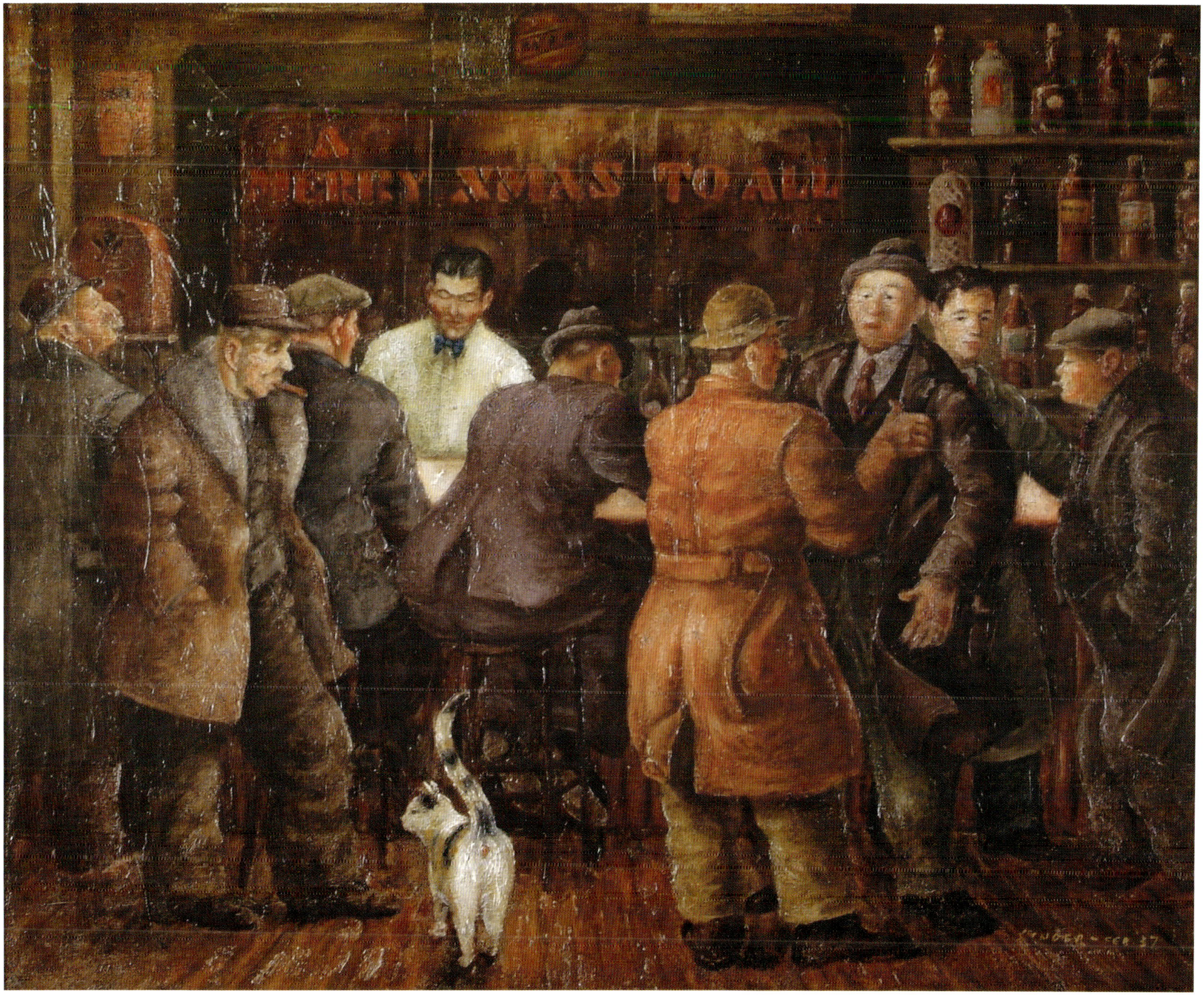

Fig. 26. *Charlie's Christmas Eve,* 1937. Oil, 22 x 27. Courtesy of Lee and Barbara Maimon

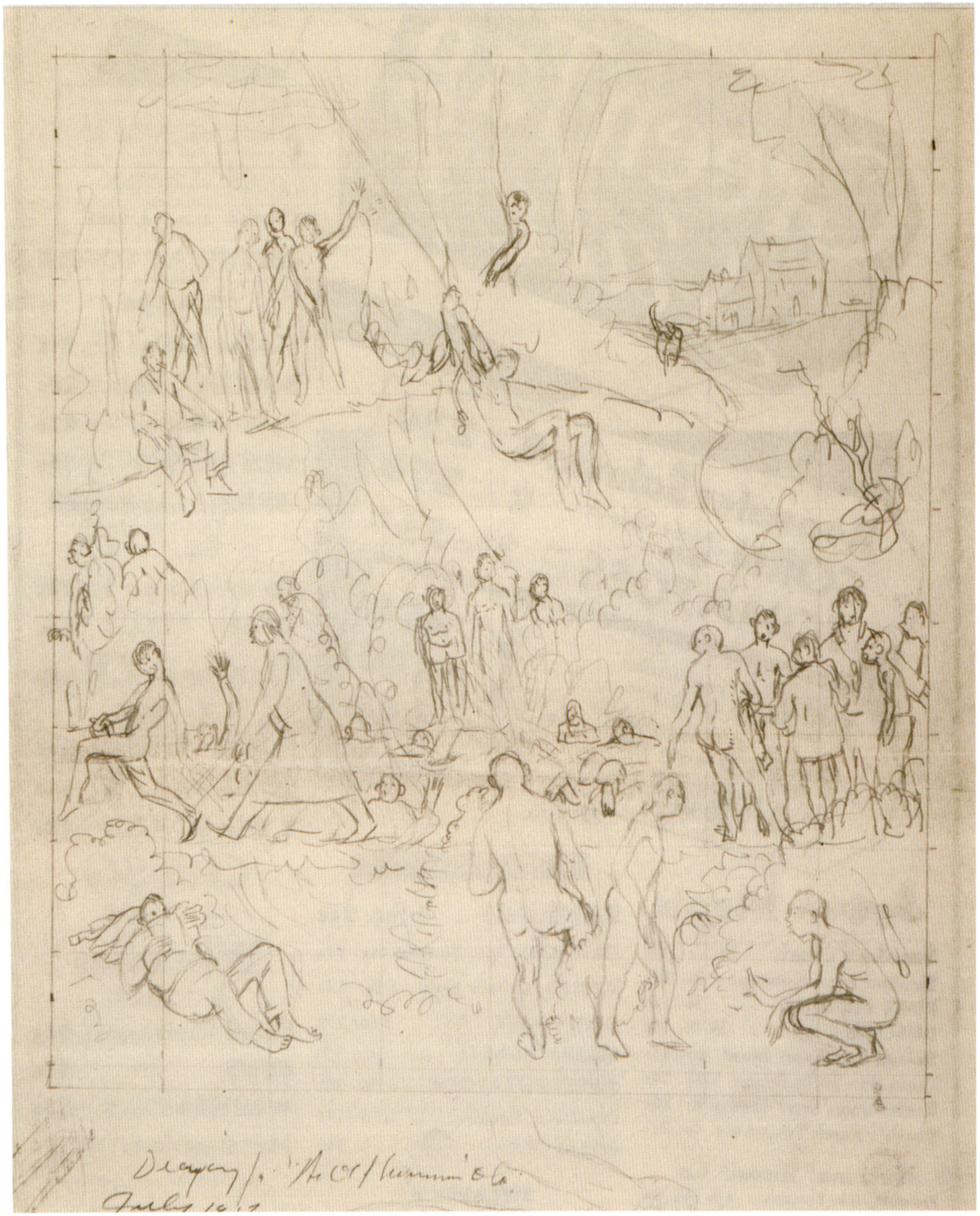

Fig. 27. *Sketch for Swimming Hole,* 1937. Graphite, 13½ x 11¼. Courtesy of Lazar's Art Gallery & Creative Framing

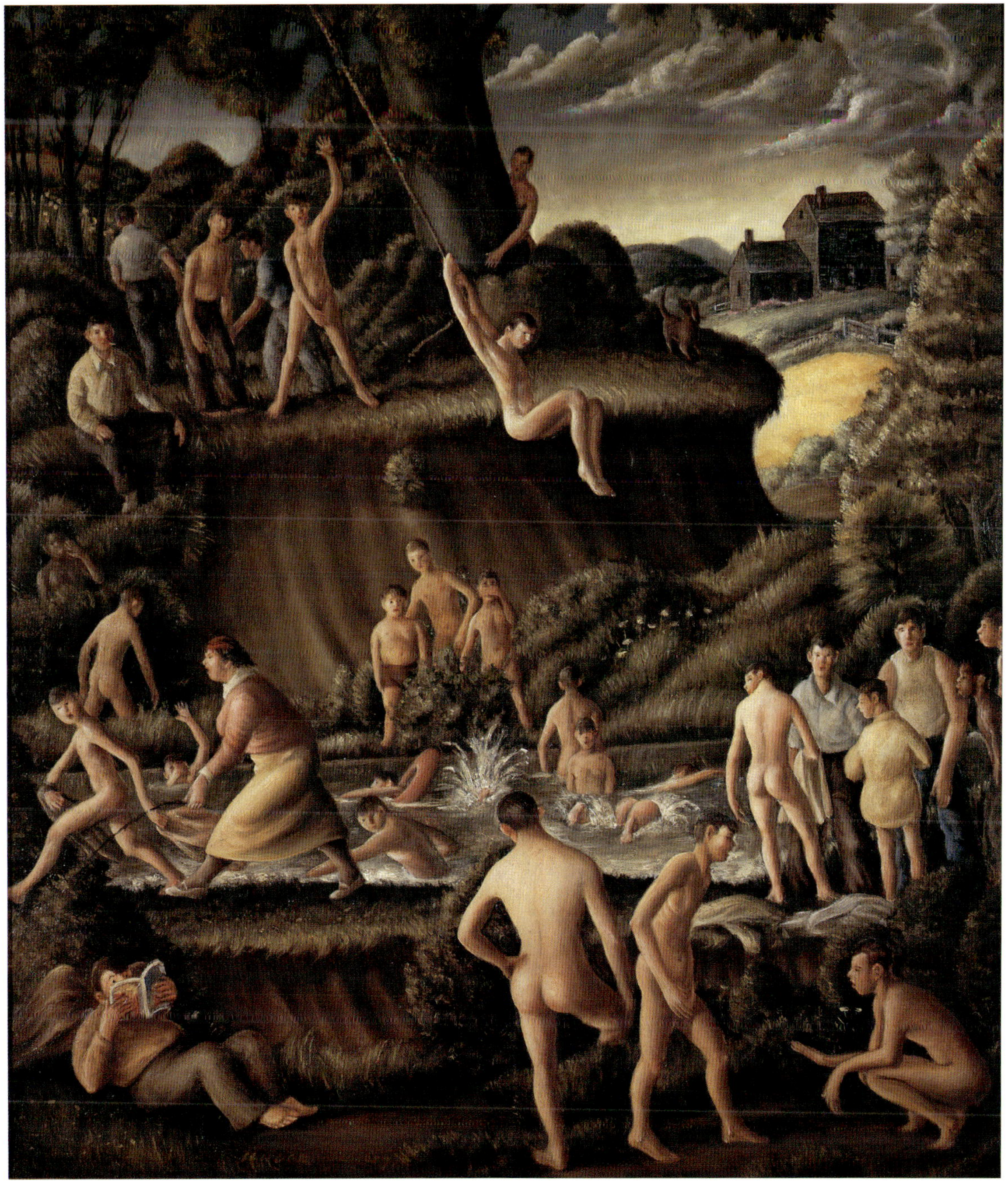

Fig. 28. *The Old Swimming Hole,* 1937. Oil, 46½ x 40½. Columbus Museum of Art, gift of Orlando A. Miller

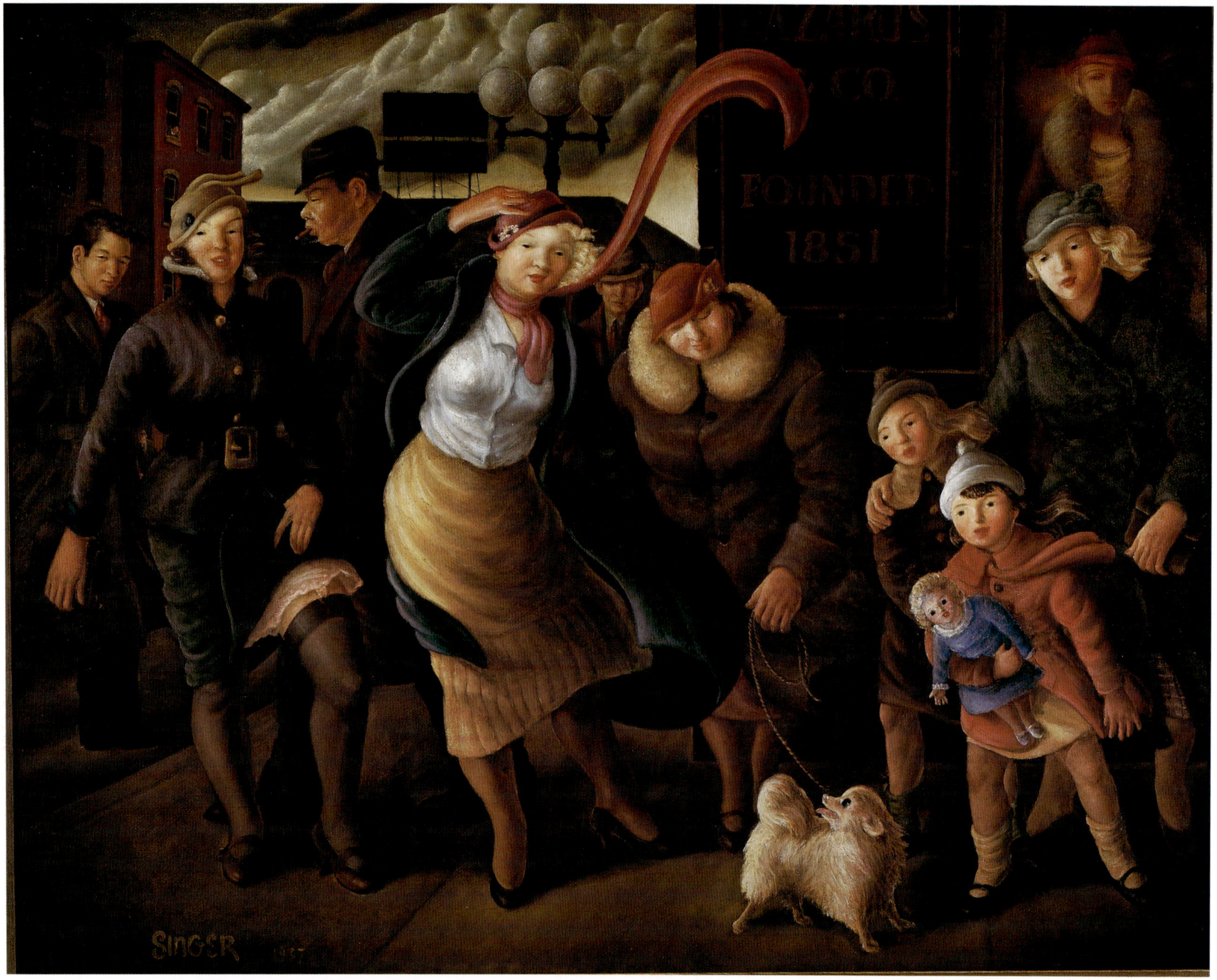

Fig. 29. *Wind on the Avenue,* 1937. Oil, 40 x 50. Columbus Museum of Art, Howald Fund

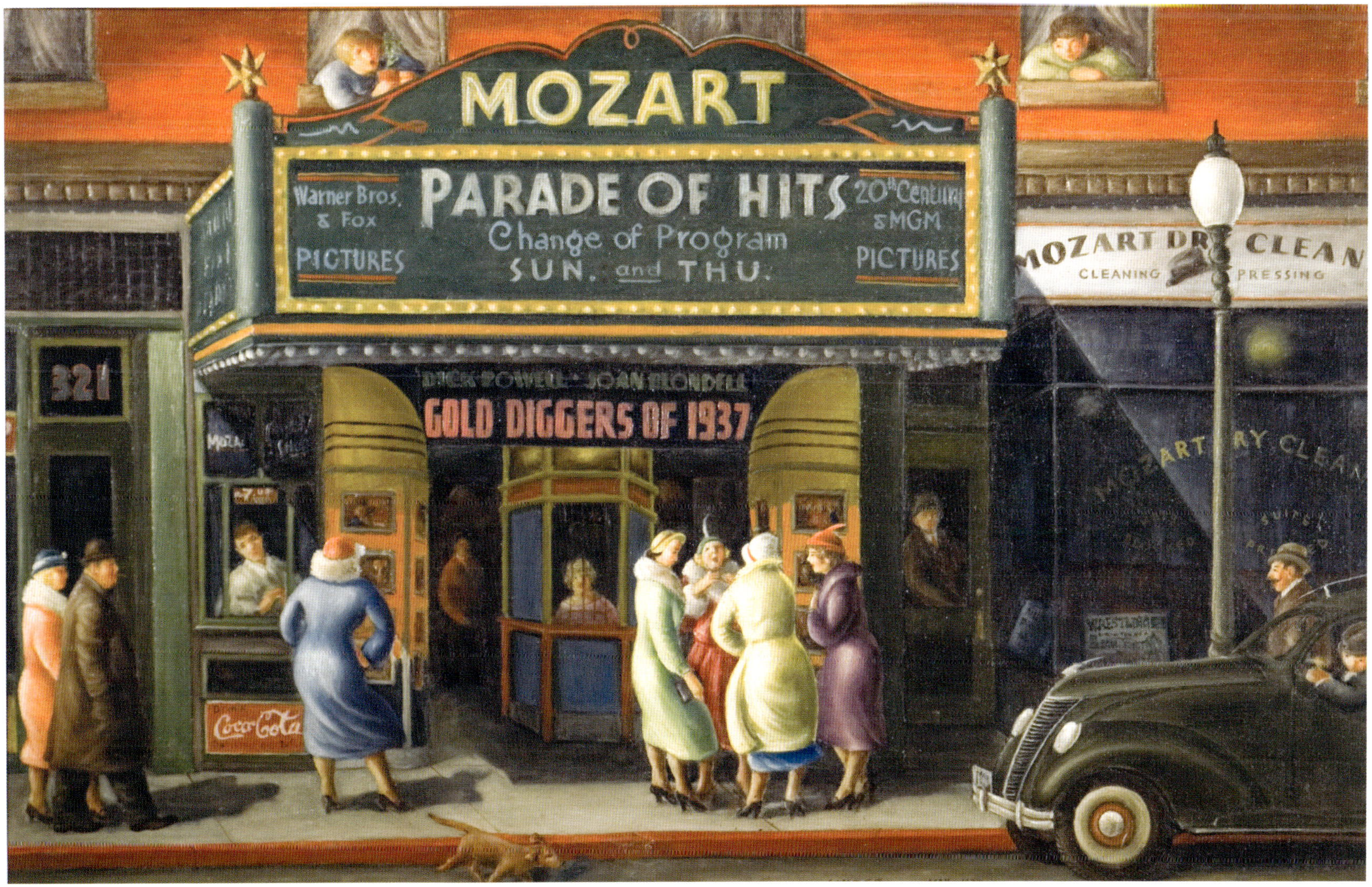

Fig. 30. *The Mozart, (Canton)*, 1937. Oil, 40 x 60. Courtesy of a private collector

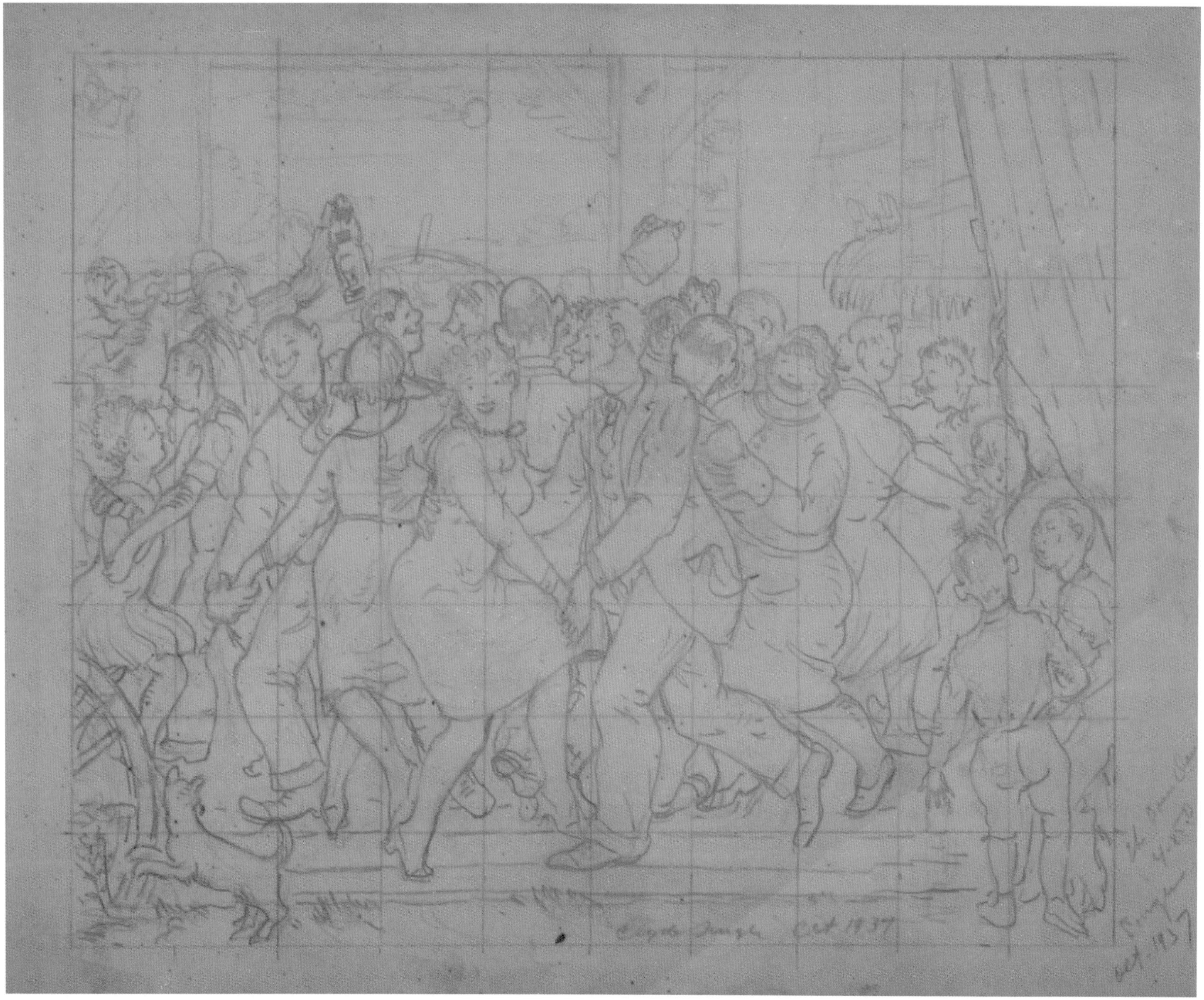

Fig. 31. *Sketch for Barn Dance*, 1937. Graphite, 5 x 7. Courtesy of Thomas W. Darling

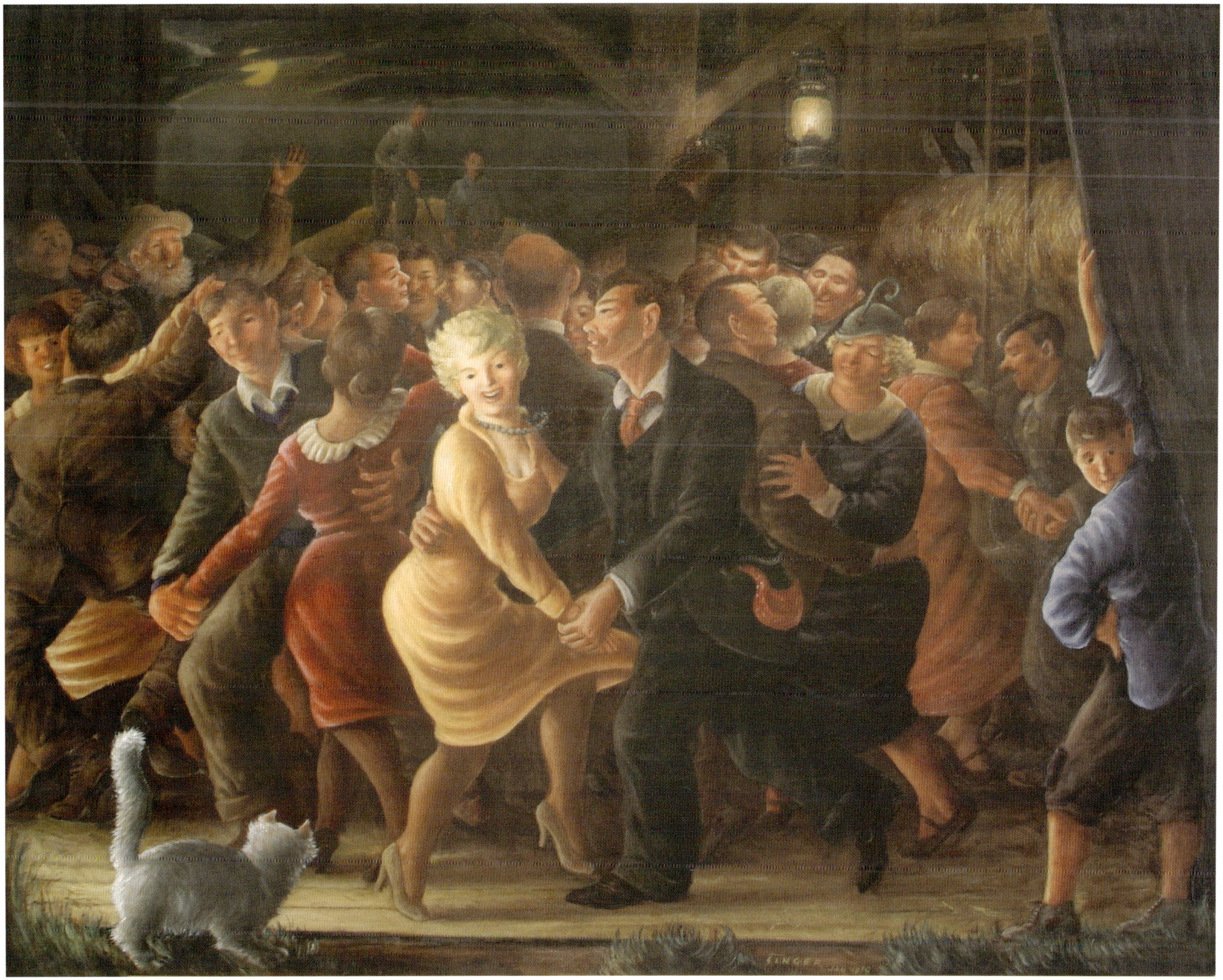

Fig. 32. *Barn Dance,* 1938. Oil, 40 x 50. Courtesy of Thomas W. Darling

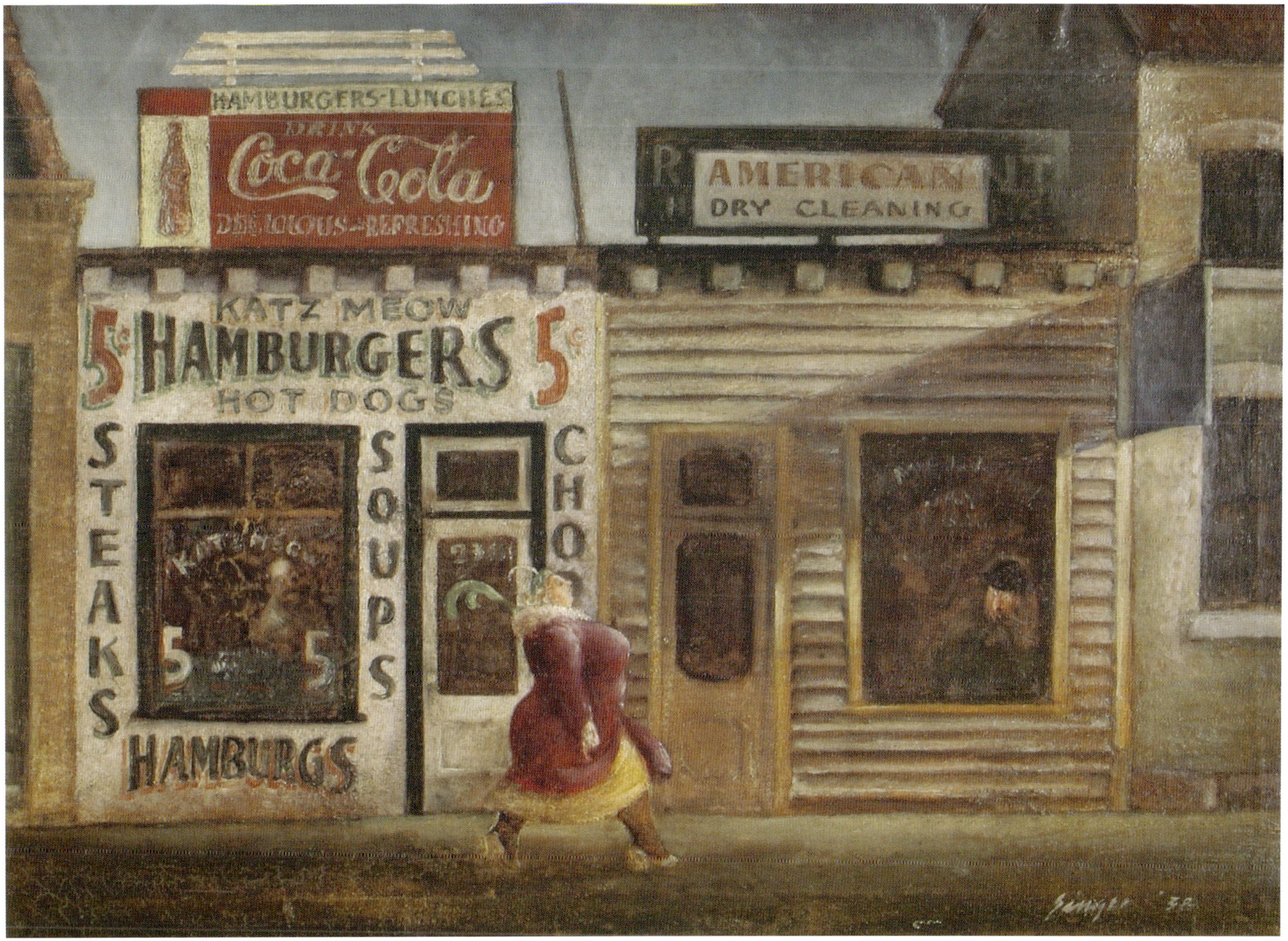

Fig. 33. *Katz Meow,* 1938. Oil, 20 x 29. Courtesy of Jack and Pat Adamson, Zoar, Ohio

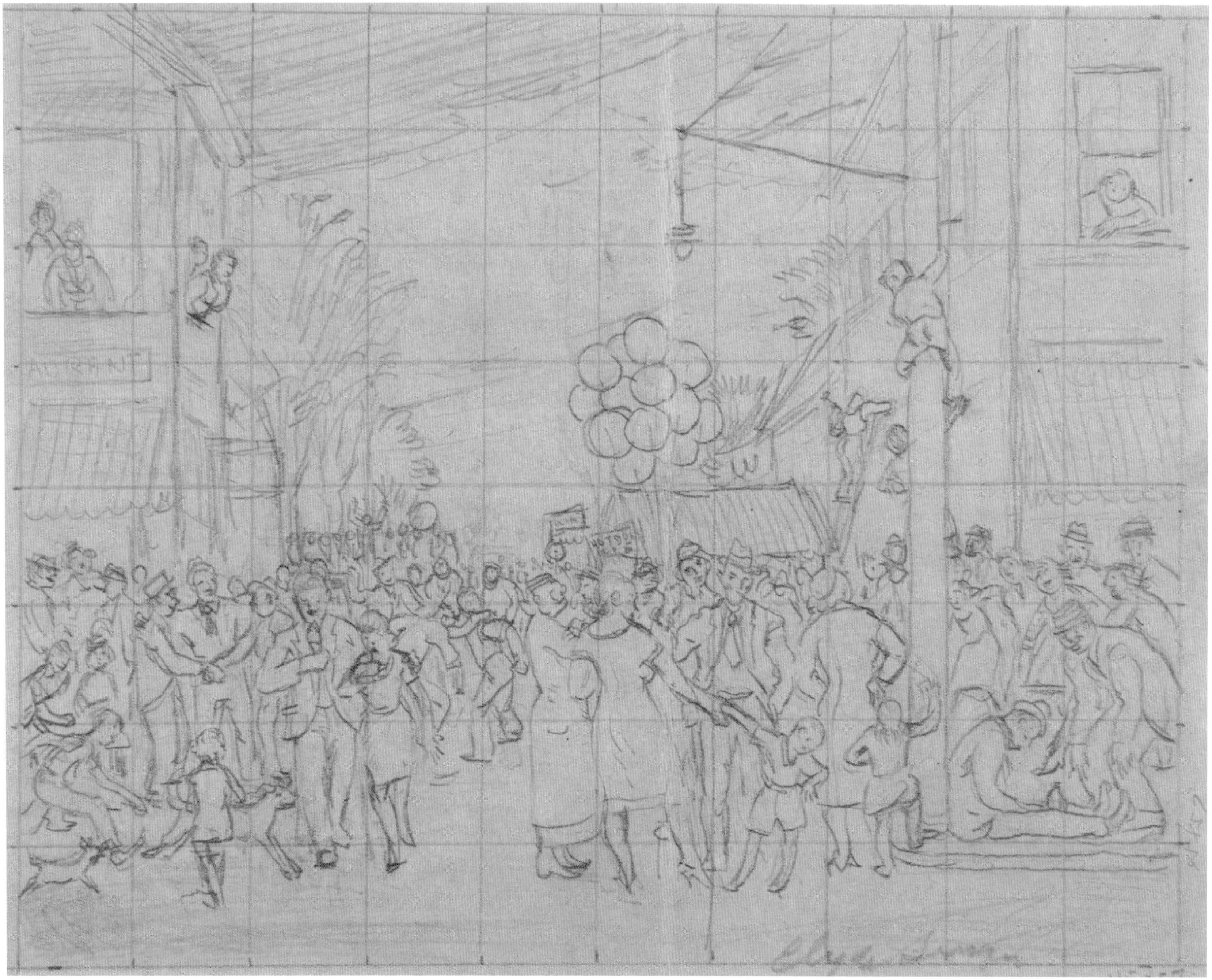

Fig. 34. *Sketch for Homecoming.* Graphite, 8¼ x 10½. Courtesy of Lazar's Art Gallery & Creative Framing

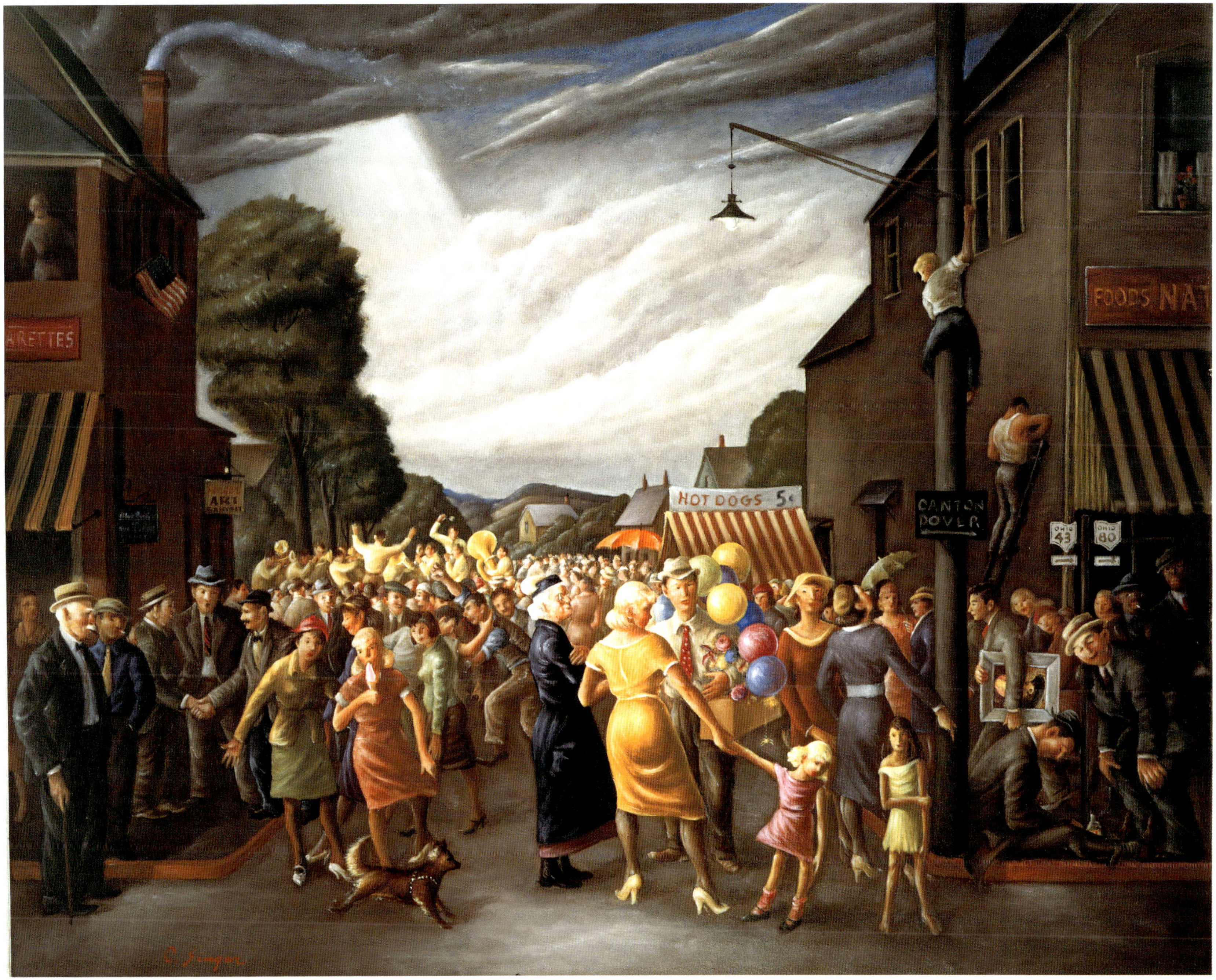

Fig. 35. *Homecoming (Malvern)*, 1939. Oil, 45 x 57. Courtesy of Michael Lawlor

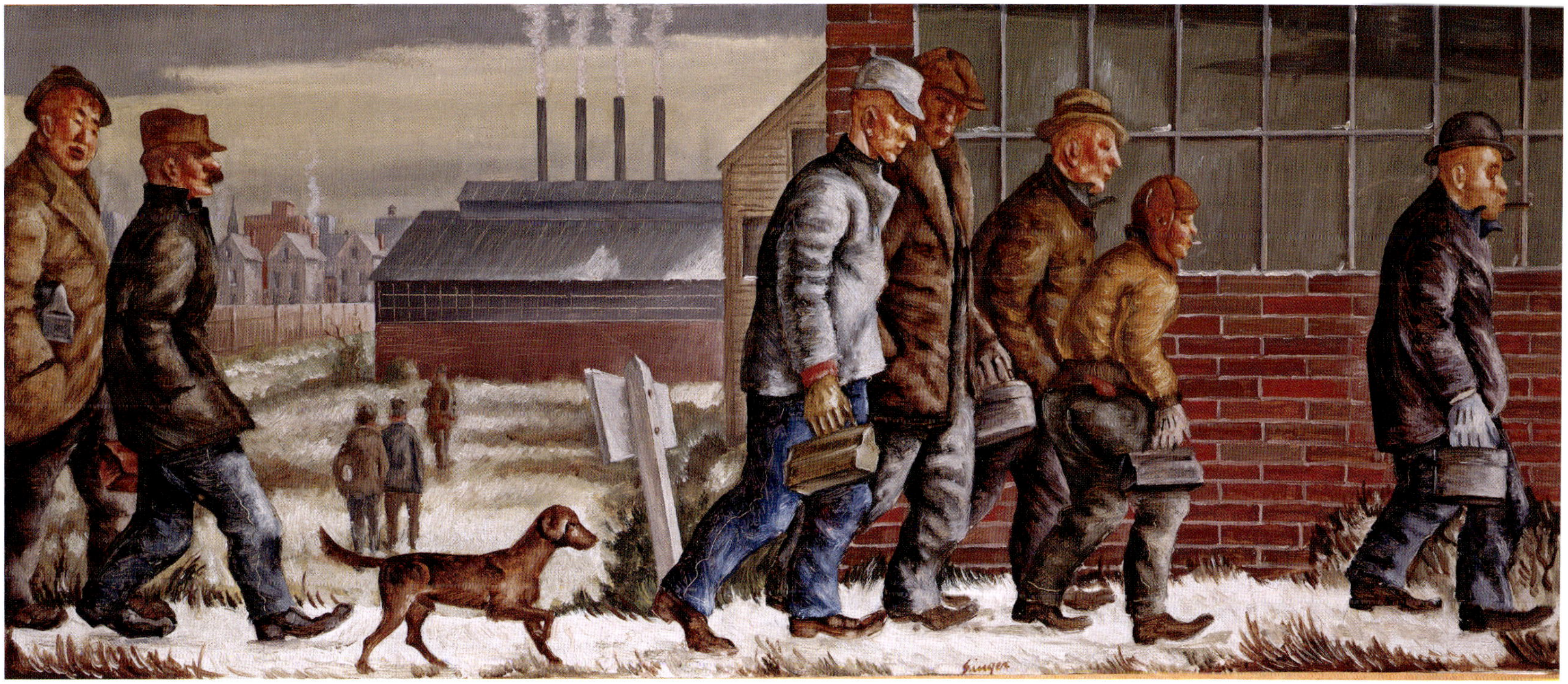

Fig. 36. *Mill Workers* mural study, 1939. Oil, 14 x 30. Courtesy of a private collector

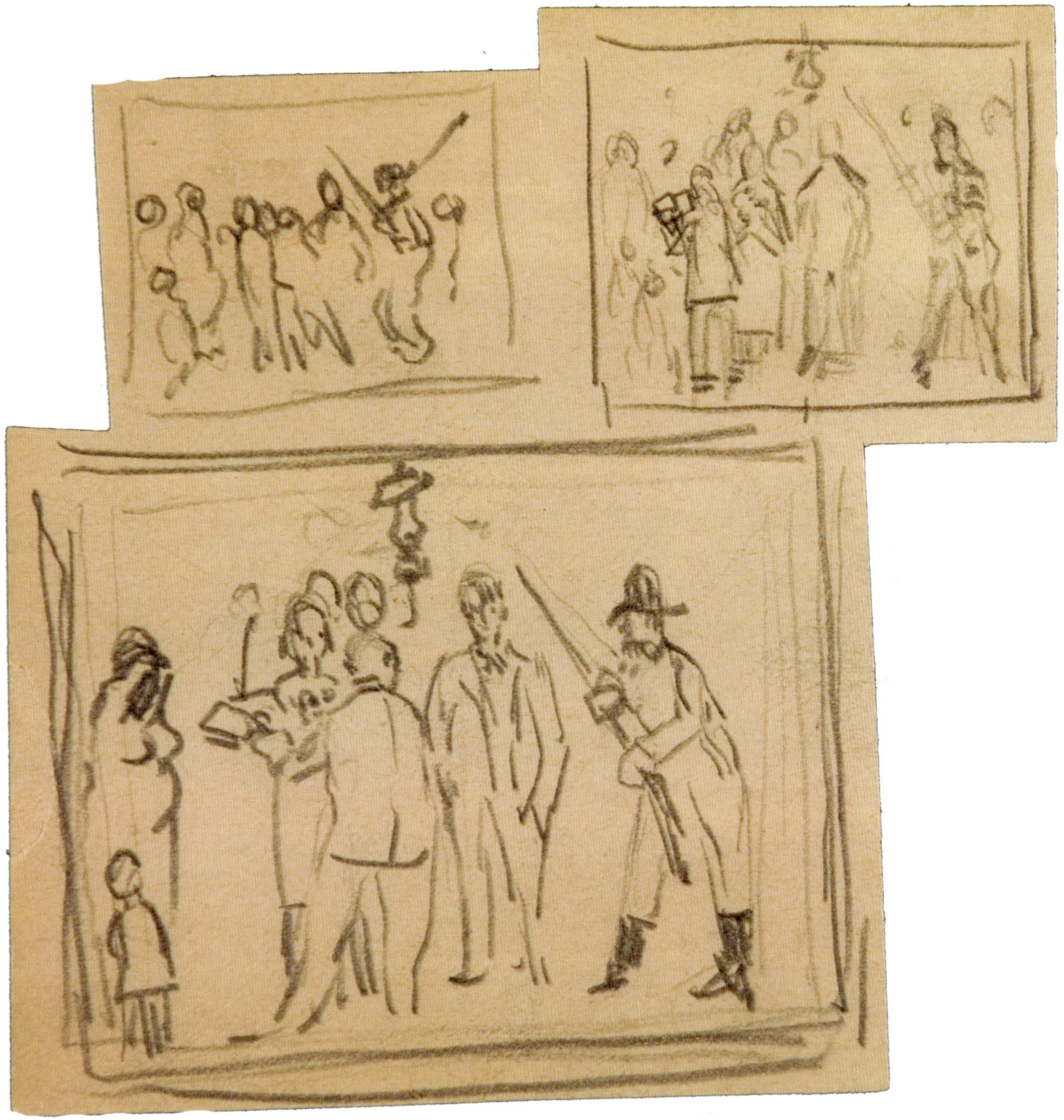

Fig. 37. *Sketches for Shotgun Wedding*. Graphite, 5 x 5. Courtesy of Lazar's Art Gallery & Creative Framing

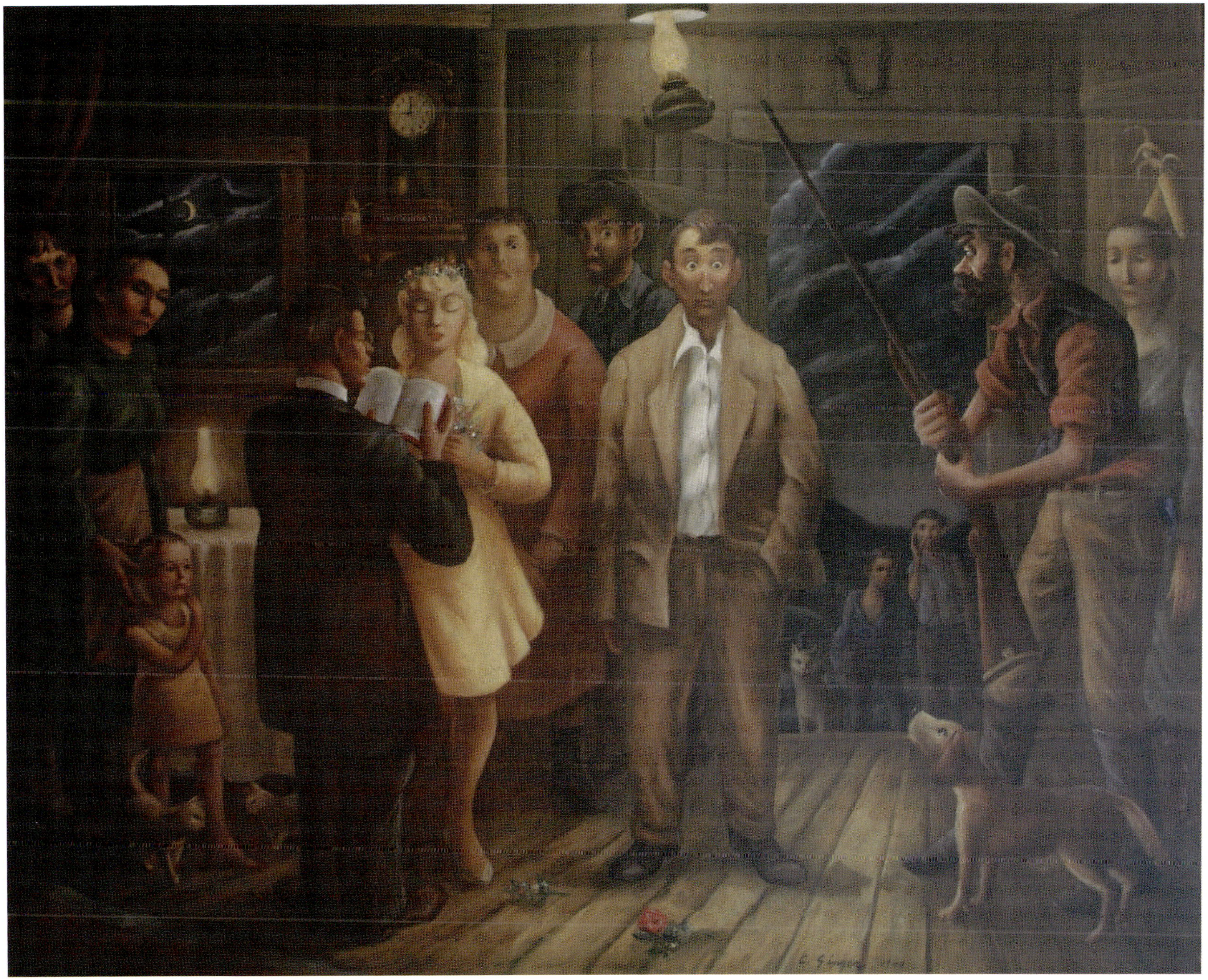

Fig. 38. *Shotgun Wedding,* 1940. Oil, 40 x 50. Courtesy of Thomas W. Darling

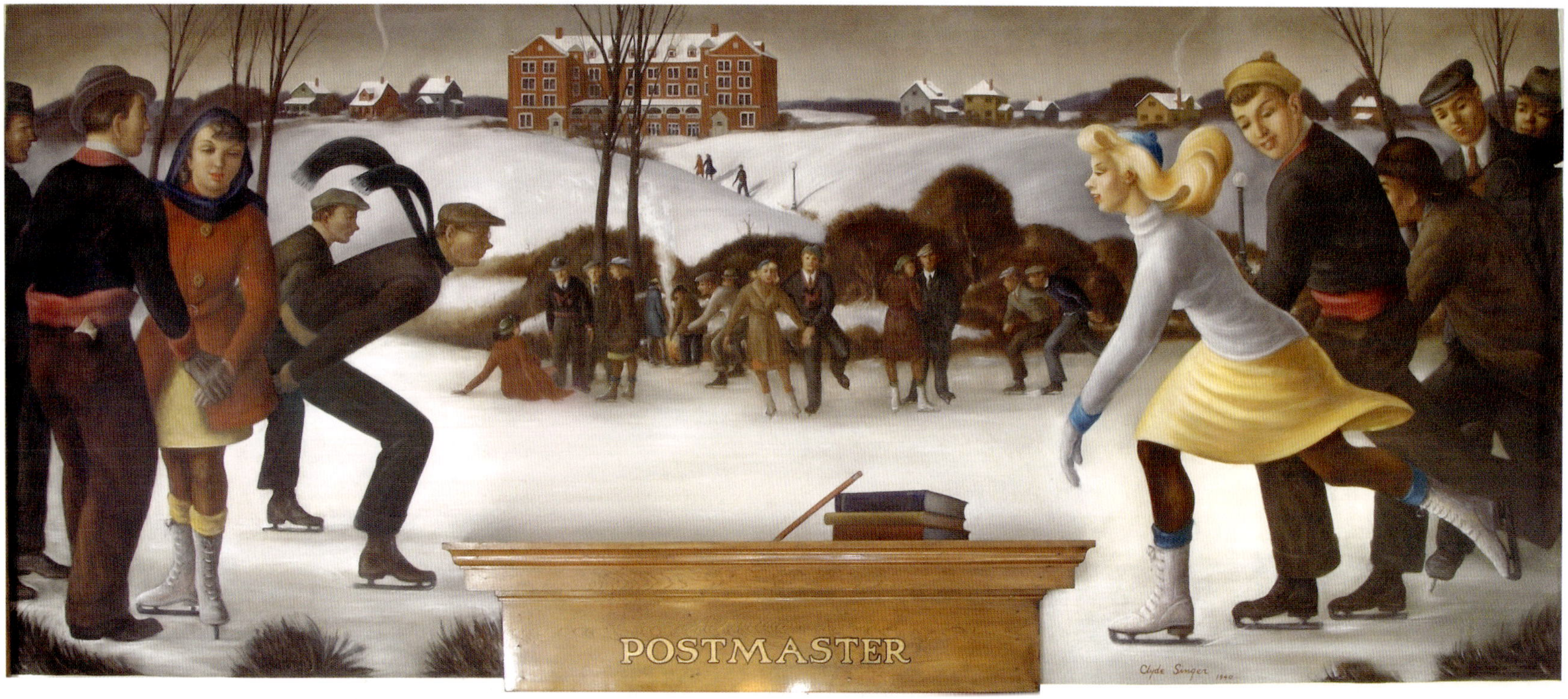

Fig. 39. *Skaters* (mural in the New Concord Post Office), 1940. Oil, 12 x 5 feet. Courtesy of New Concord Post Office

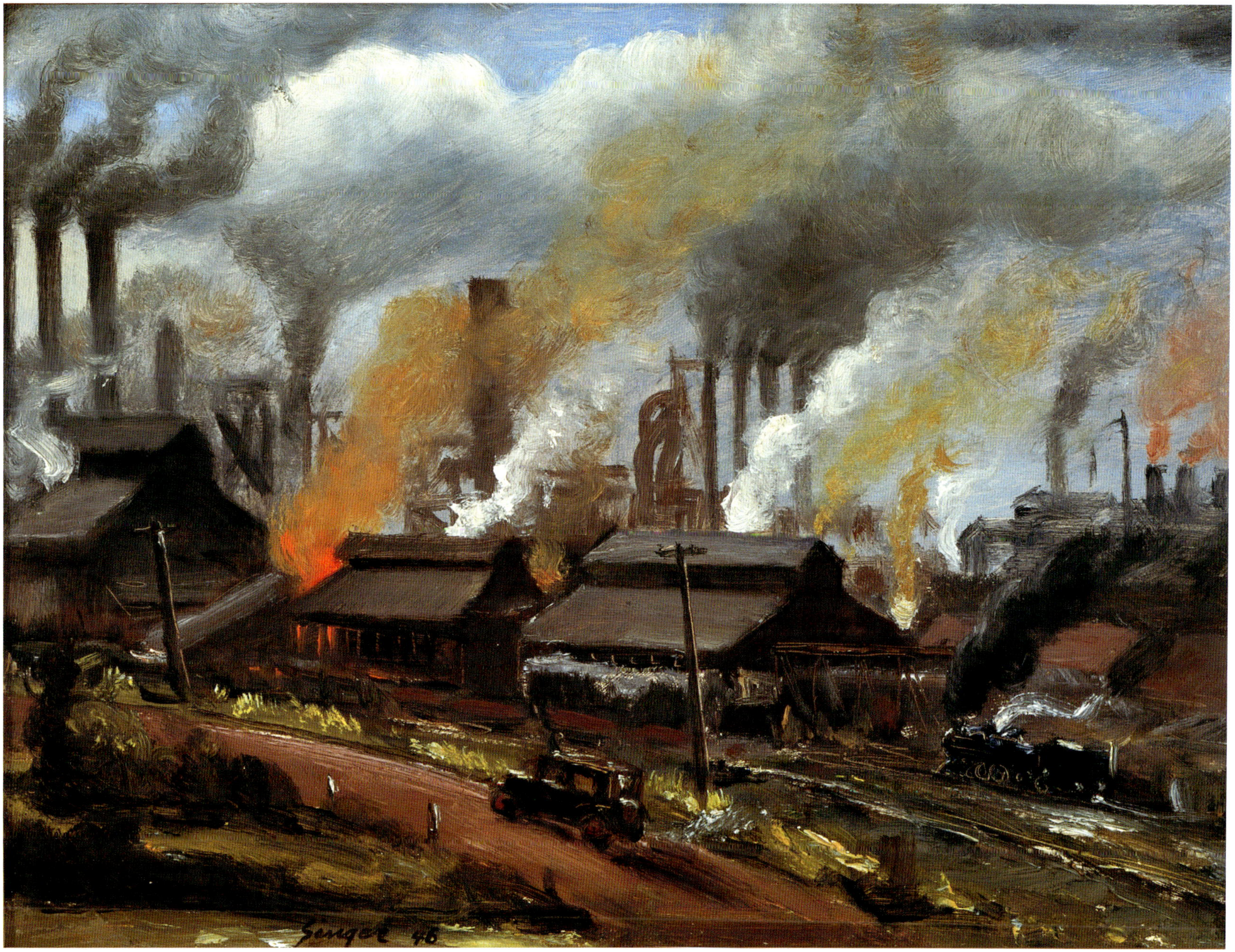

Fig. 40. *Steel Mill & Train Going Down the Tracks,* 1946. Oil, 12 x 16. Courtesy of a private collector

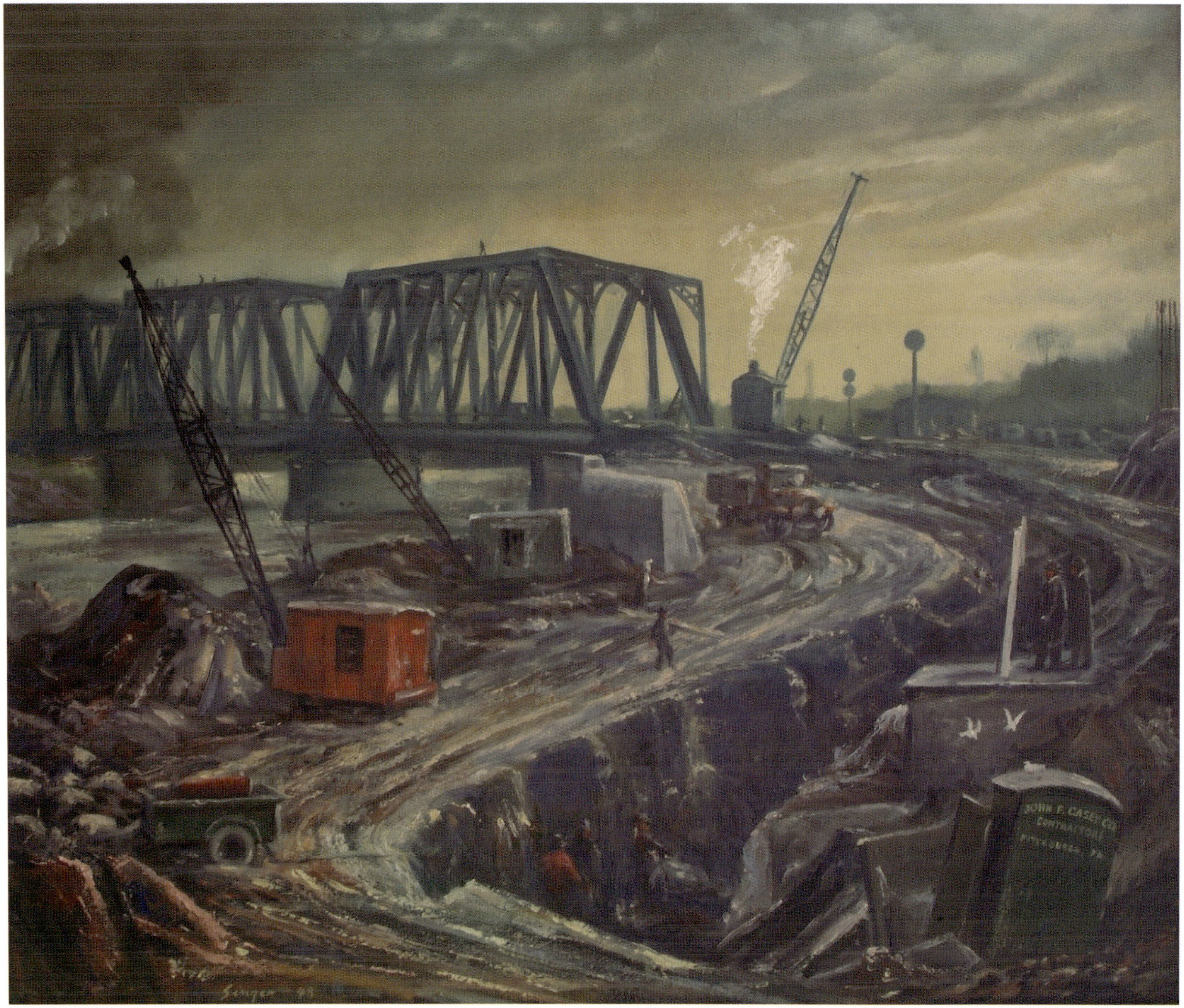

Fig. 41. *Massillon Bridge Project,* 1948. Oil, 30 x 36. Collection of the Massillon Museum, Baldwin Purchase Award

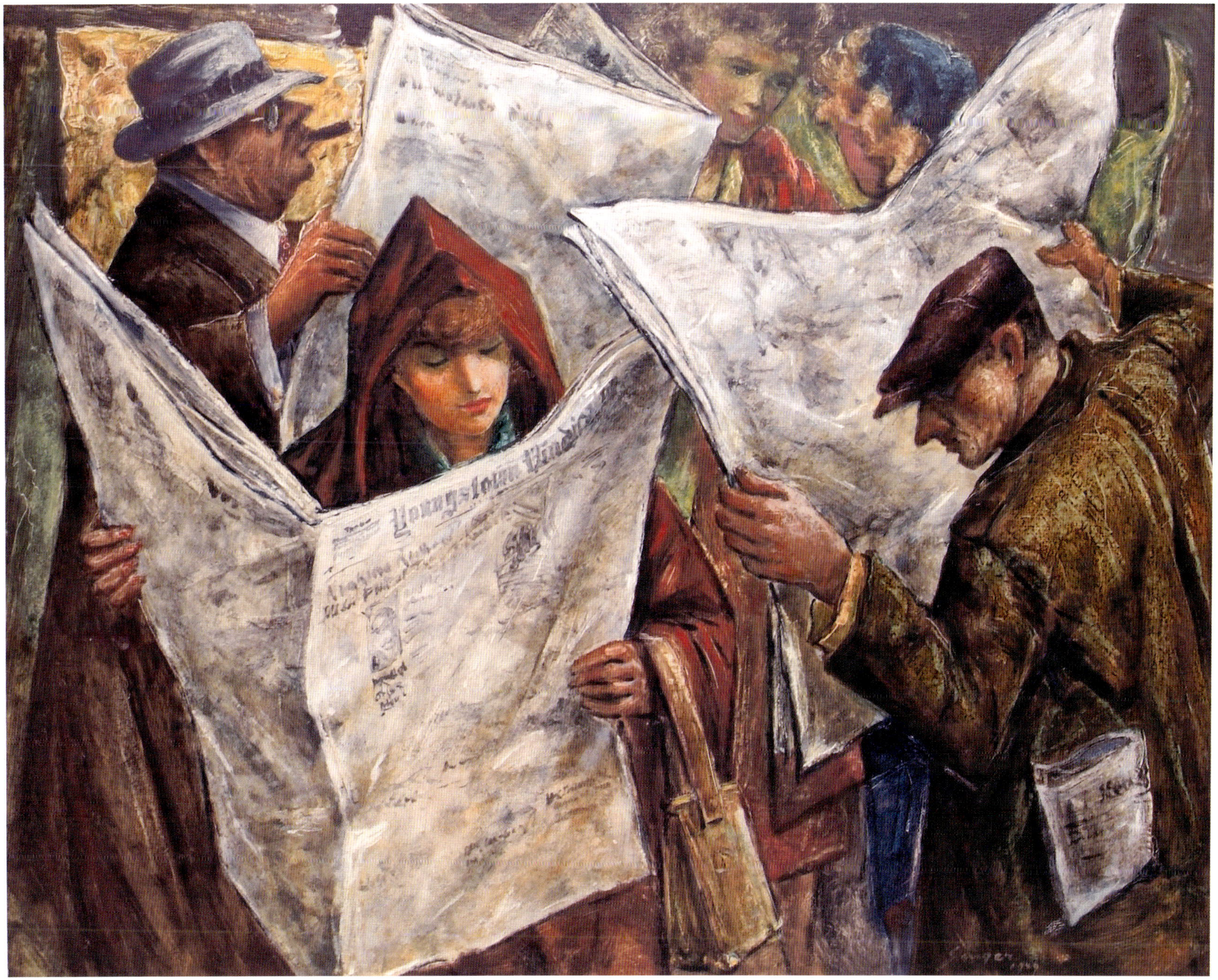

Fig. 42. *Early Edition,* 1949. Oil, 37½ x 29½. Canton Museum of Art

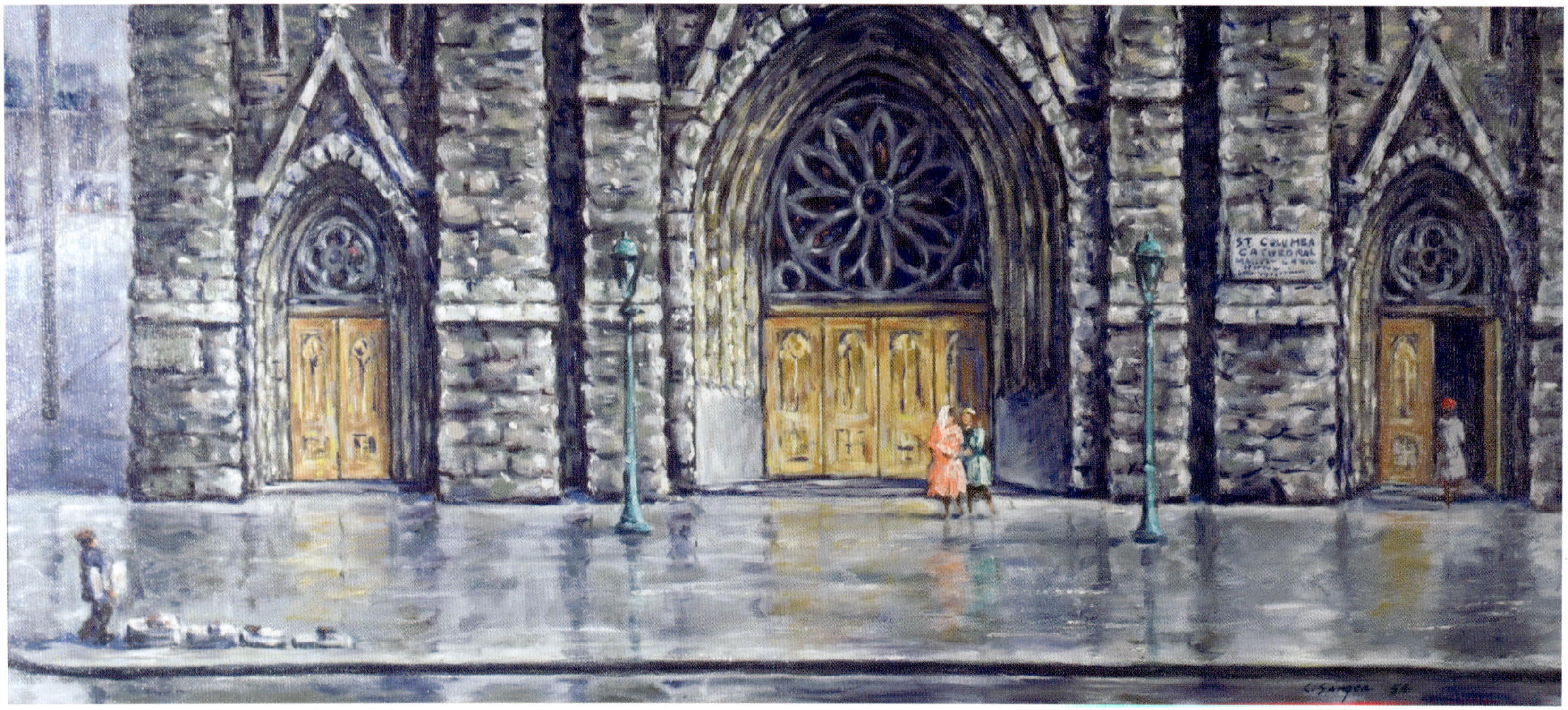

Fig. 43. *St. Columba's Cathedral Doors,* 1954. Oil, 17 x 40. Courtesy of Robert and Lesa Schnabel

Maitland and Marietta

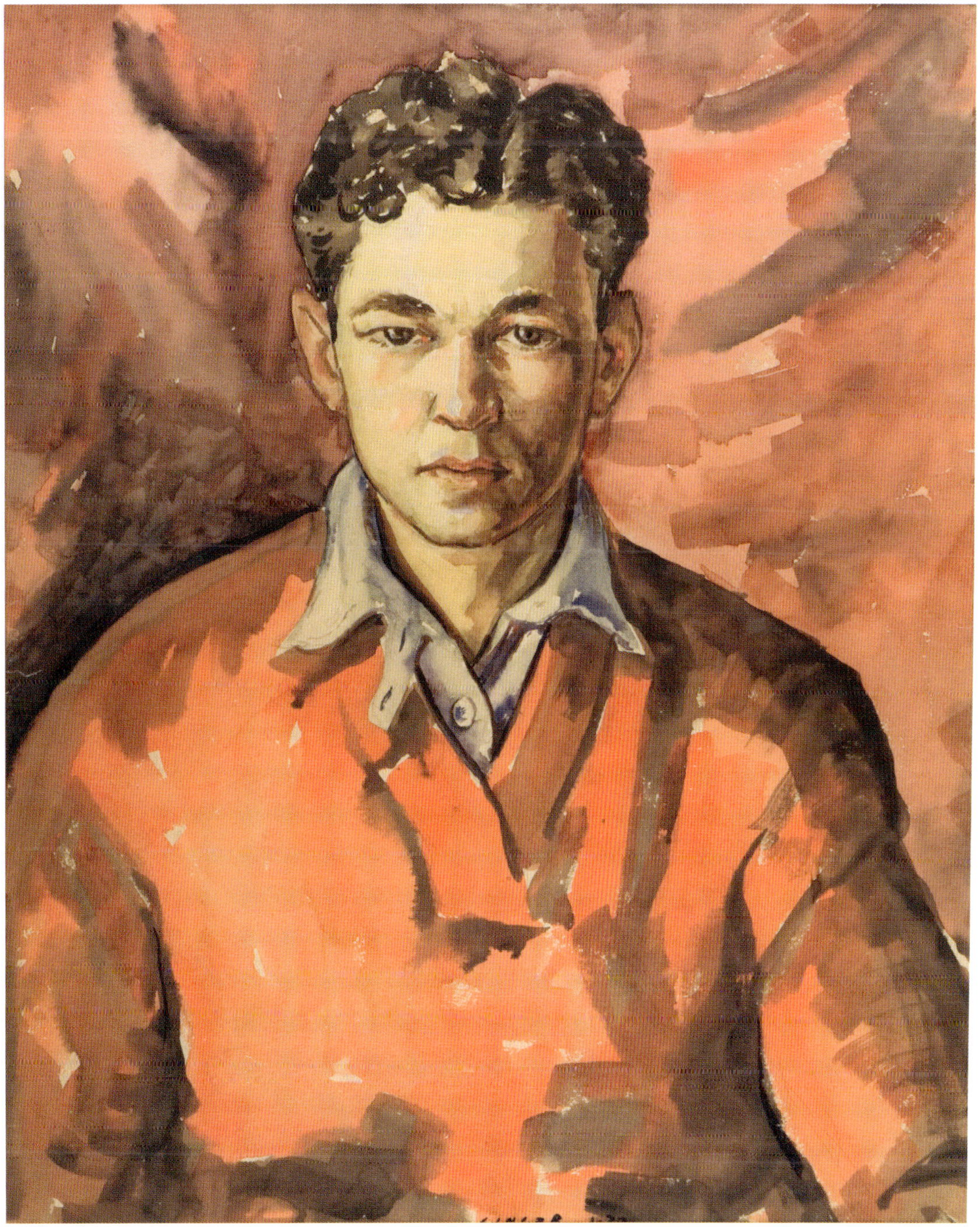

Fig. 44. *Self-Portrait,* 1932. Watercolor, 19 x 25. Courtesy of Robert Burns

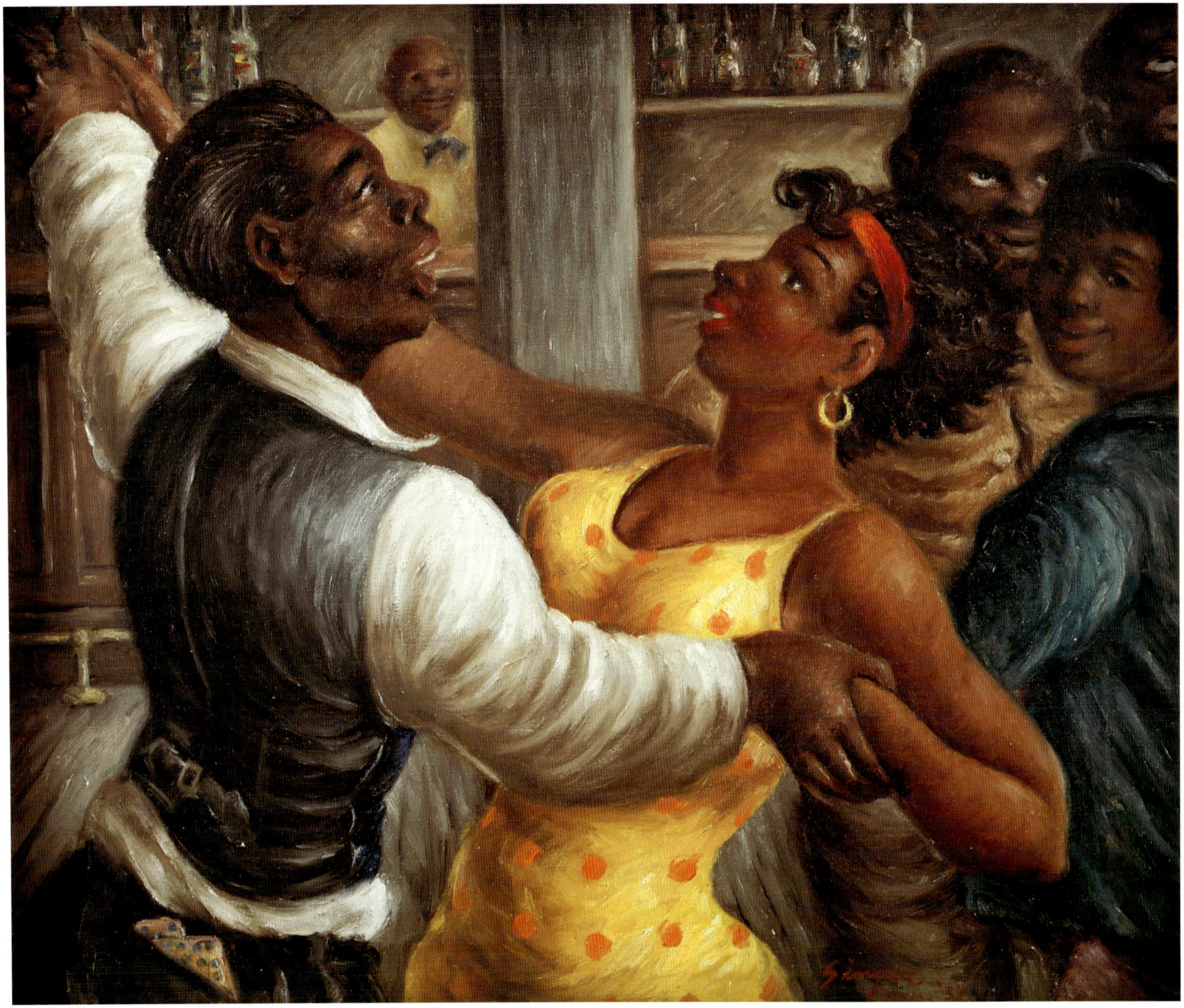

Fig. 45. *Eatonville Elite,* 1939. Oil, 19½ x 24½. Courtesy of Peter and Deon Schildhause

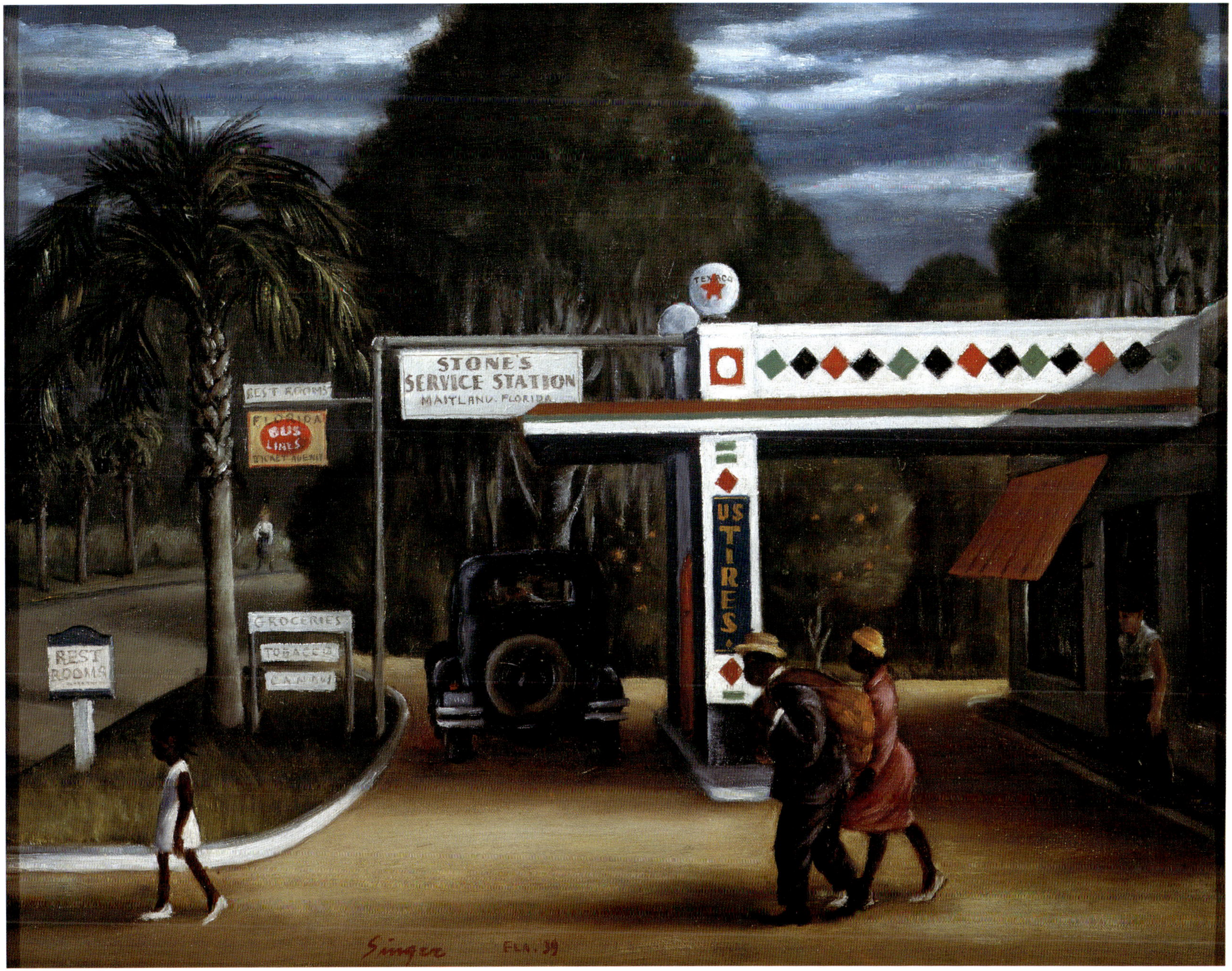

Fig. 46. *Stone's Service Station,* 1939. Oil, 20 x 26. Courtesy of Sam and Robbie Vickers, Florida Collection

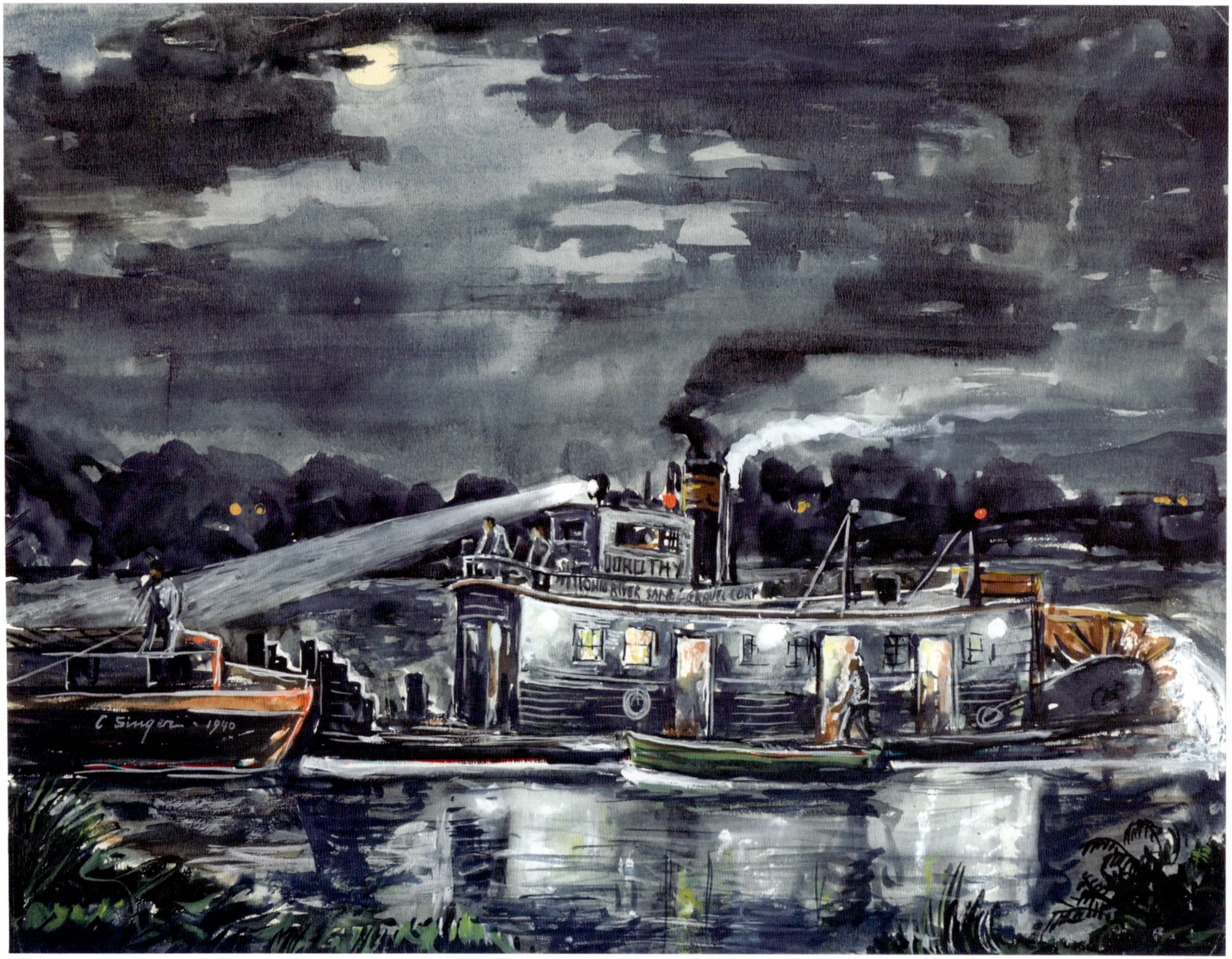

Fig. 47. *Marietta,* 1940. Watercolor, 15 x 20. Courtesy of a private collector

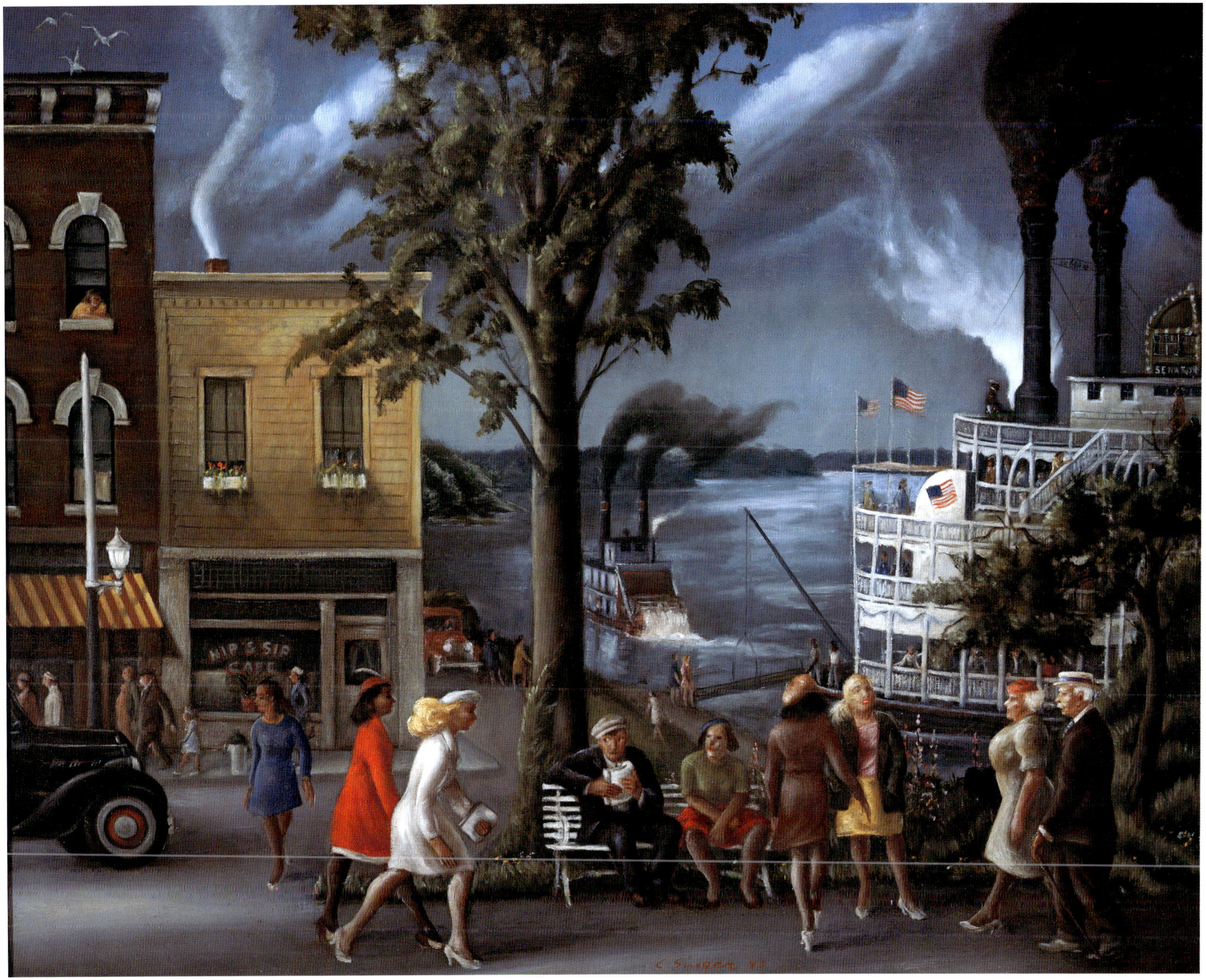

Fig. 48. *Down by the Ohio,* 1940. Oil, 40 x 50. Courtesy of Michael Lawlor

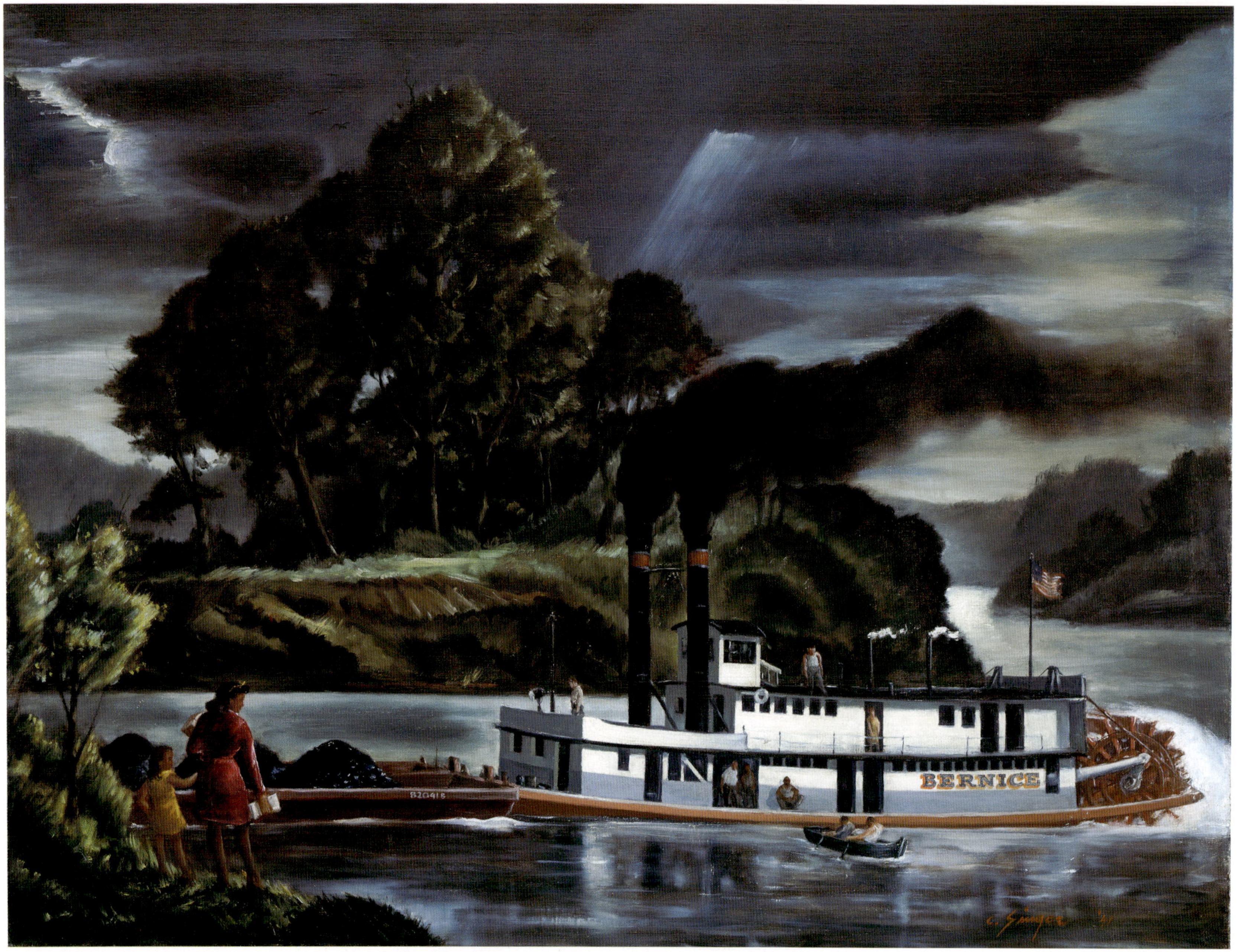

Fig. 49. *Steamboat on the Ohio,* 1941. Oil, 36 x 48. Courtesy of Wes Nedblake

Clyde Singer's New York

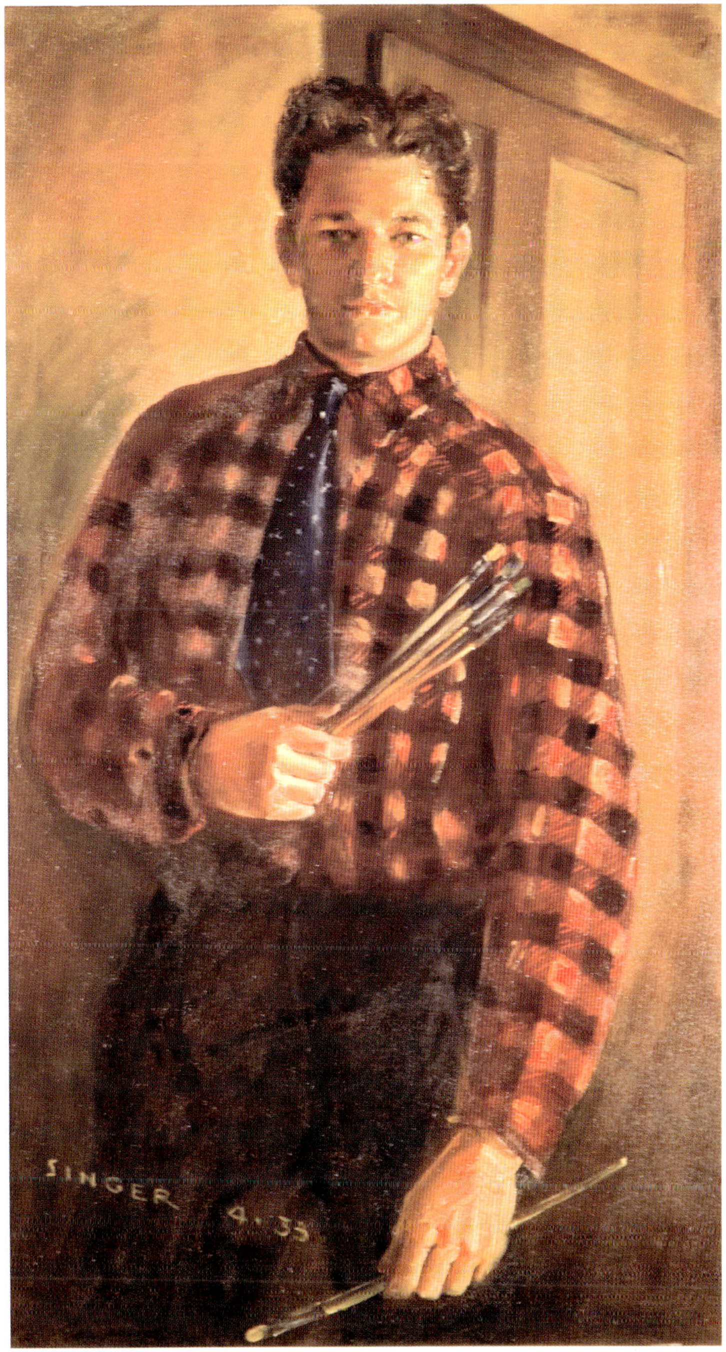

Fig. 50. *Self-Portrait,* 1933. Oil, 48 x 28. Courtesy of a private collector

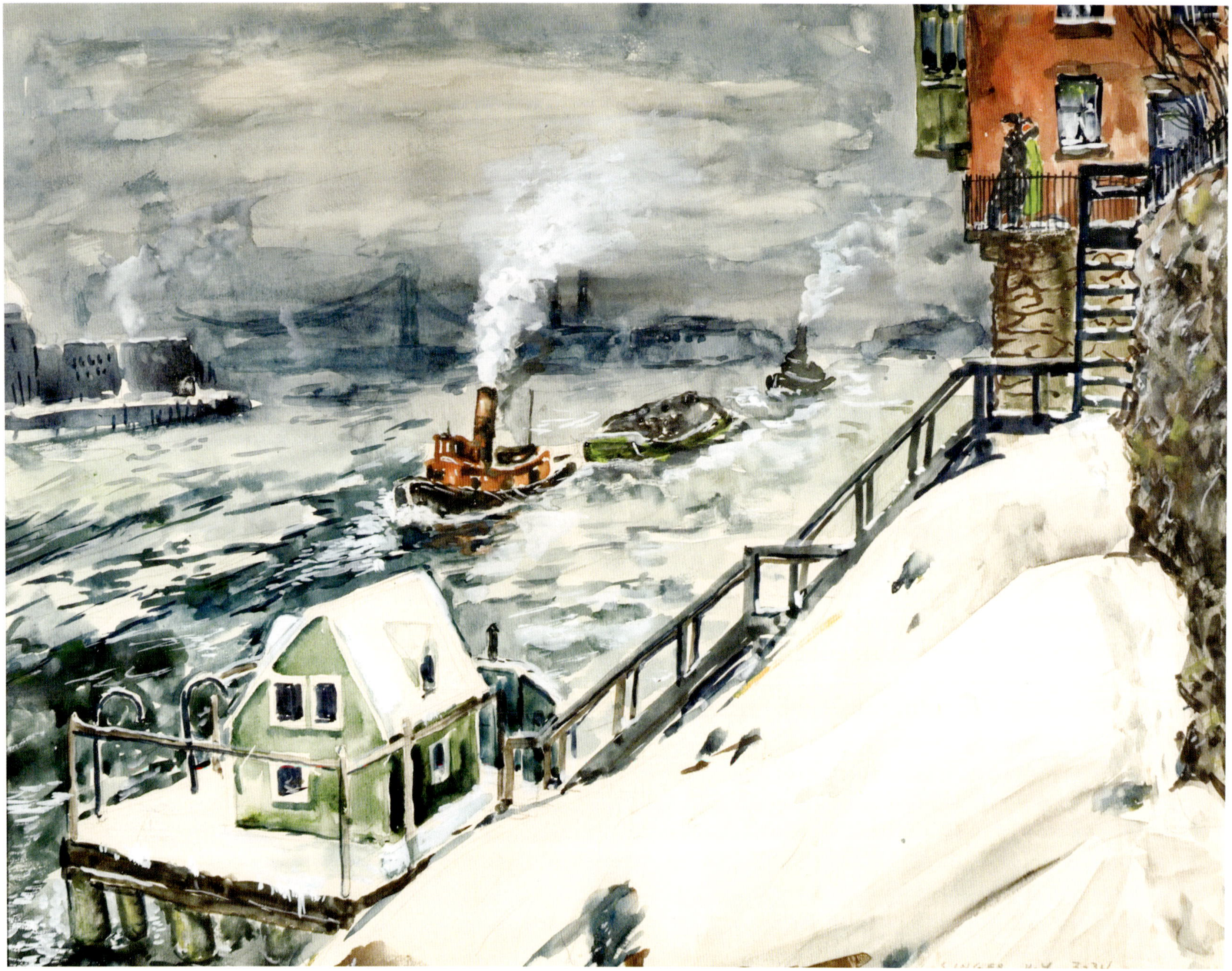

Fig. 51. *Tugboats in Winter,* 1934. Watercolor, 15 x 19. Courtesy of a private collector

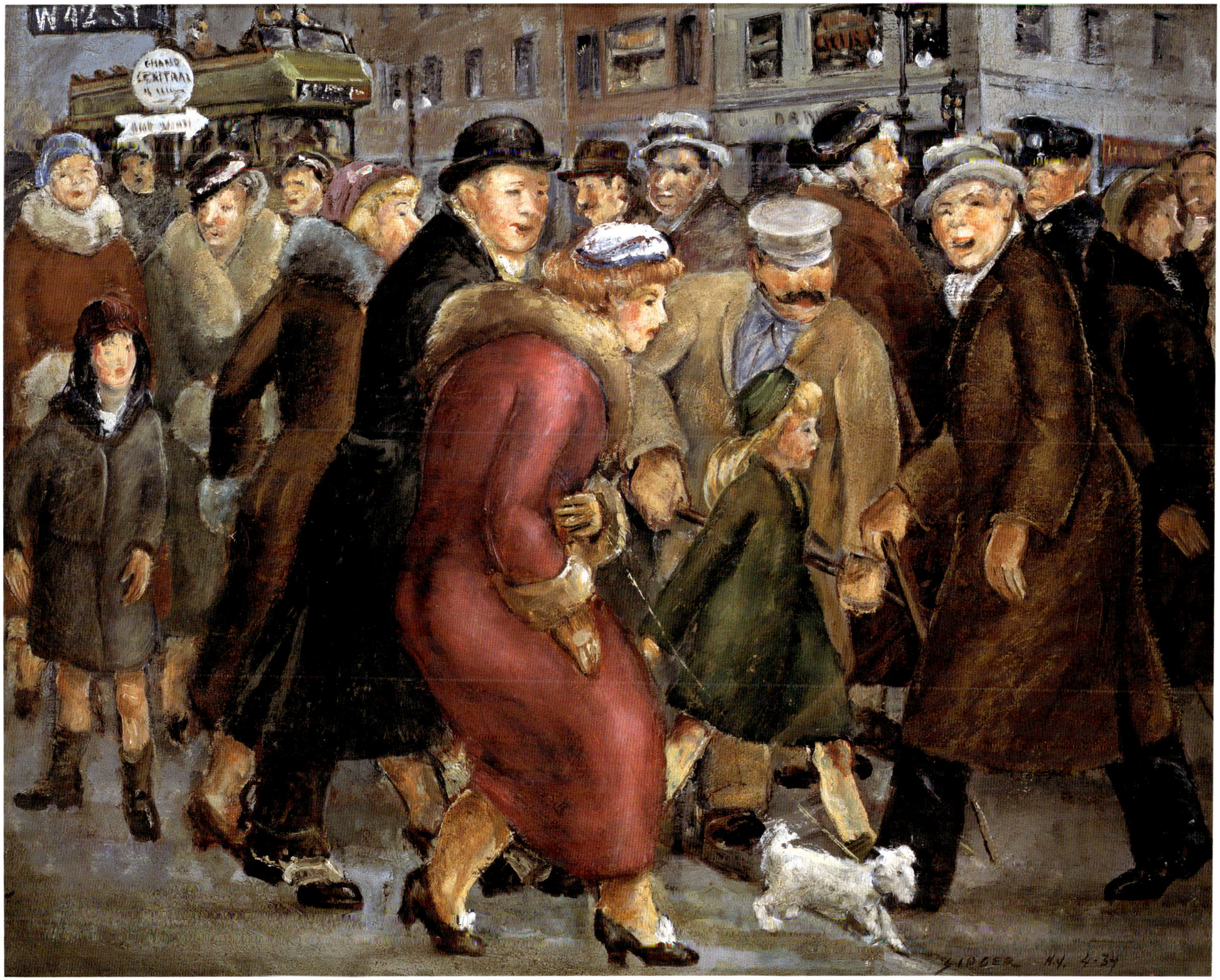

Fig. 52. *42nd Street Crowd,* 1934. Oil, 24 x 30. Courtesy of Ed and Karen Ogul, Franklin, Michigan

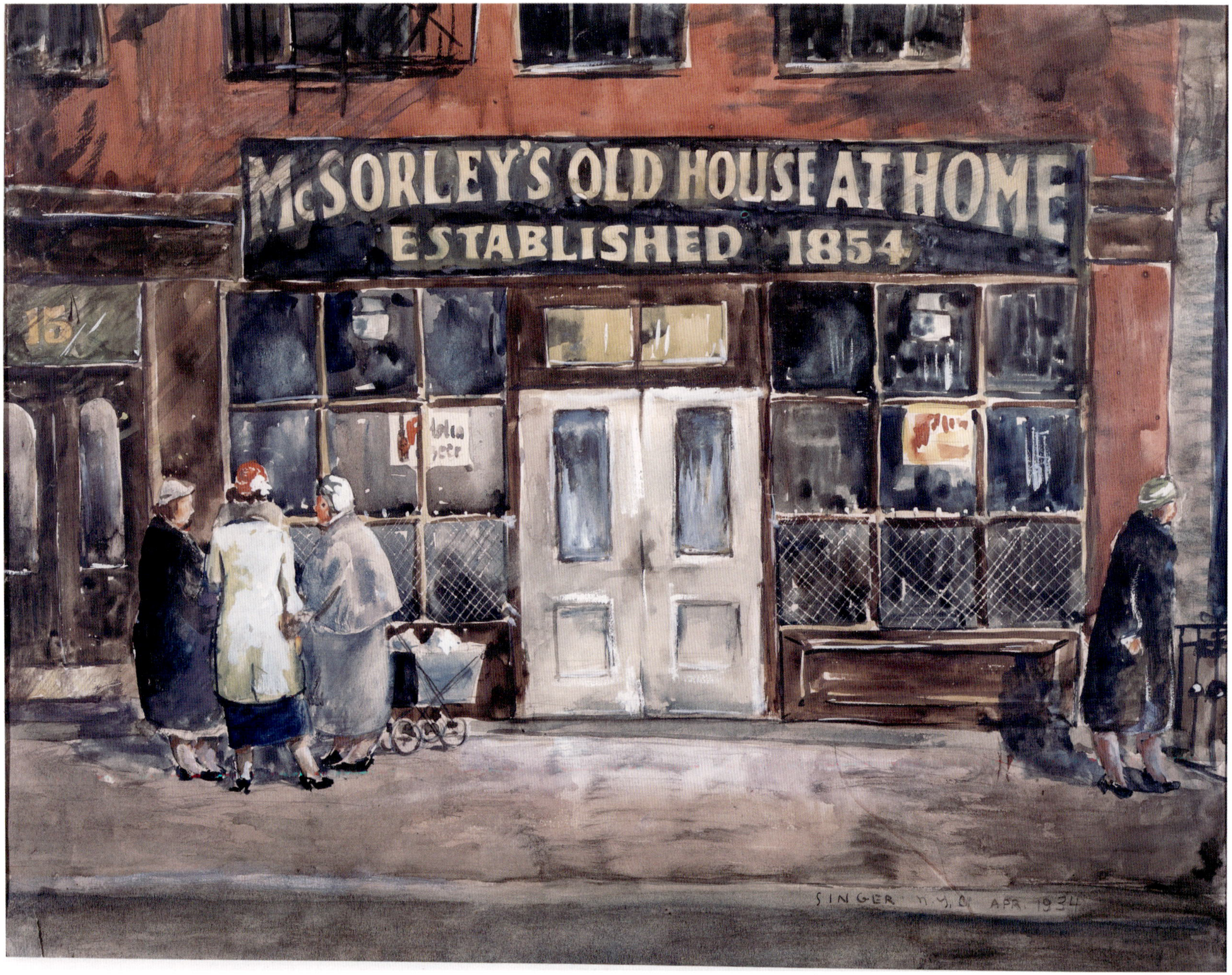

Fig. 53. *McSorley's on Sunday,* 1934. Watercolor, 15¾ x 20¼. The Butler Institute of American Art, gift of Drs. Paul and Laura Mesaros

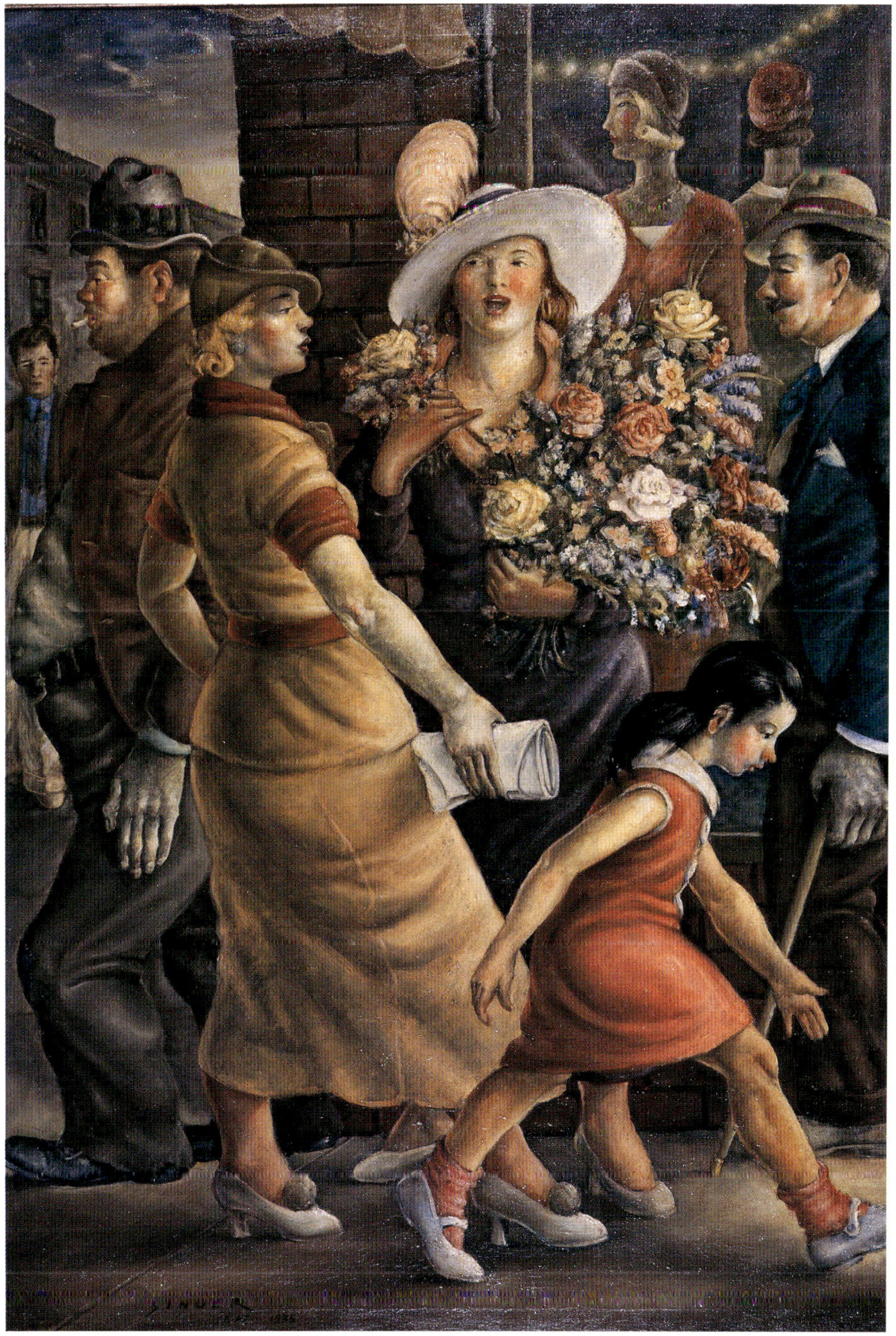

Fig. 54. *The Flower Vendor,* 1935. Oil, 58 x 40. The Butler Institute of American Art

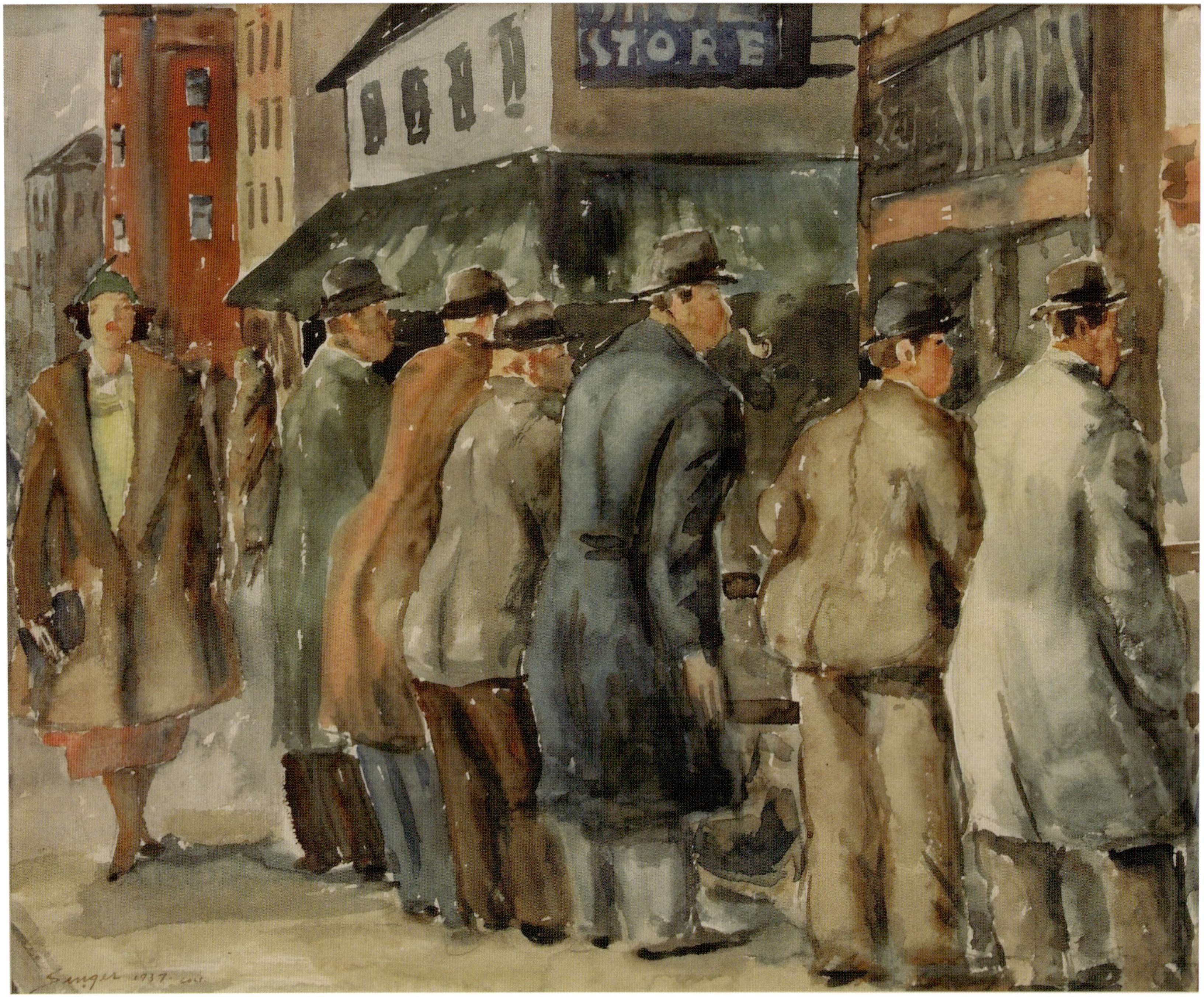

Fig. 55. *On Lookers,* 1937. Watercolor, 11½ x 14¼. Canton Museum of Art, given in memory of Austin Lynch and Mary K. Lynch

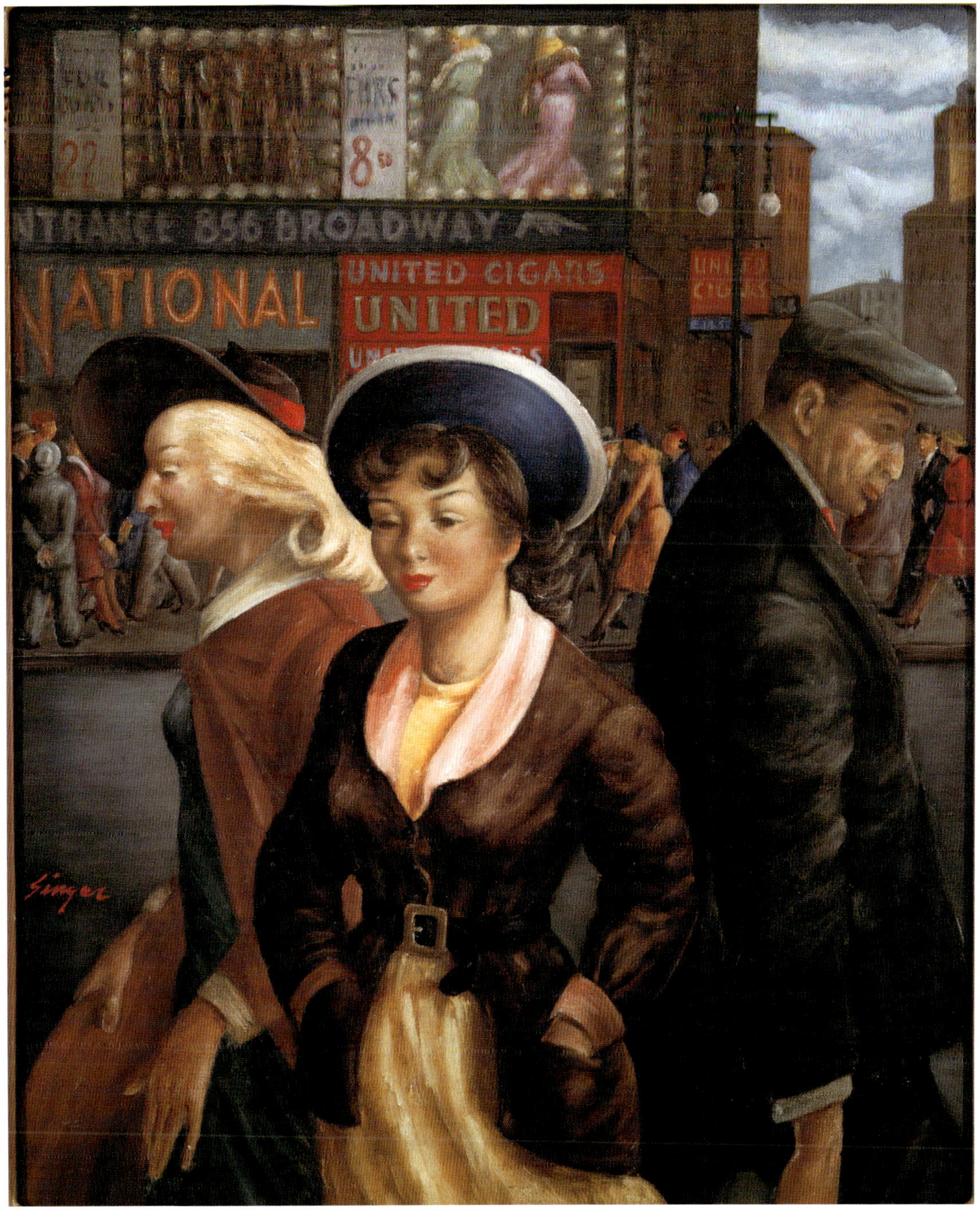

Fig. 56. *On 14th Street,* 1938. Oil, 30 x 24. Courtesy of Michael Lawlor

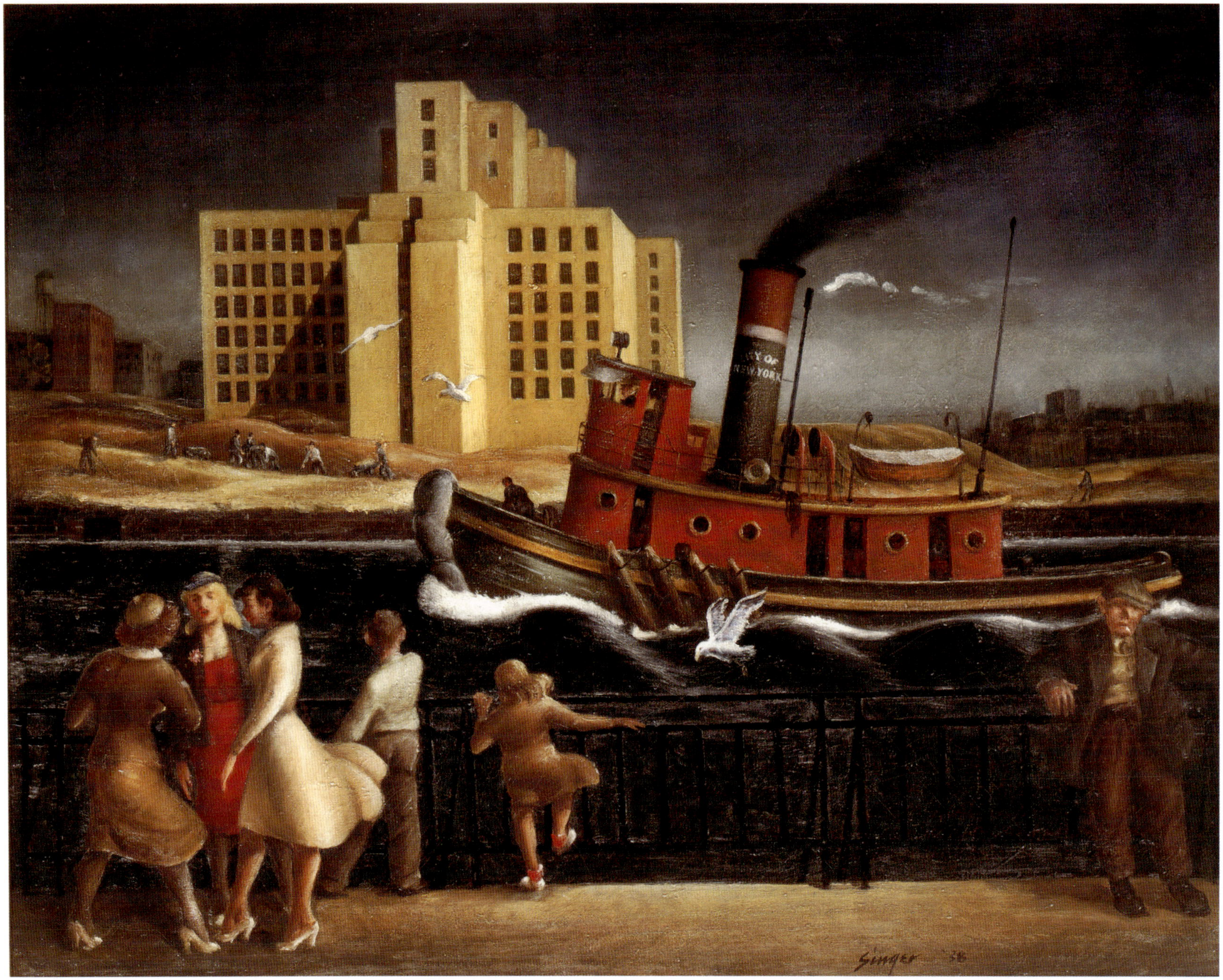

Fig. 57. *East River, New York,* 1938. Oil, 32 x 40. Courtesy of Bruce and Susan Lueck

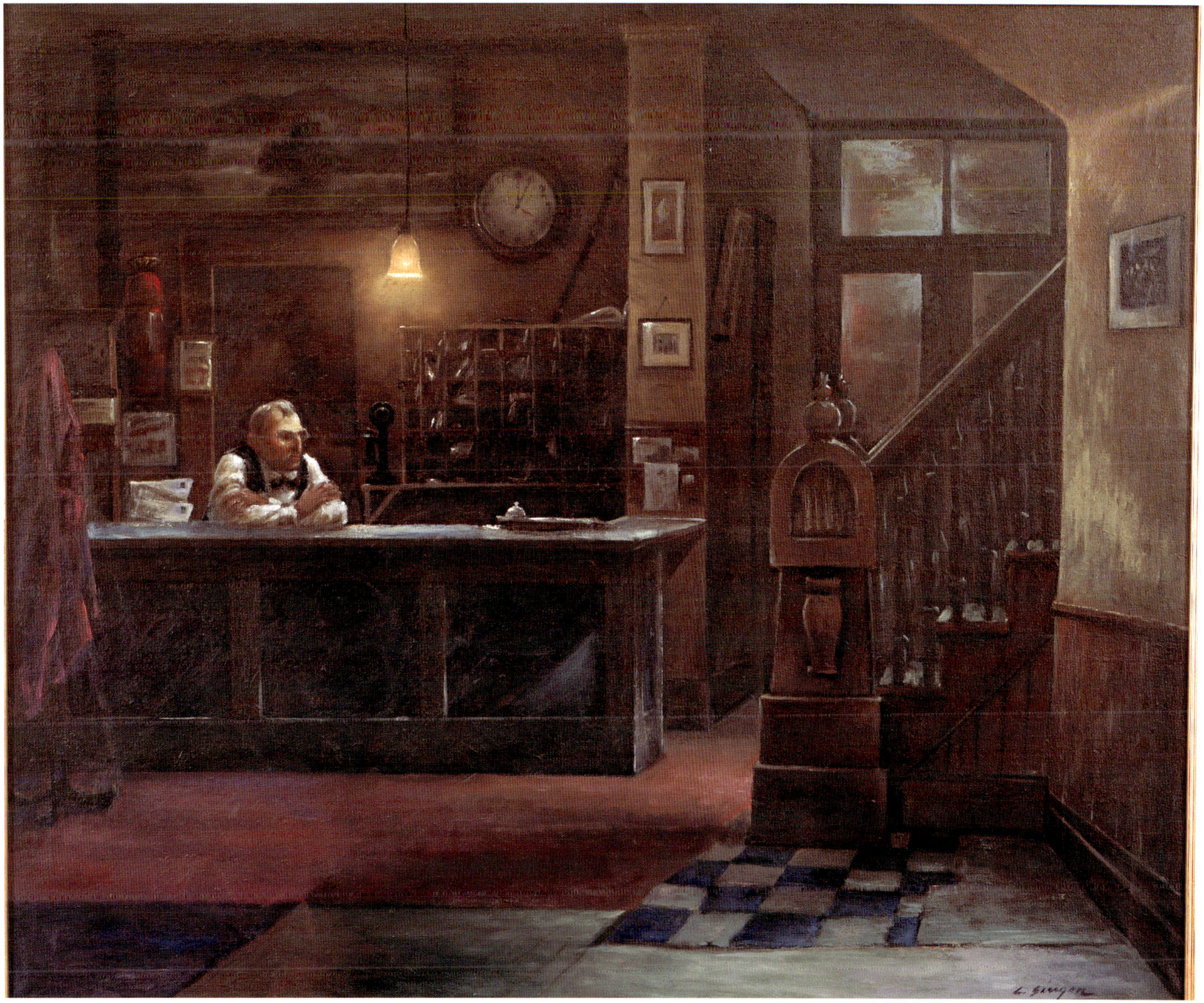

Fig. 58. *Hotel Lobby,* 1947–60. Oil, 28 x 46. Courtesy of a private collector

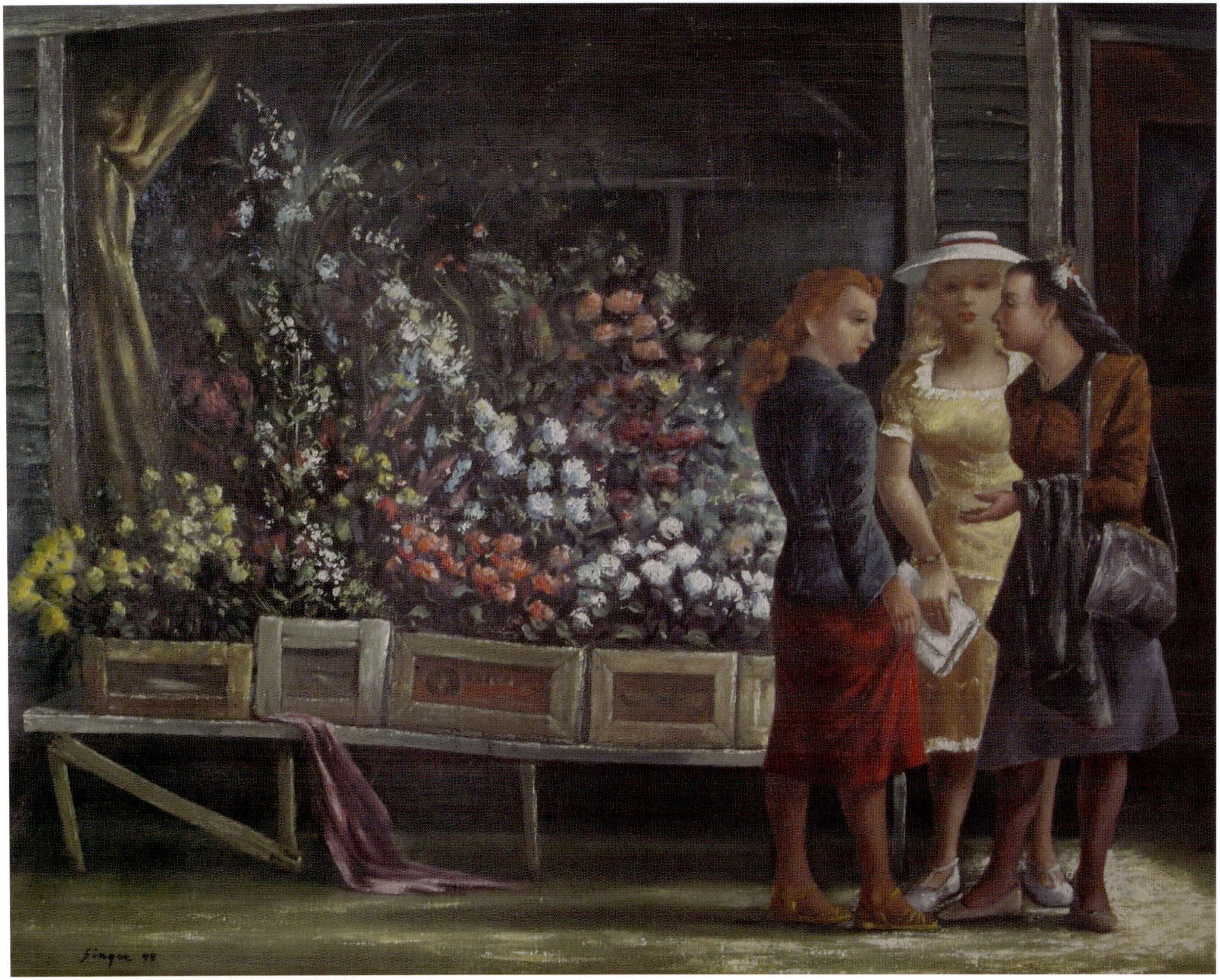

Fig. 59. *Flower Shop,* 1948. Oil, 37 x 48. Courtesy of Donald "Pete" Slates

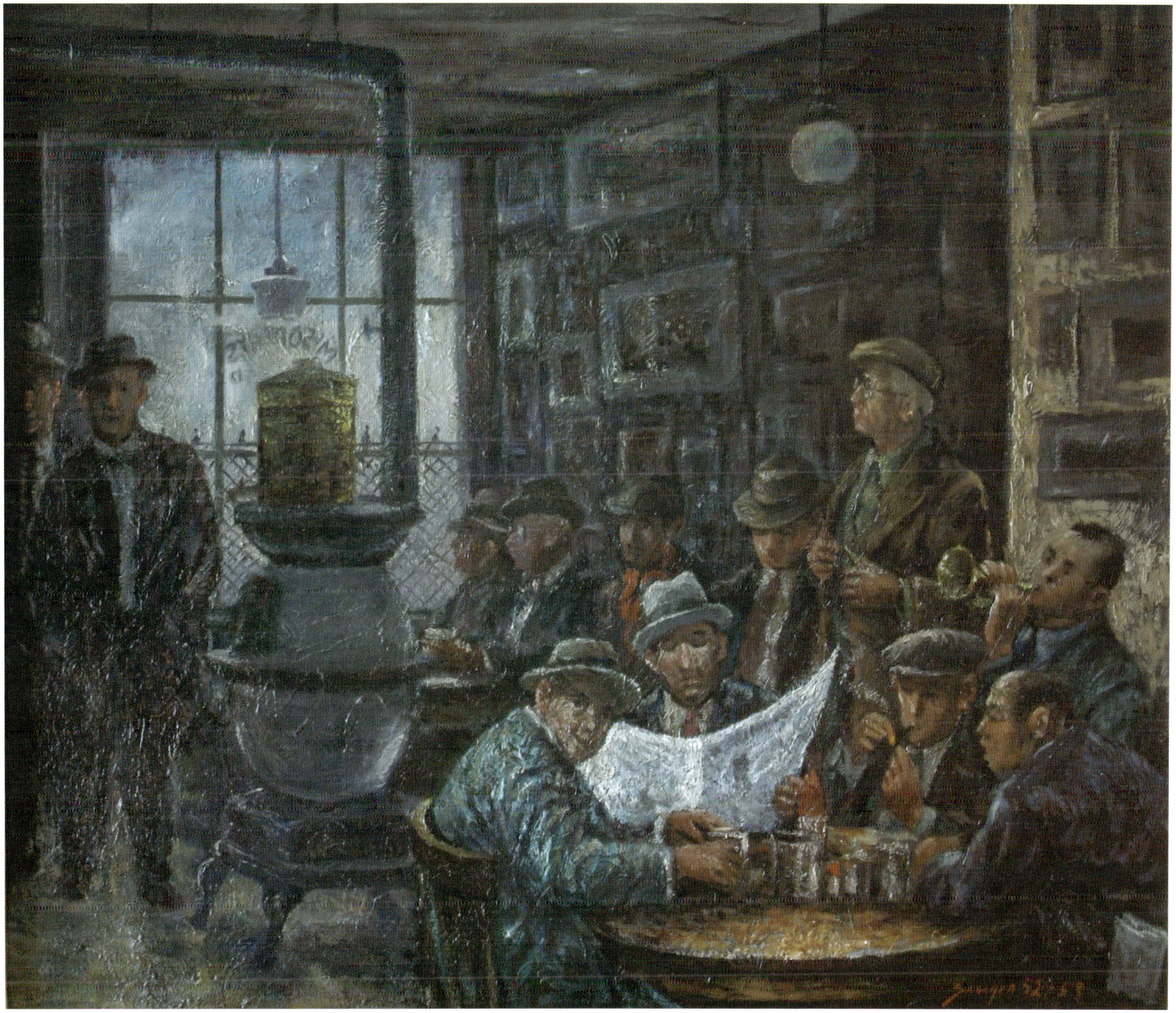

Fig. 60. *Washington's Birthday,* 1952–53. Oil, 18 x 20. Courtesy of Thomas W. Darling

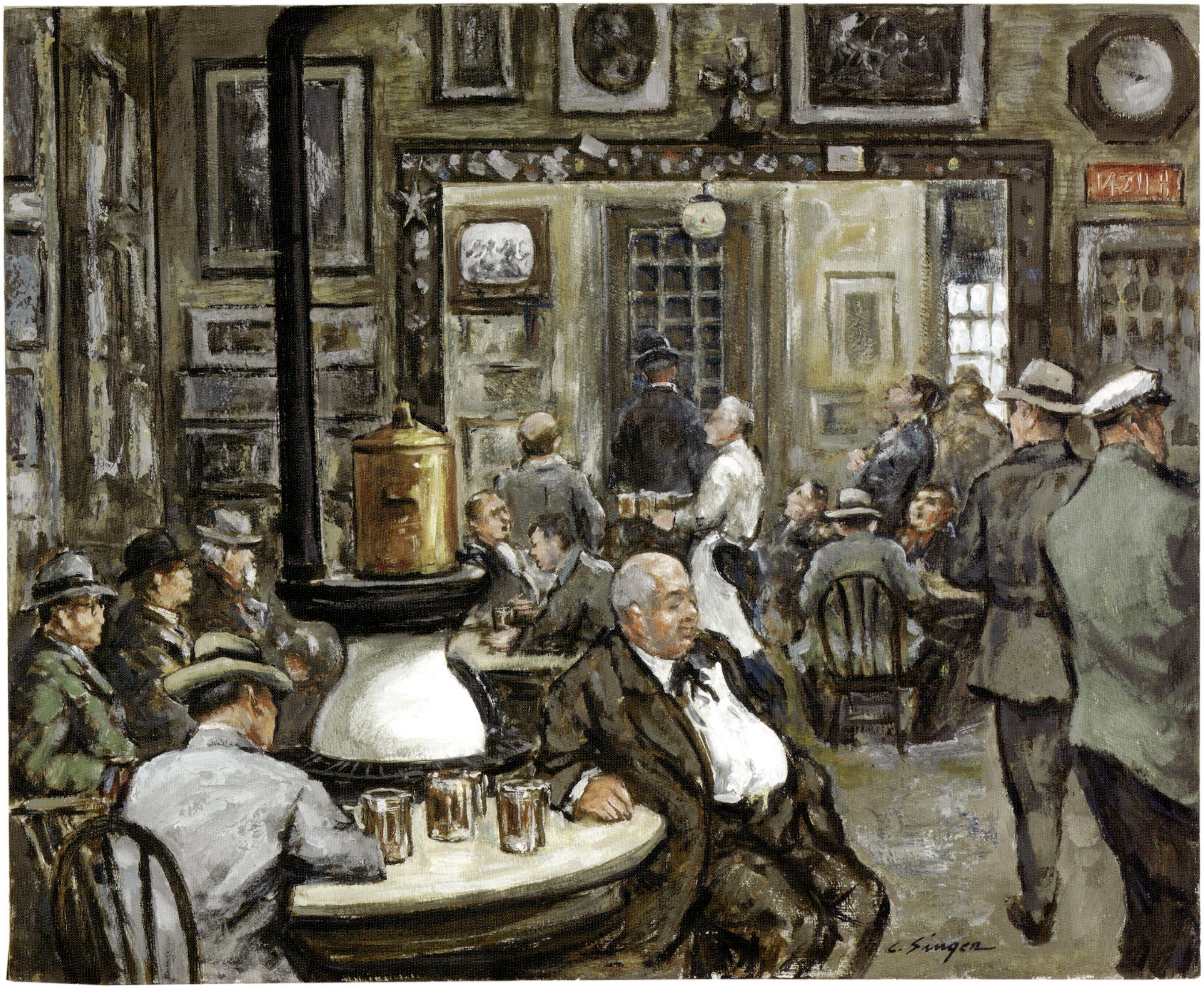

Fig. 61. *Football Saturday at McSorley's,* 1960. Casein, 15 x 19. Courtesy of a private collector

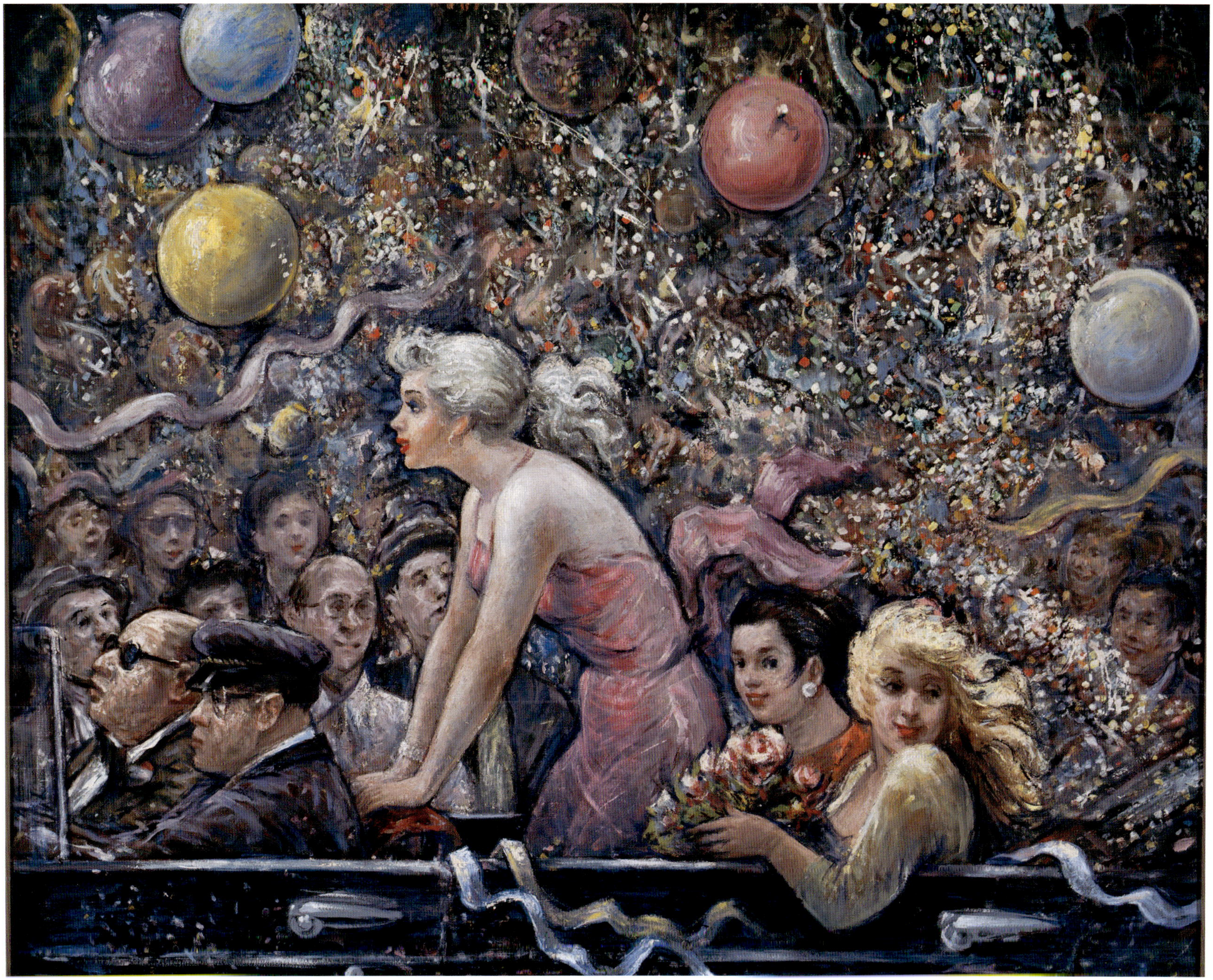

Fig. 62. *Parade*, 1965. Oil, 39¼ x 49¼. Courtesy of The Butler Institute of American Art, gift of Joseph Erdelac

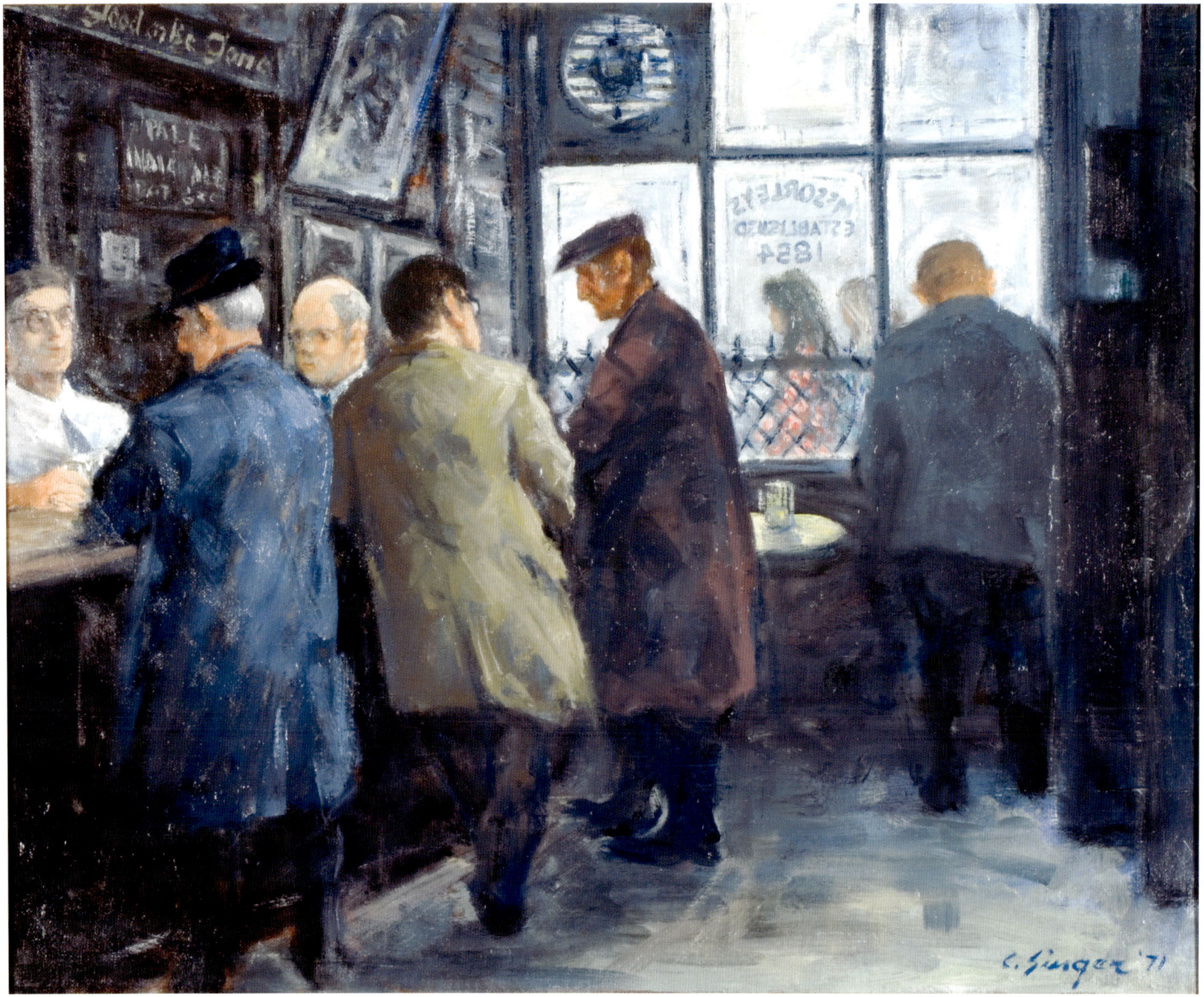

Fig. 63. *McSorley's: 5 Customers,* 1971. Oil, 18 x 20. Courtesy of Dr. Michael and Sue Lehmiller

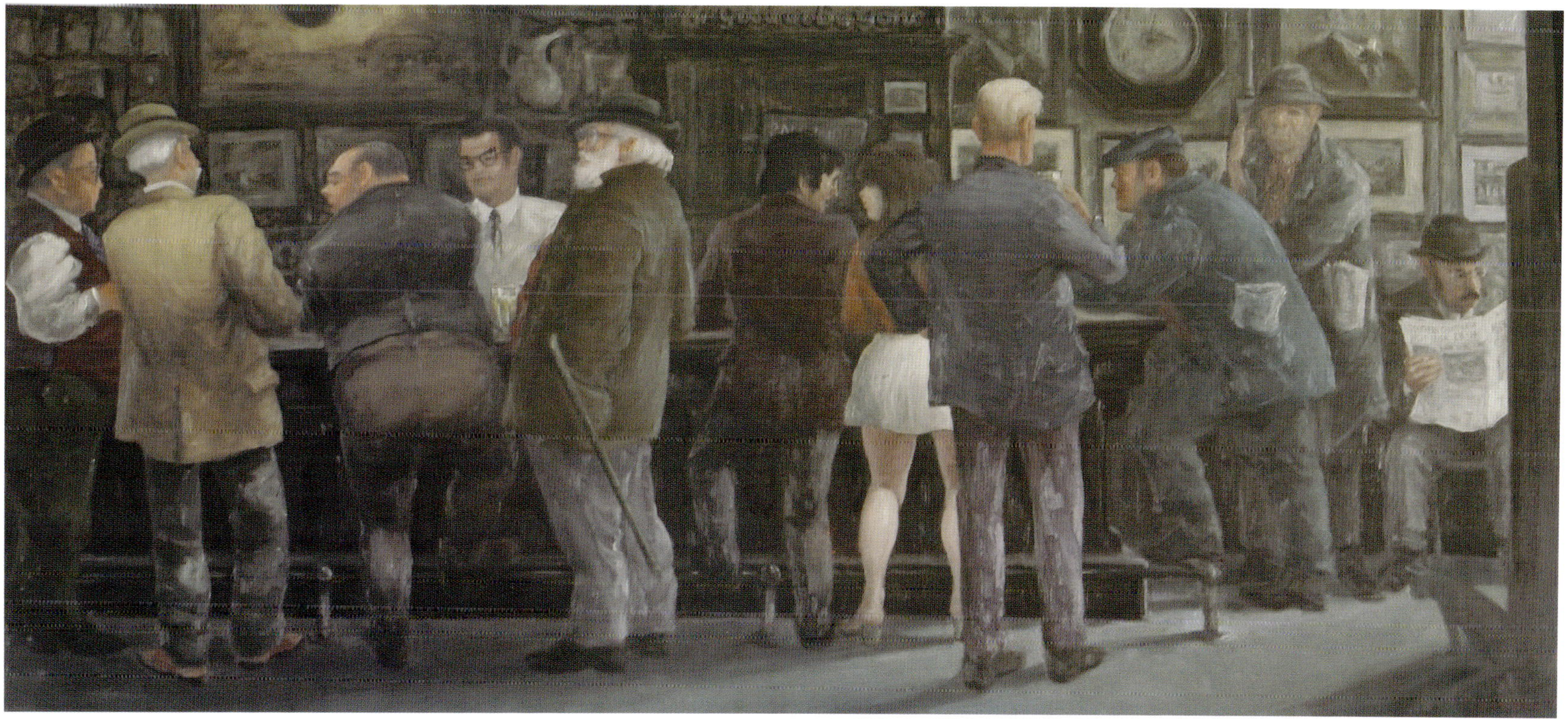

Fig. 64. *McSorley's First Team,* 1971. Oil, 18 x 40. Courtesy of Donald "Pete" Slates

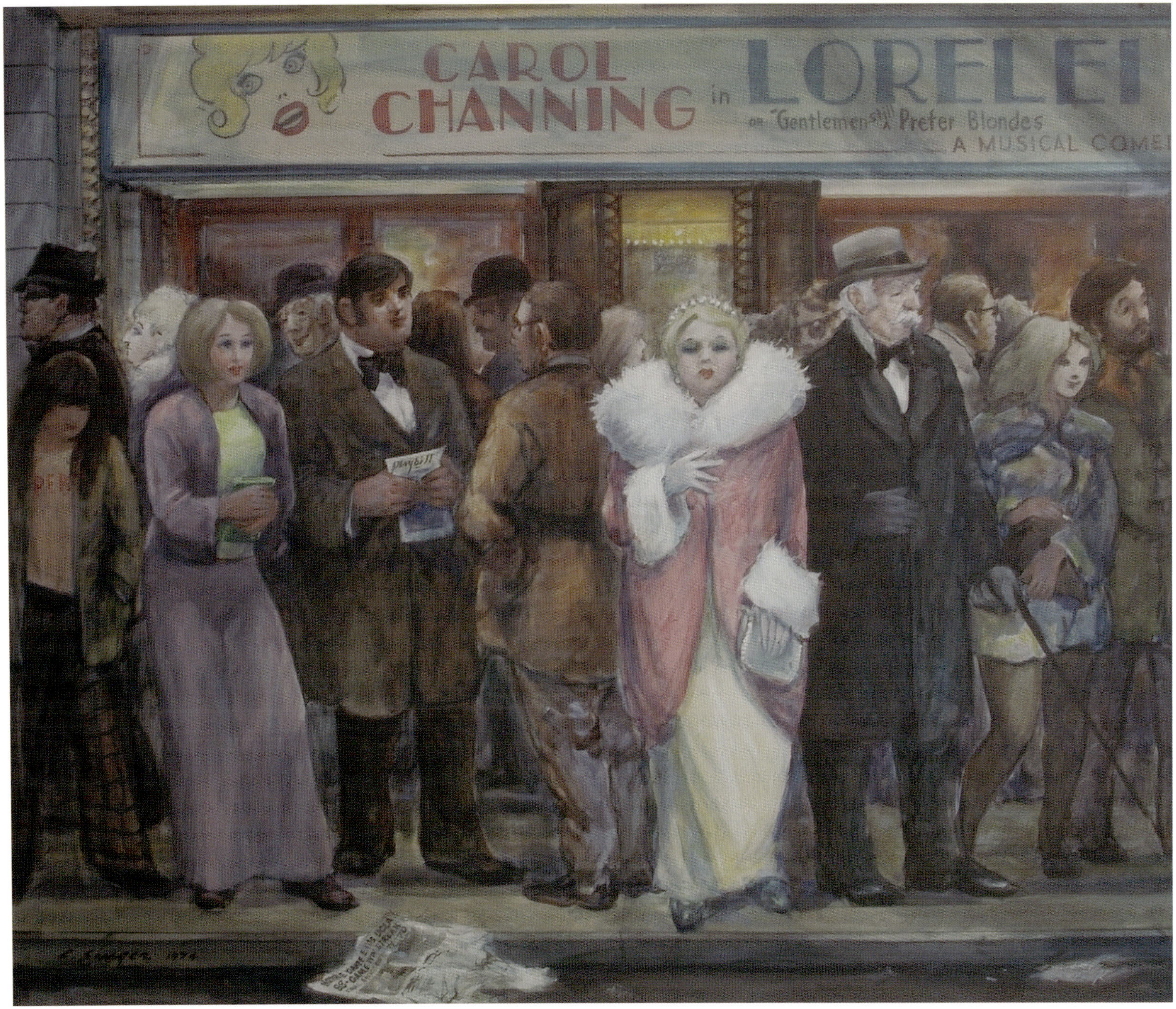

Fig. 65. *Broadway,* 1974. Oil, 28 x 33. Courtesy of Mr. and Mrs. James M. Conley

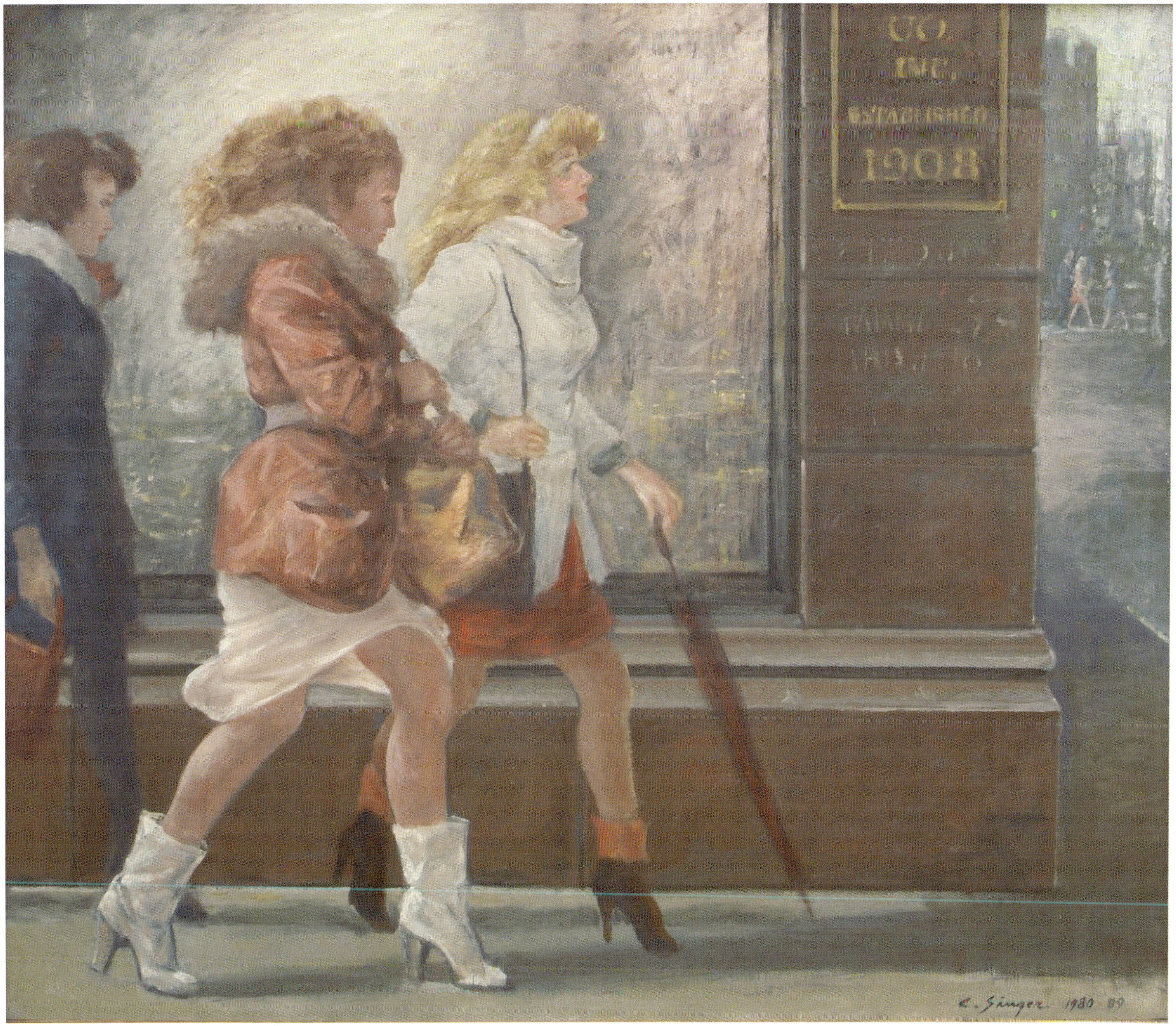

Fig. 66. *Brownstone*, 1980. Oil, 31 x 37½. Courtesy of Mr. and Mrs. Paul Herron

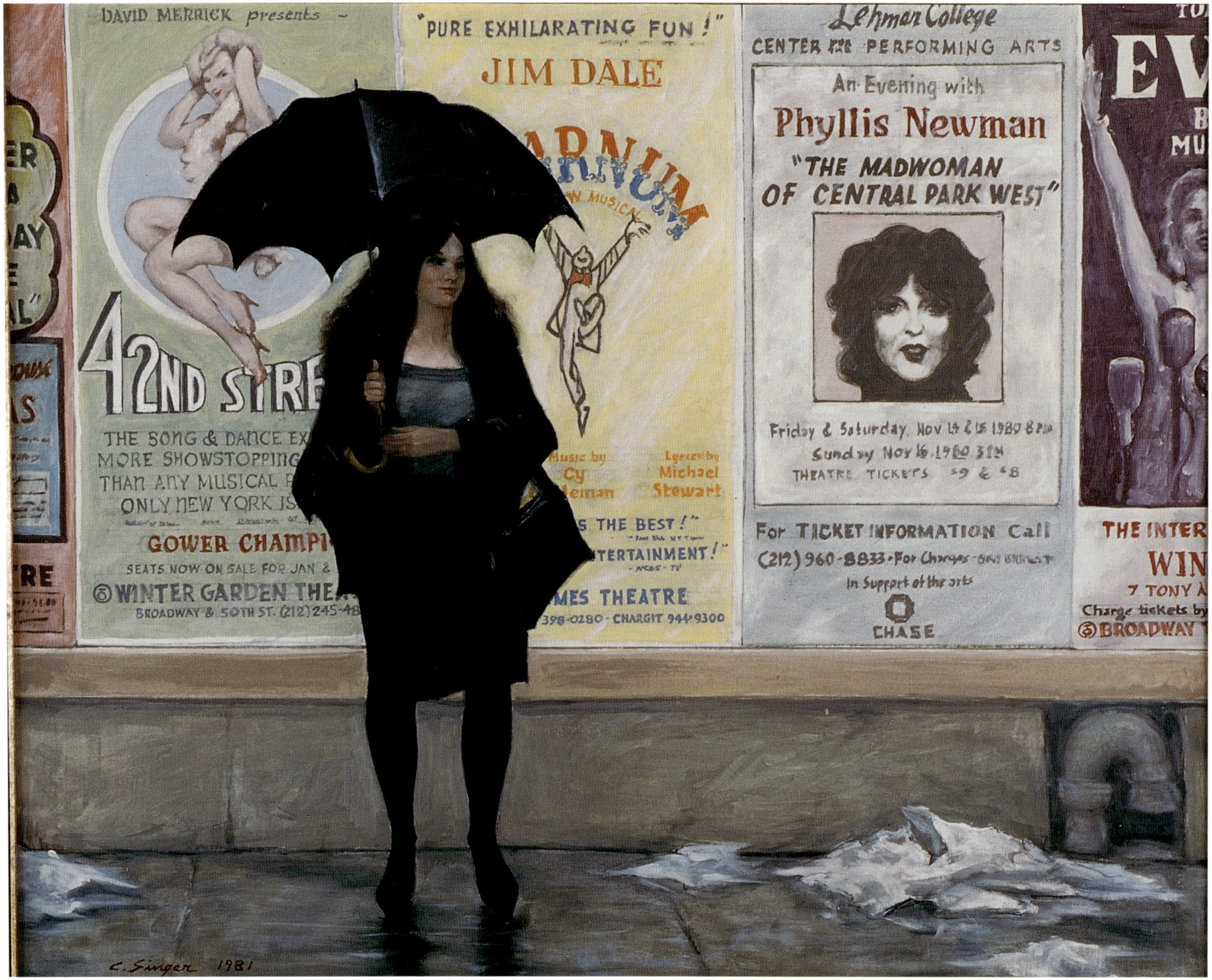

Fig. 67. *Waiting in the Rain,* 1981. Oil, 33 x 41. Courtesy of Ann and Stuart Wallack

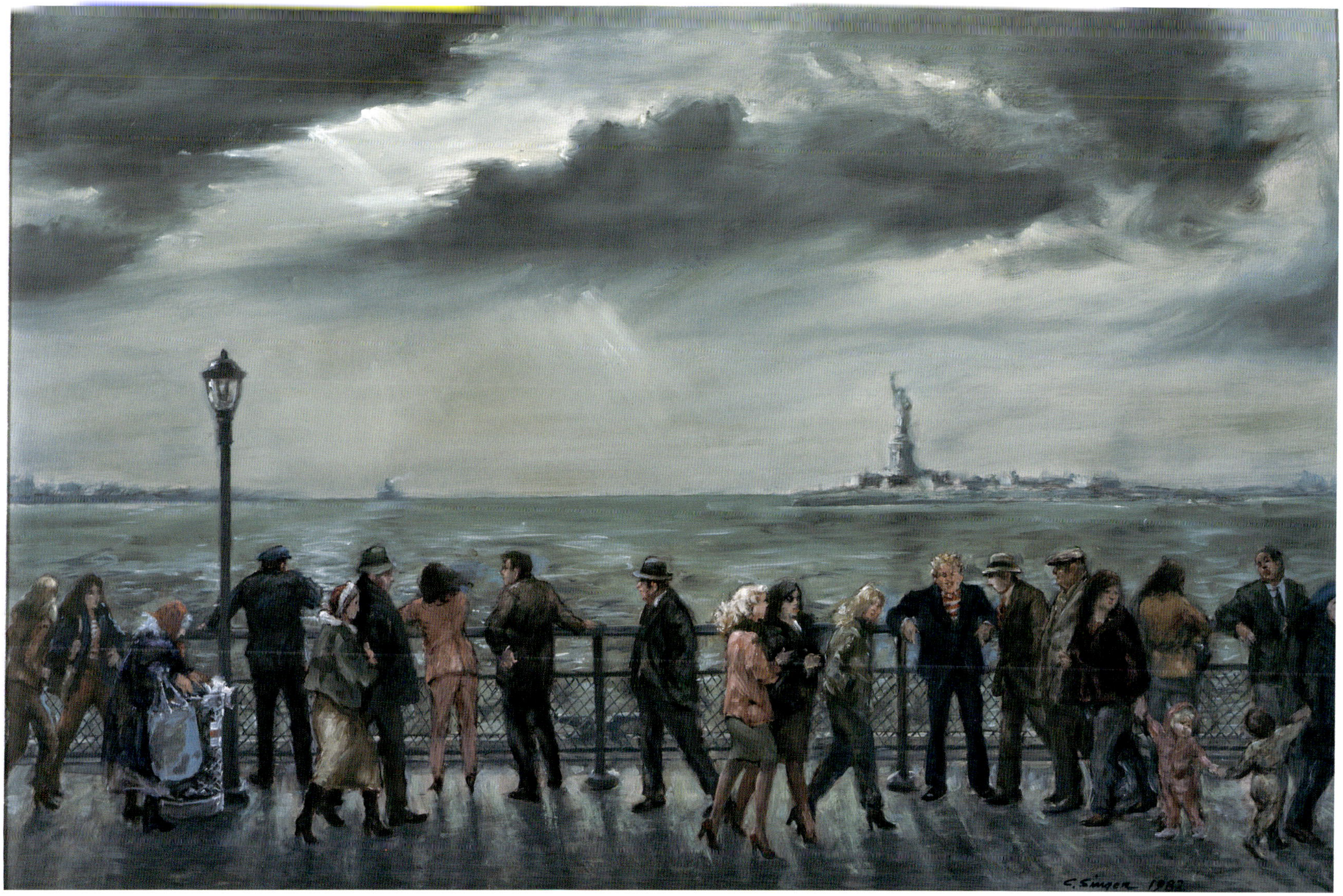

Fig. 68. *Battery Park, Statue of Liberty,* 1982. Oil, 25 x 40. Courtesy of Dr. and Mrs. Albert B. Cinelli

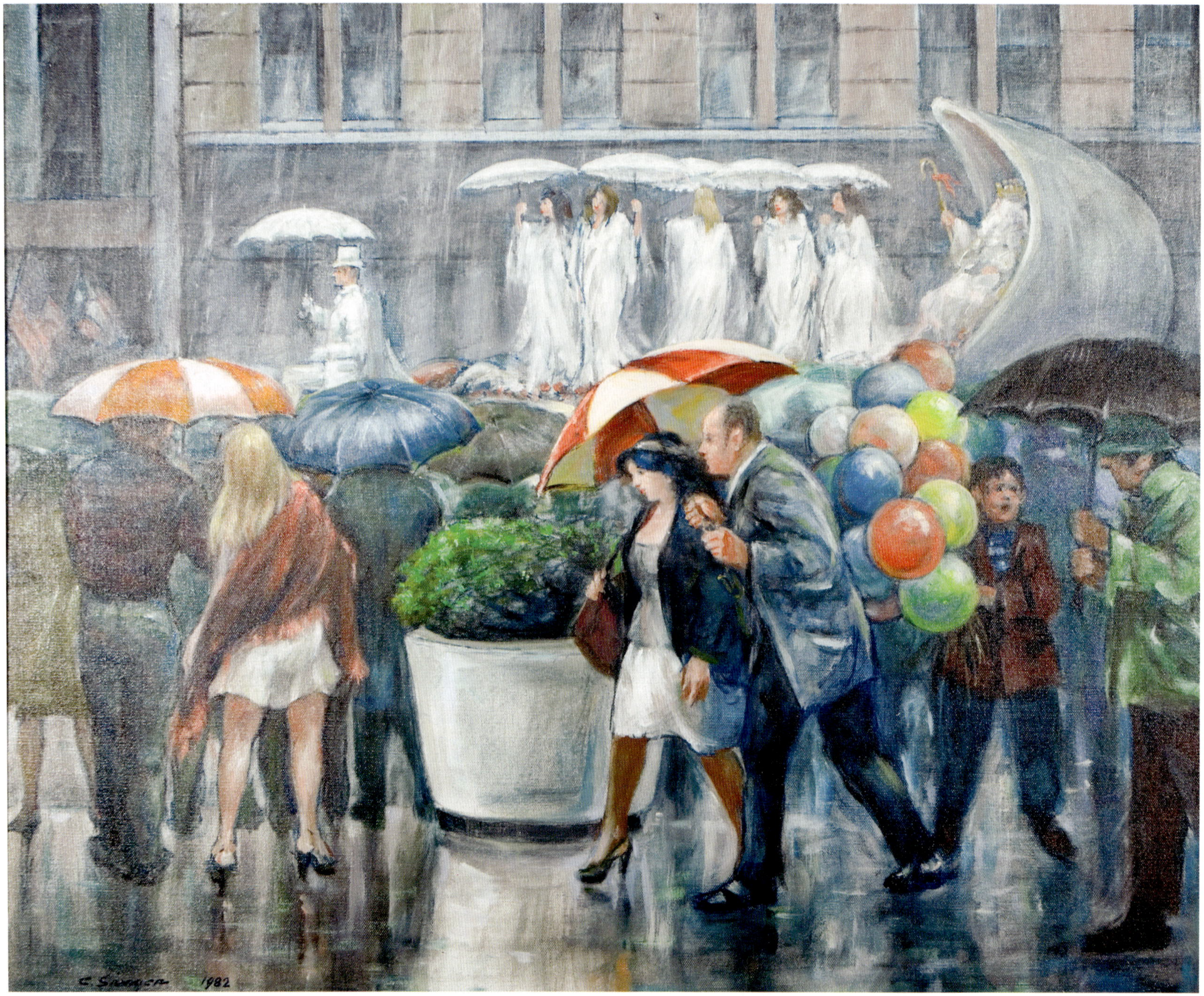

Fig. 69. *5th Avenue Parade,* 1982. Oil, 24 x 30. Courtesy of Mr. and Mrs. Donald J. Geis

Profiles and Portraits

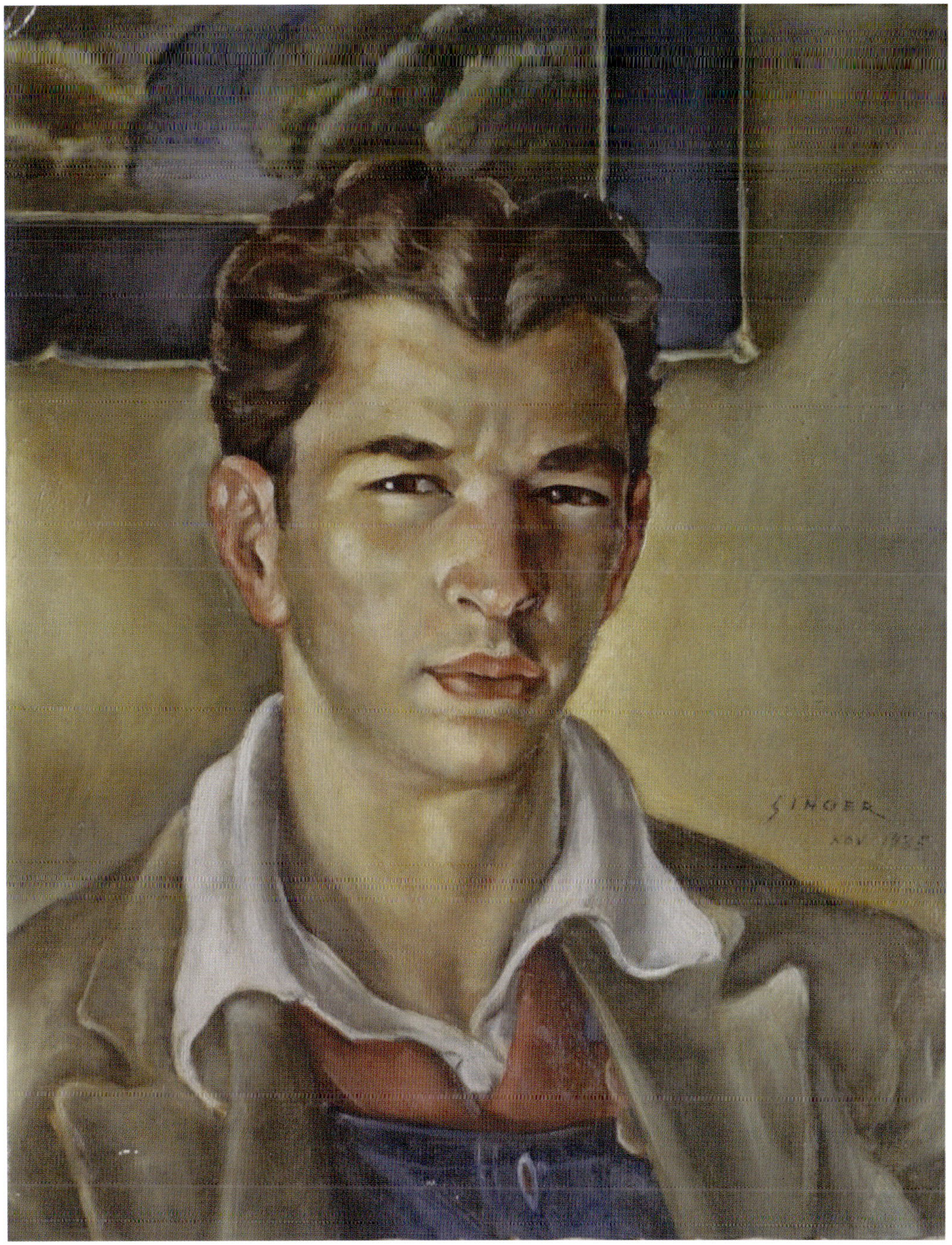

Fig. 70. *Self-Portrait,* 1935. Oil, 16 x 20. Courtesy of the Massillon Museum, gift of Albert Hise

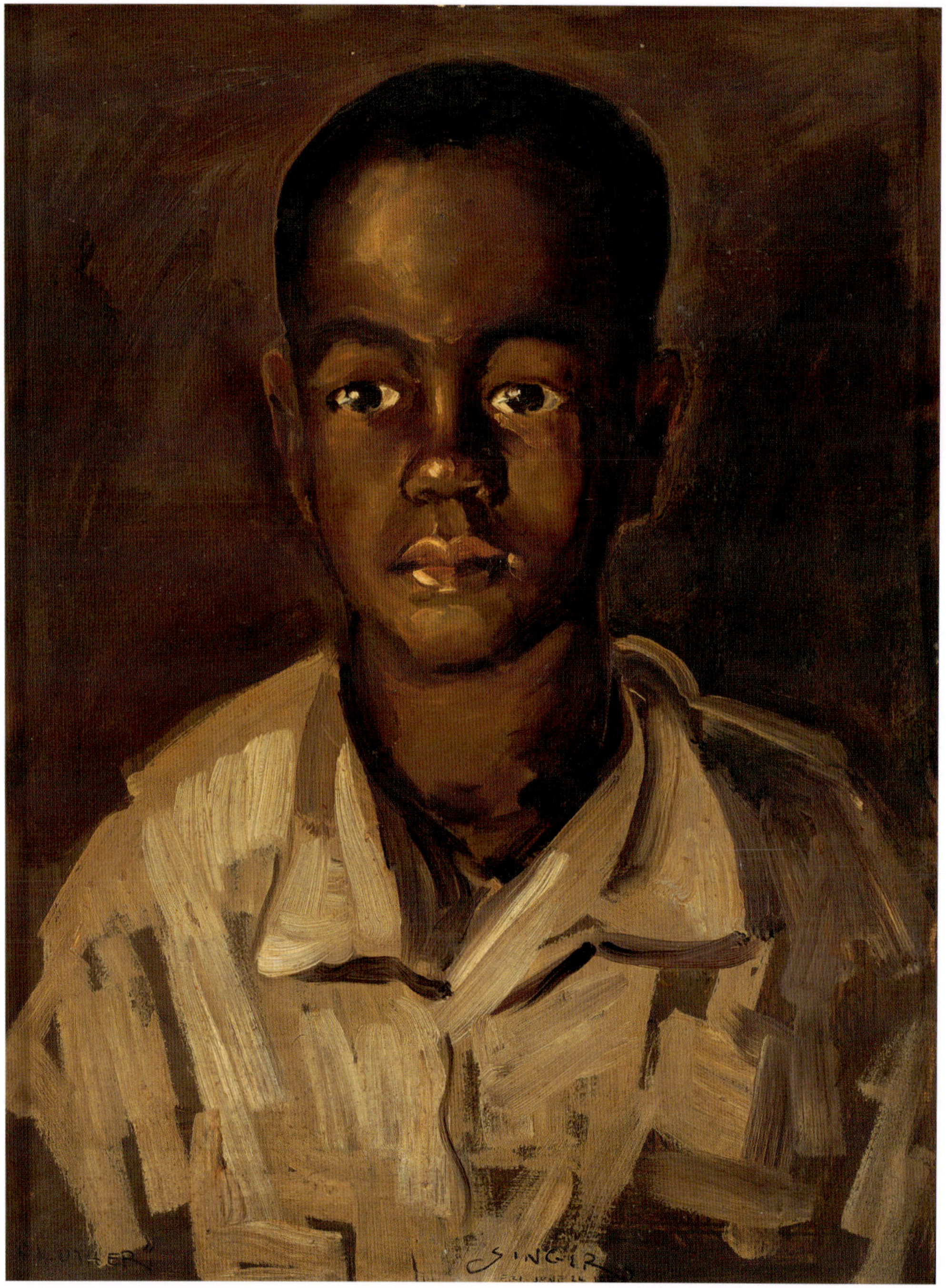

Fig. 71. *Luther,* 1932. Oil, 20 x 15 (painted in one hour, Friday, June 24, 1932). Courtesy of Ed and Karen Ogul, Franklin, Michigan

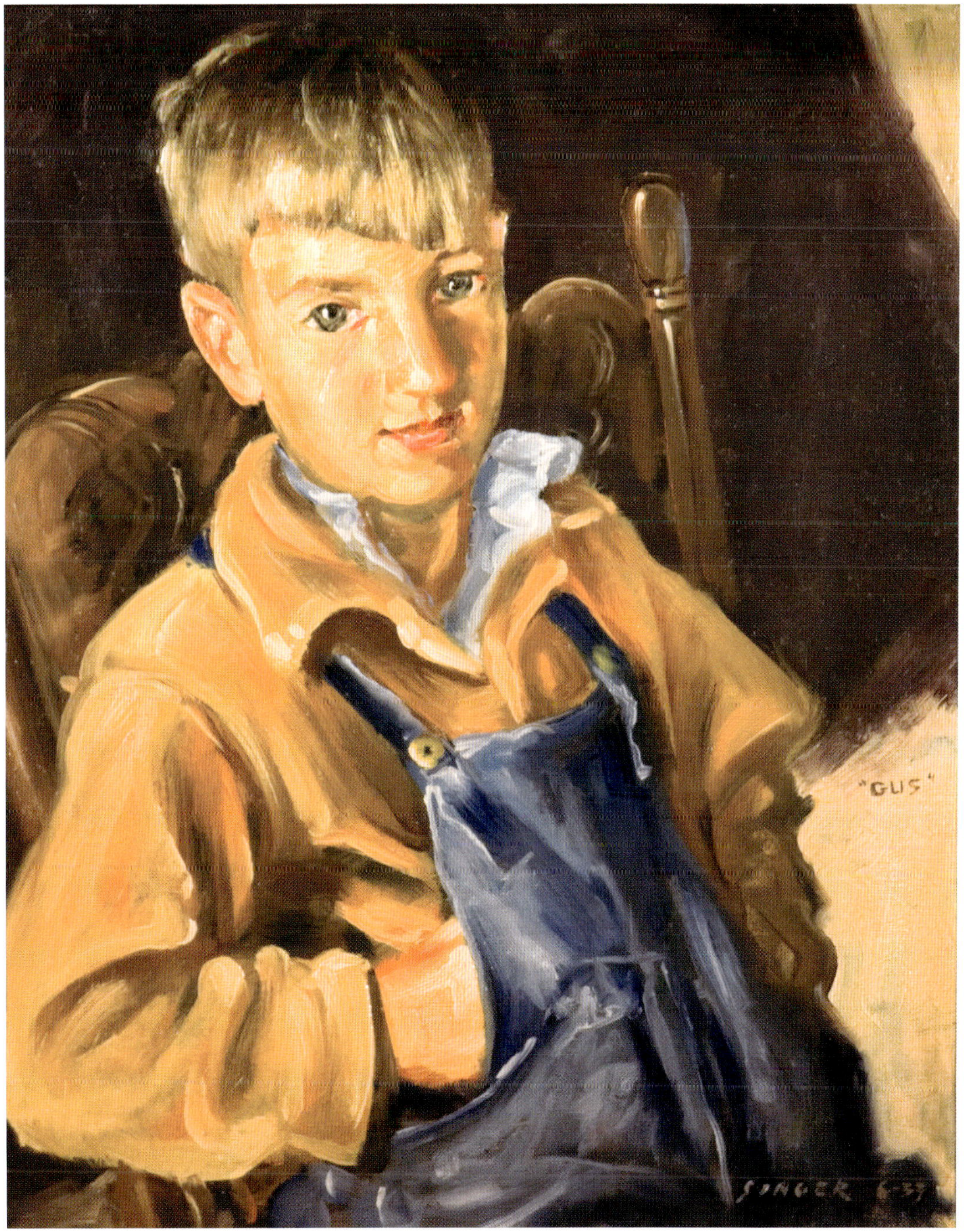

Fig. 72. *Gus,* 1933. Oil, 23 x 19. Courtesy of a private collector

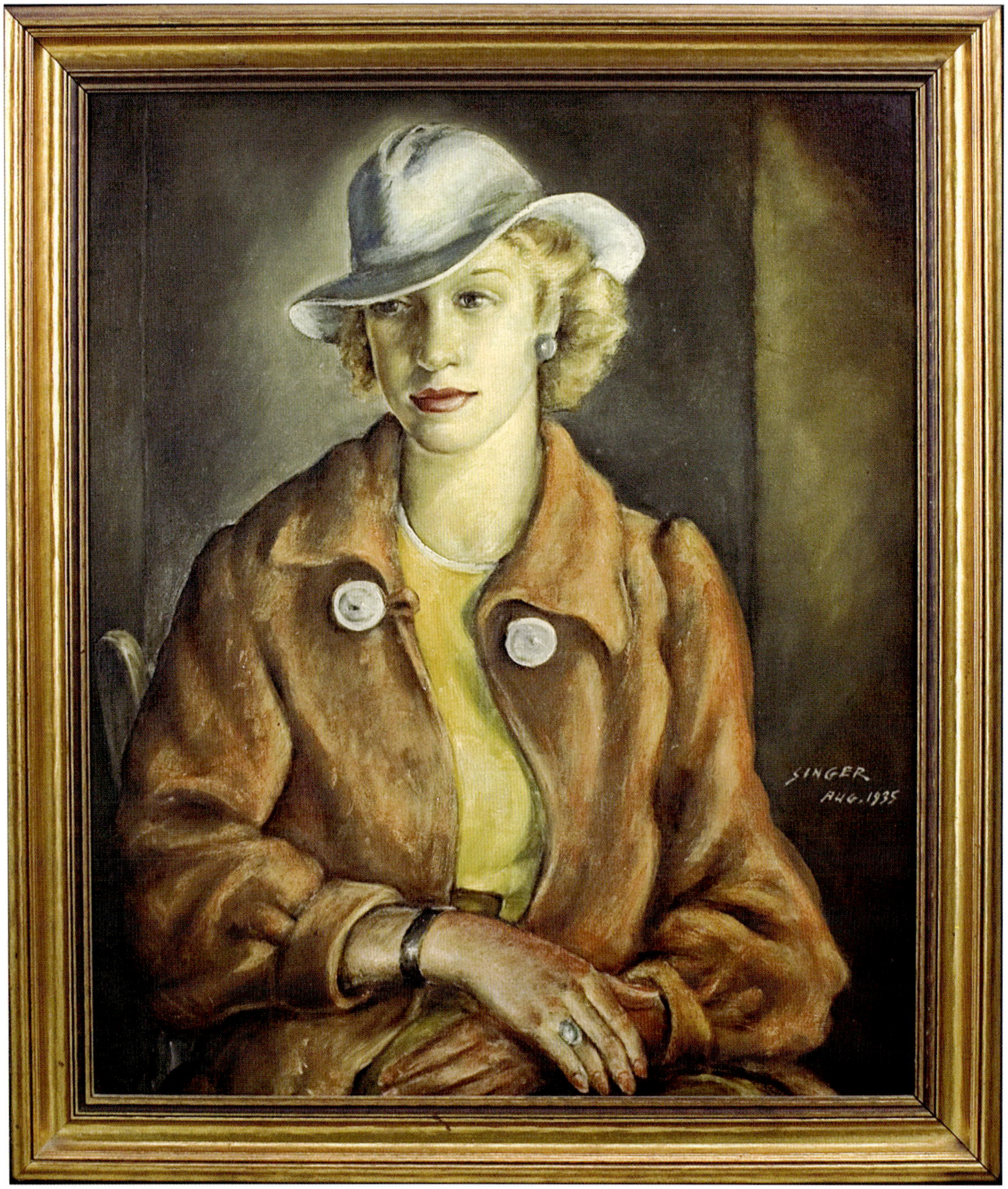

Fig. 73. *Portrait of Doris Singer,* 1935. Oil, 30½ x 25½. Courtesy of a private collector

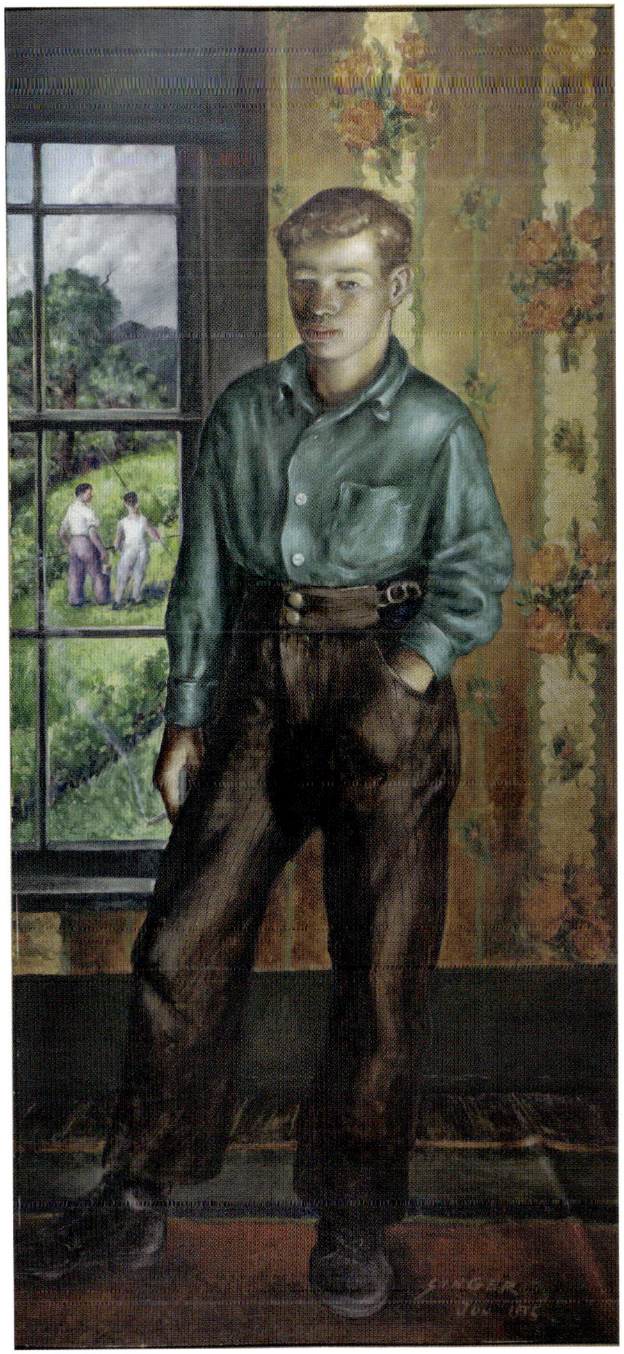

Fig. 74. *Bill,* 1935. Oil, 68 x 31¾. Courtesy of the Pennsylvania Academy of the Fine Arts, Philadelphia, John Lambert Fund

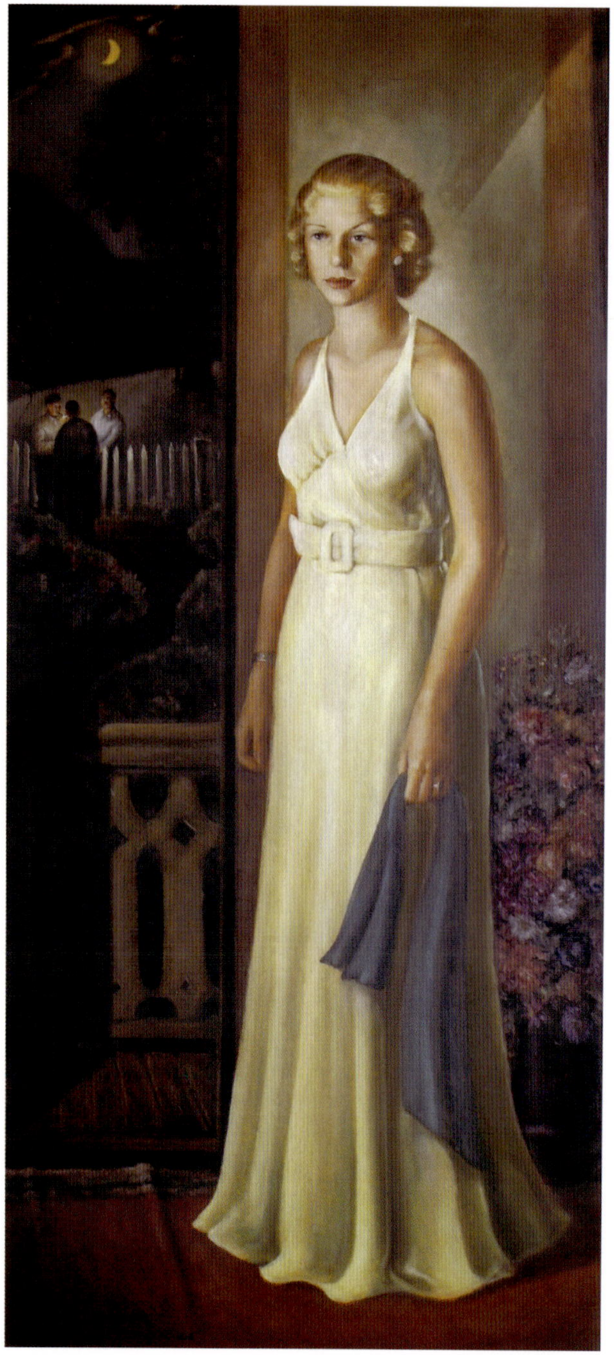

Fig. 75. *Doris Singer,* 1936. Oil, 77 x 35¼. Courtesy of a private collector

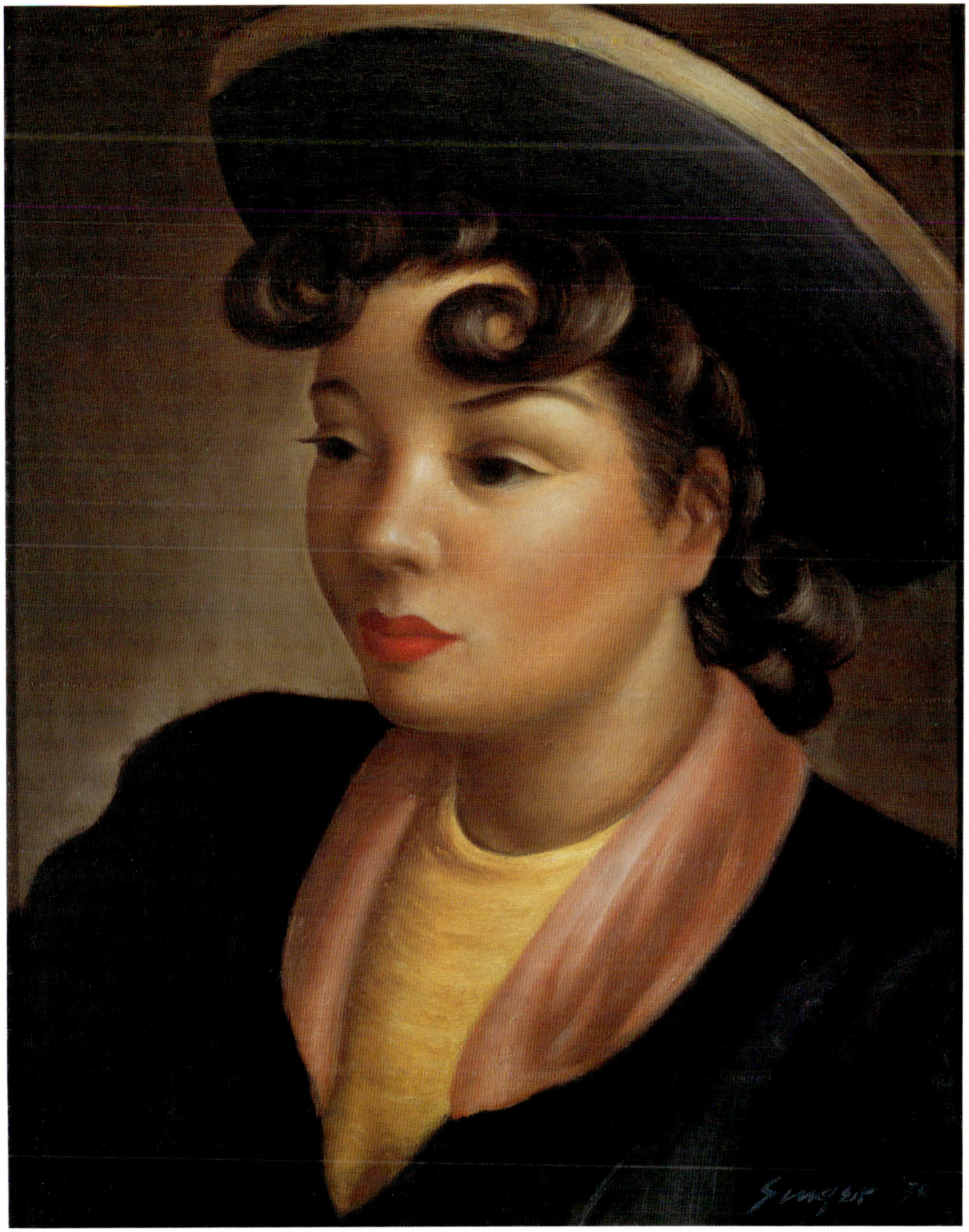

Fig. 76. *Marion,* 1938. Oil, 20 x 16. Courtesy of Ed and Karen Ogul, Franklin, Michigan

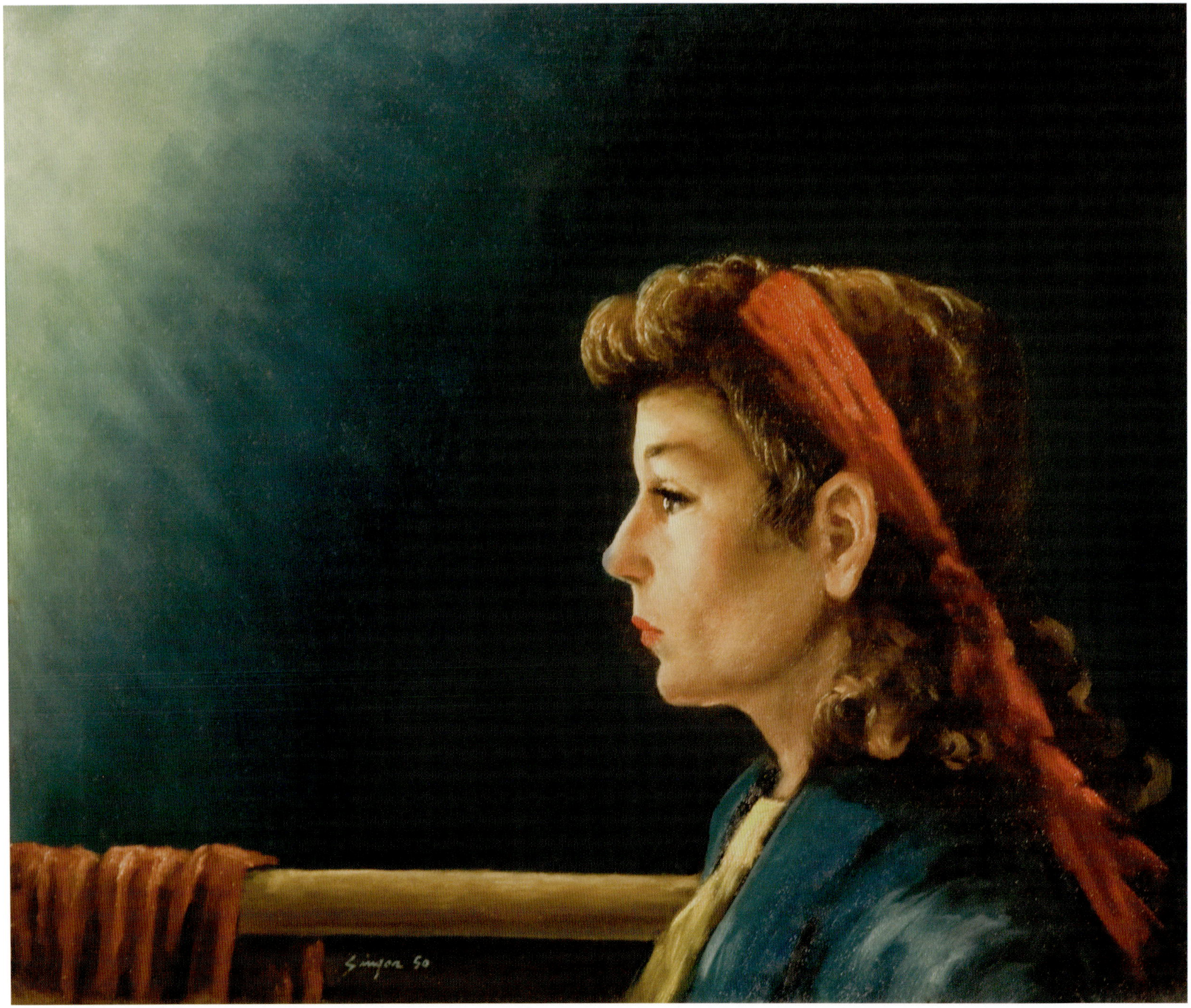

Fig. 77. *Mrs. Clyde Singer,* 1950. Oil, 15 x 20. Courtesy of a private collector

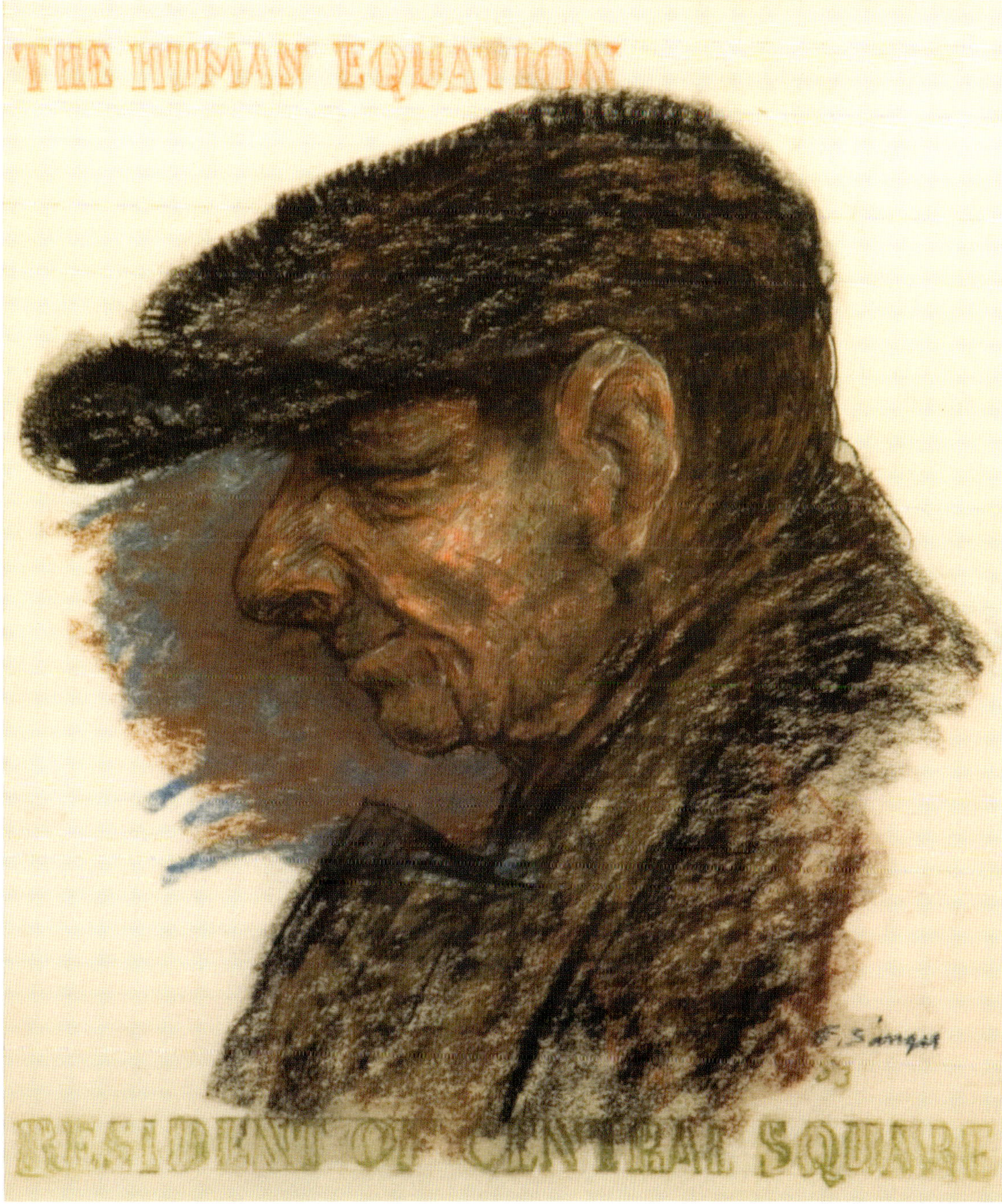

Fig. 78. *The Human Equation*, 1953. Charcoal/Pastel, 17 x 14. Courtesy of a private collector

Polls, Poverty, and Protest

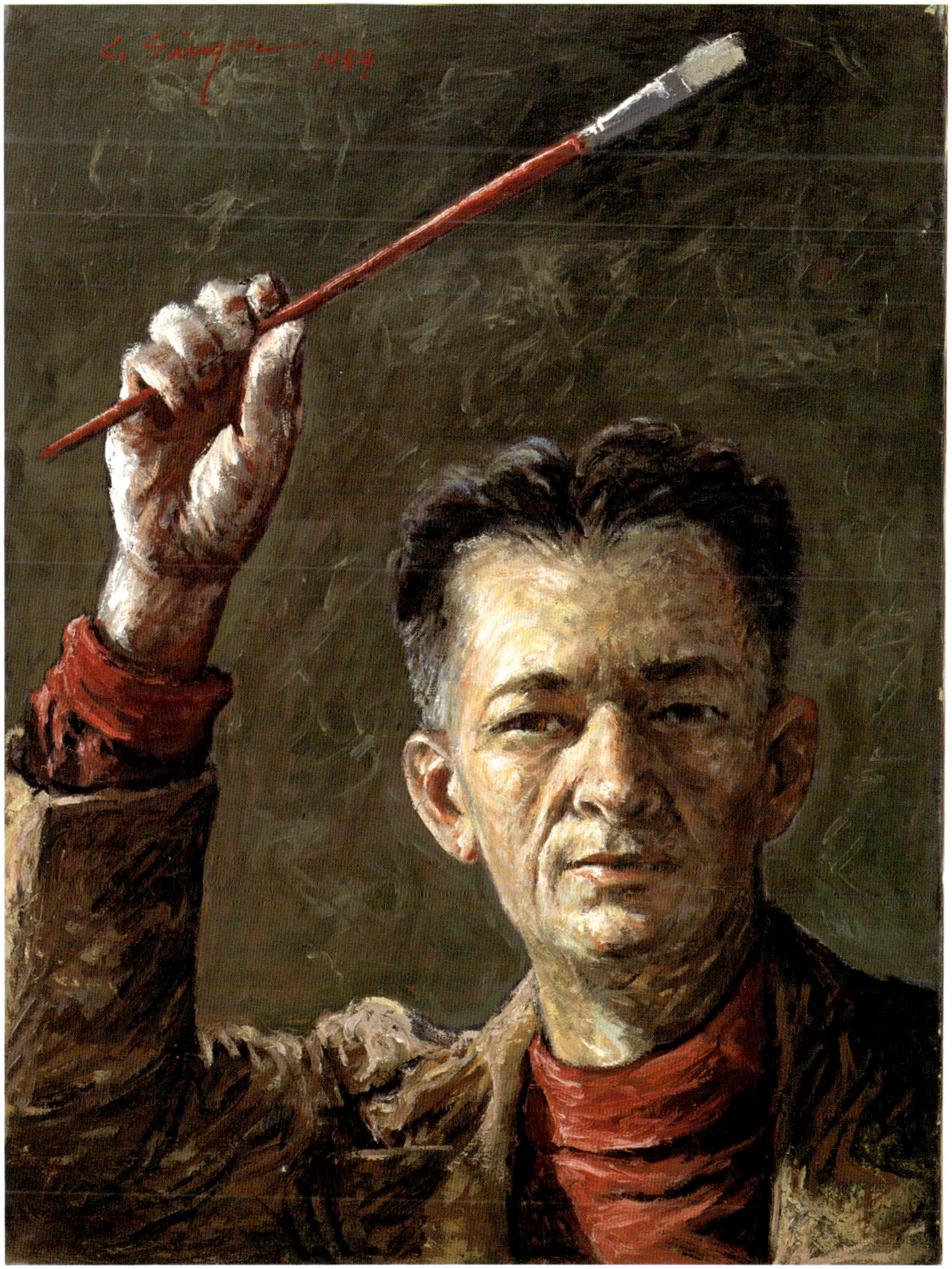

Fig. 79. *Self-Portrait #26,* 1954. Oil, 20 x 16. Courtesy of Ed and Karen Ogul, Franklin, Michigan

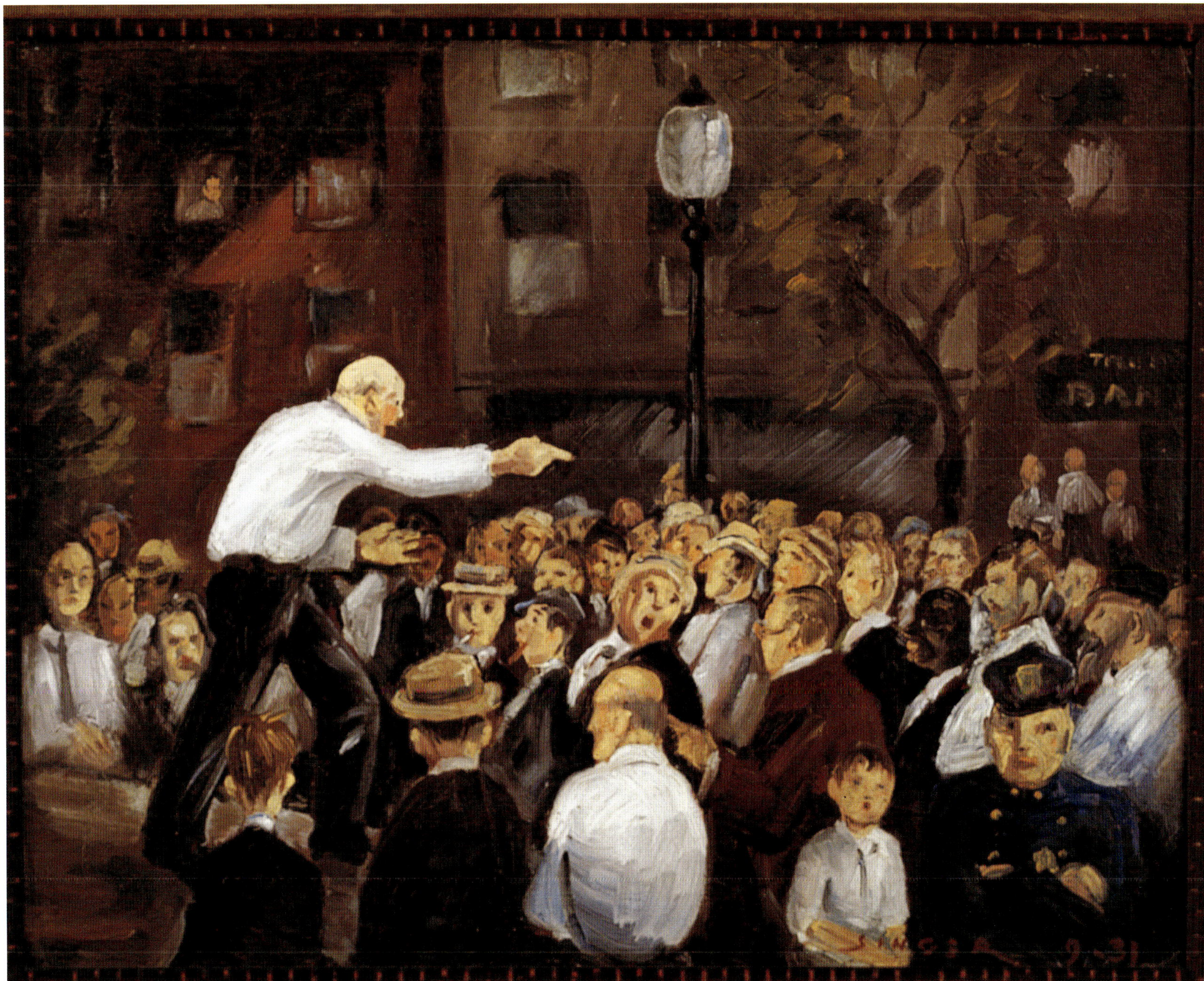

Fig. 80. *The Communist Rally in Cleveland,* 1931. Oil, 17 x 22. Courtesy of a private collector

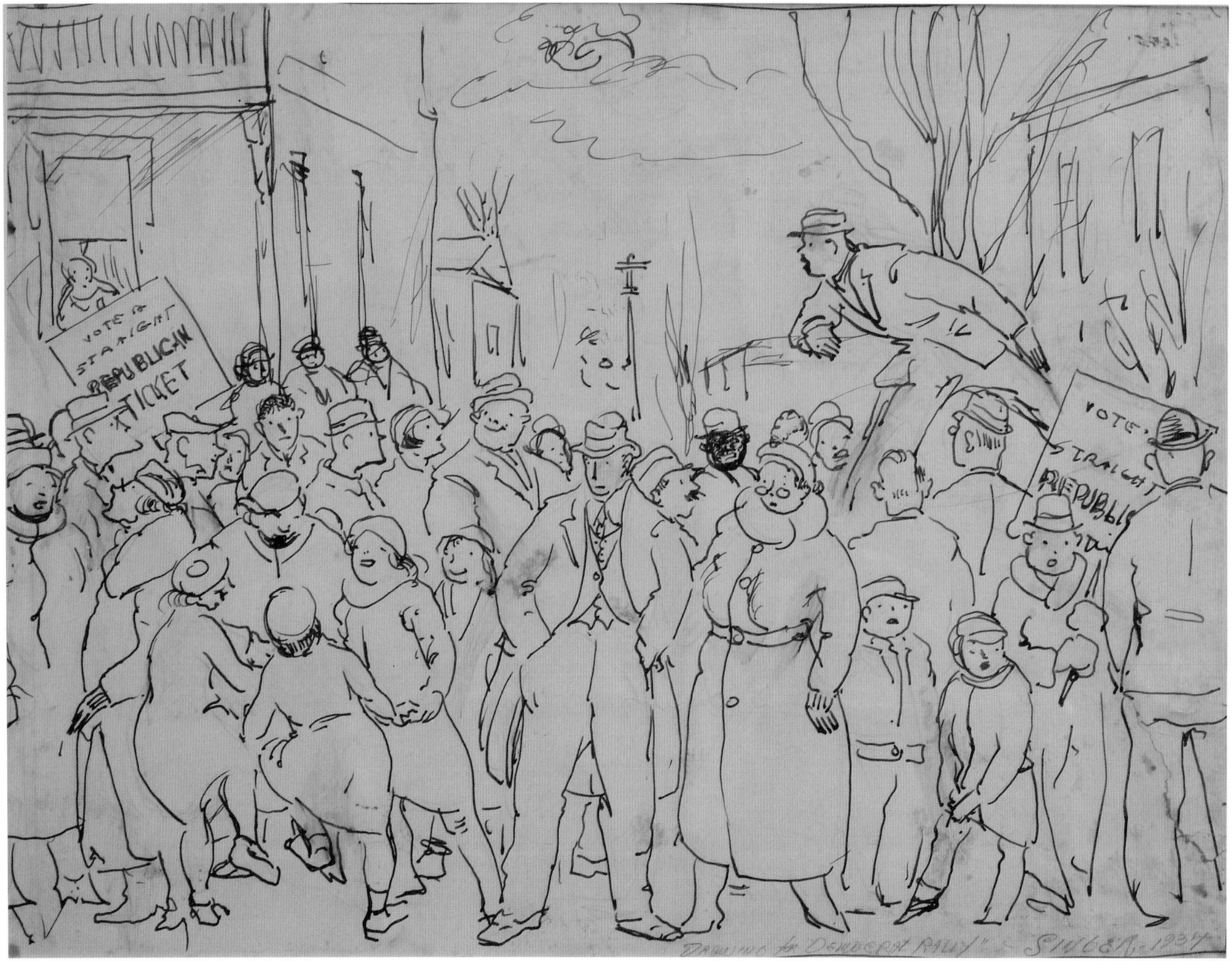

Fig. 81. *Sketch for Democrat Rally,* 1934. Graphite, 8 x 12. Courtesy of Thomas W. Darling

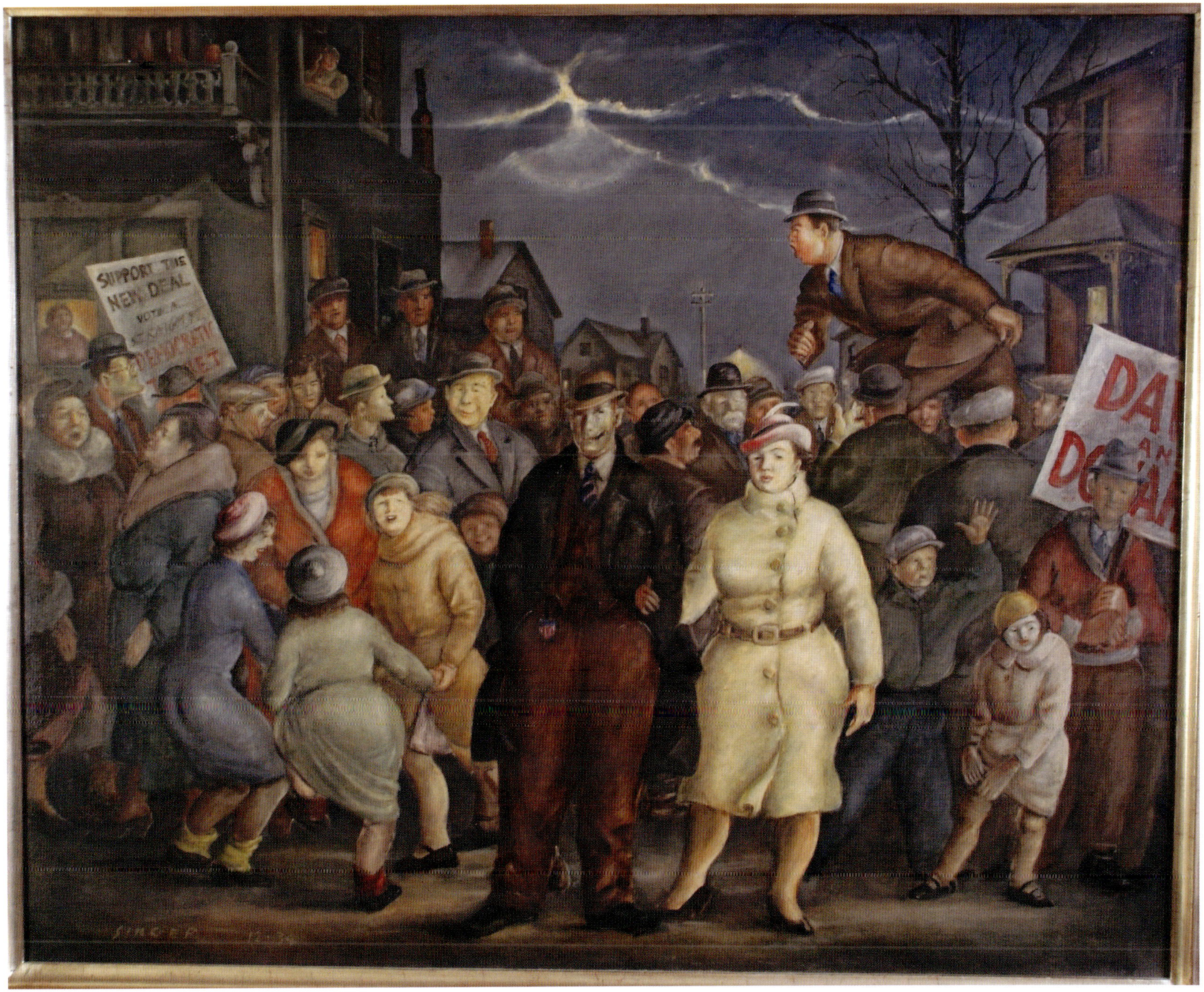

Fig. 82. *Democrat Rally,* 1935. Oil, 40 x 50. Courtesy of Lee and Barbara Maimon

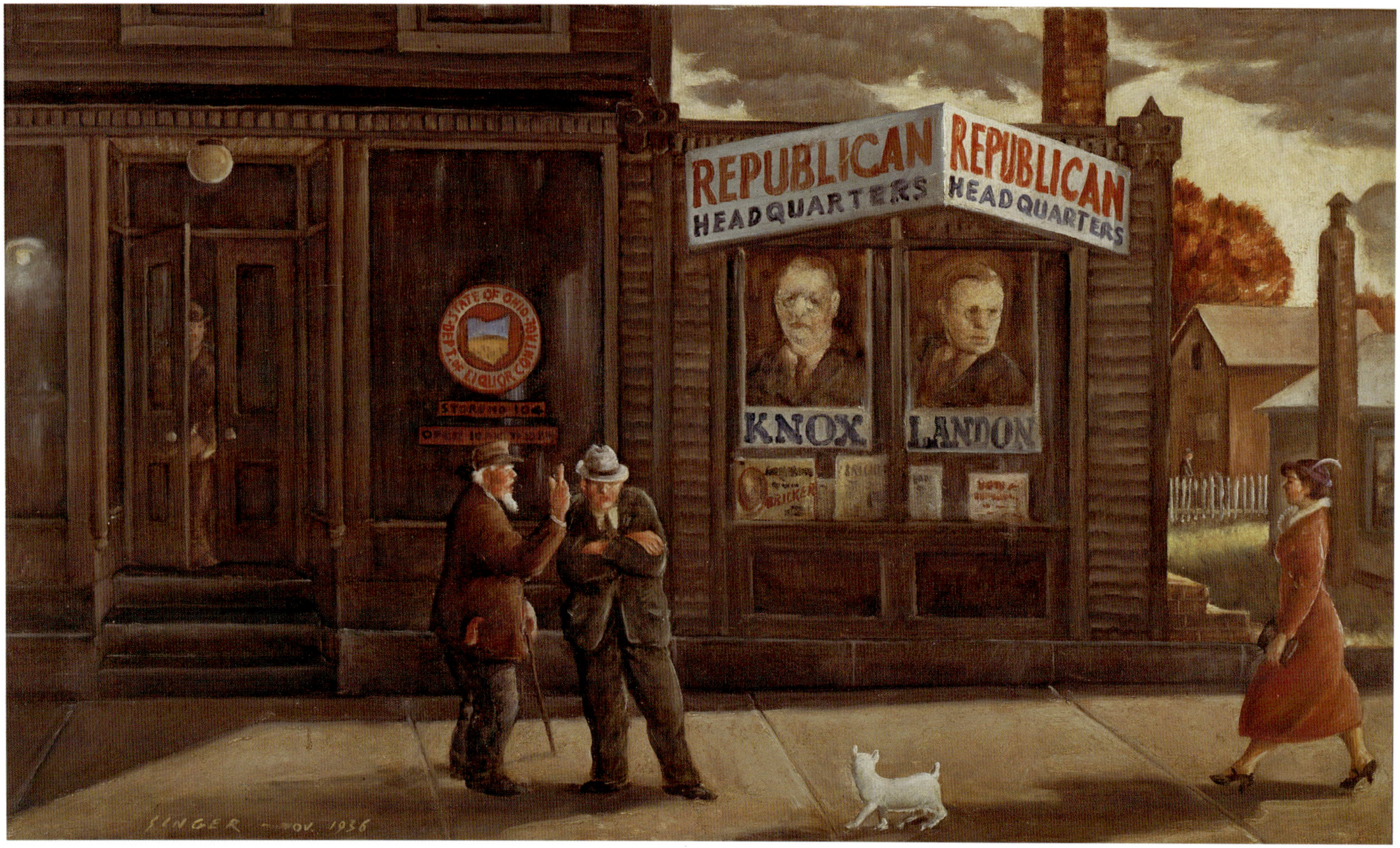

Fig. 83. *Republican Headquarters,* 1936. Oil, 20 x 36. Courtesy of a private collector

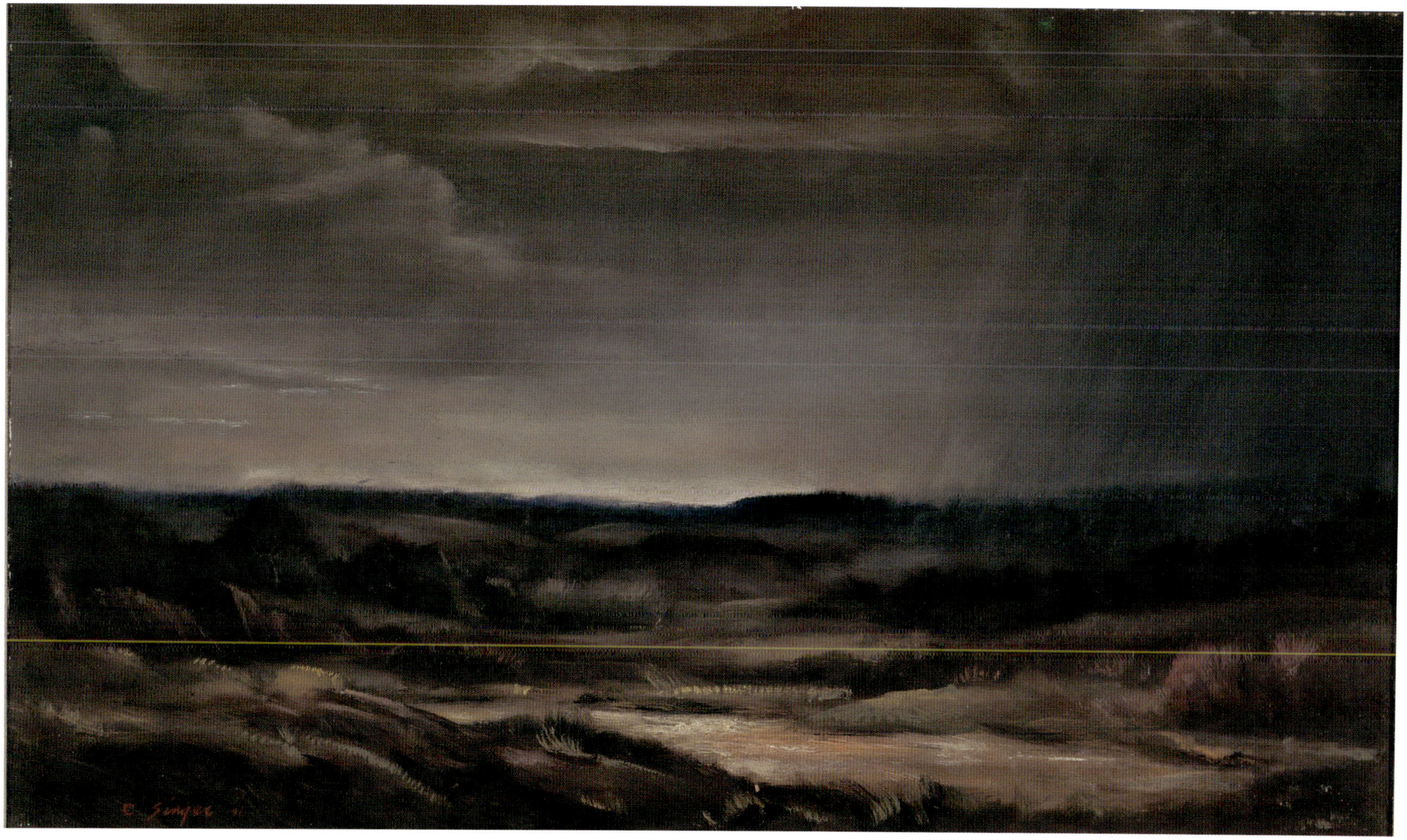

Fig. 84. *Stormy Weather,* 1941. Oil, 21 x 35½. The Butler Institute of American Art

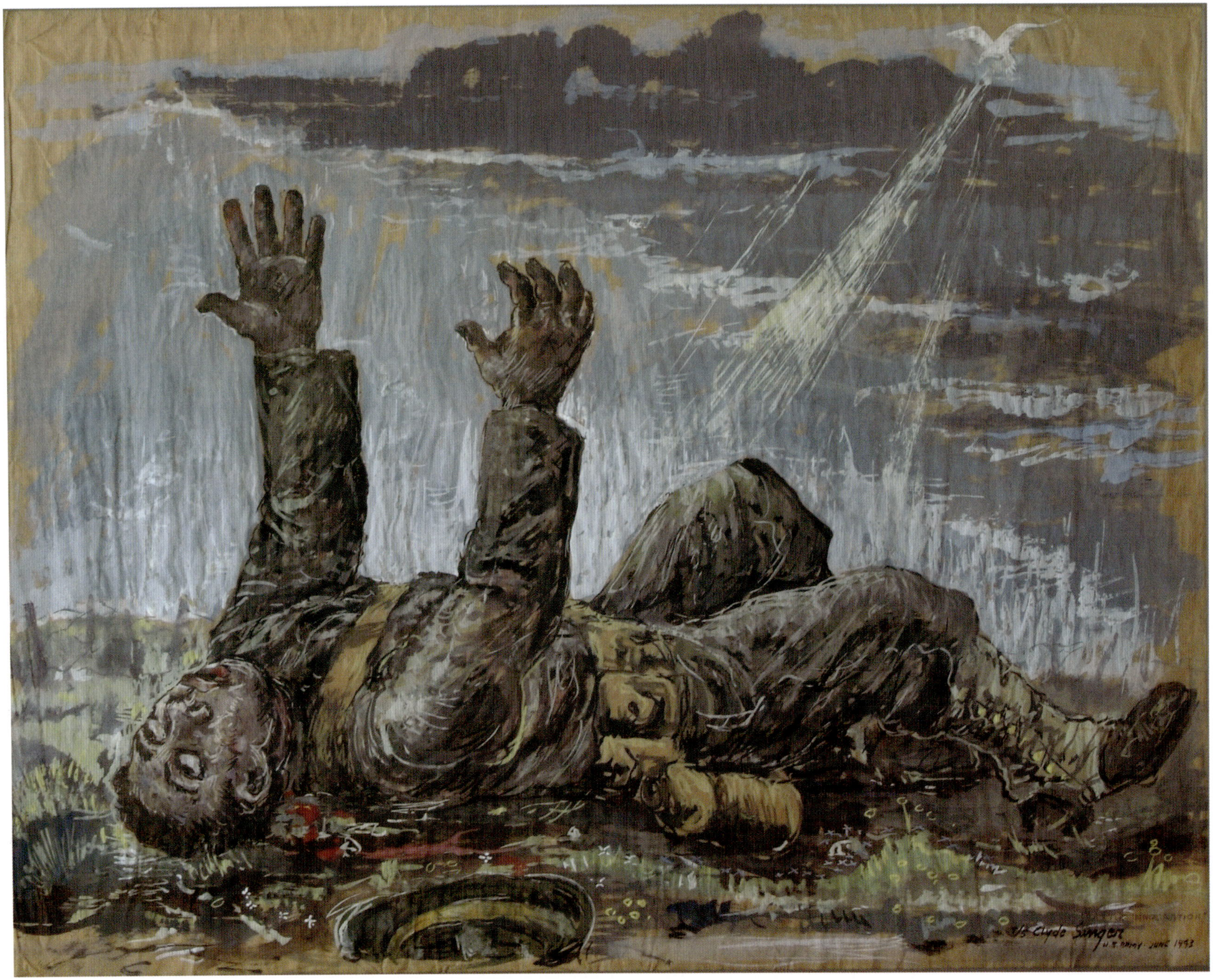

Fig. 85. *Battle Inoculation,* 1943. Gouache, 18 x 22. Courtesy of Thomas W. Darling

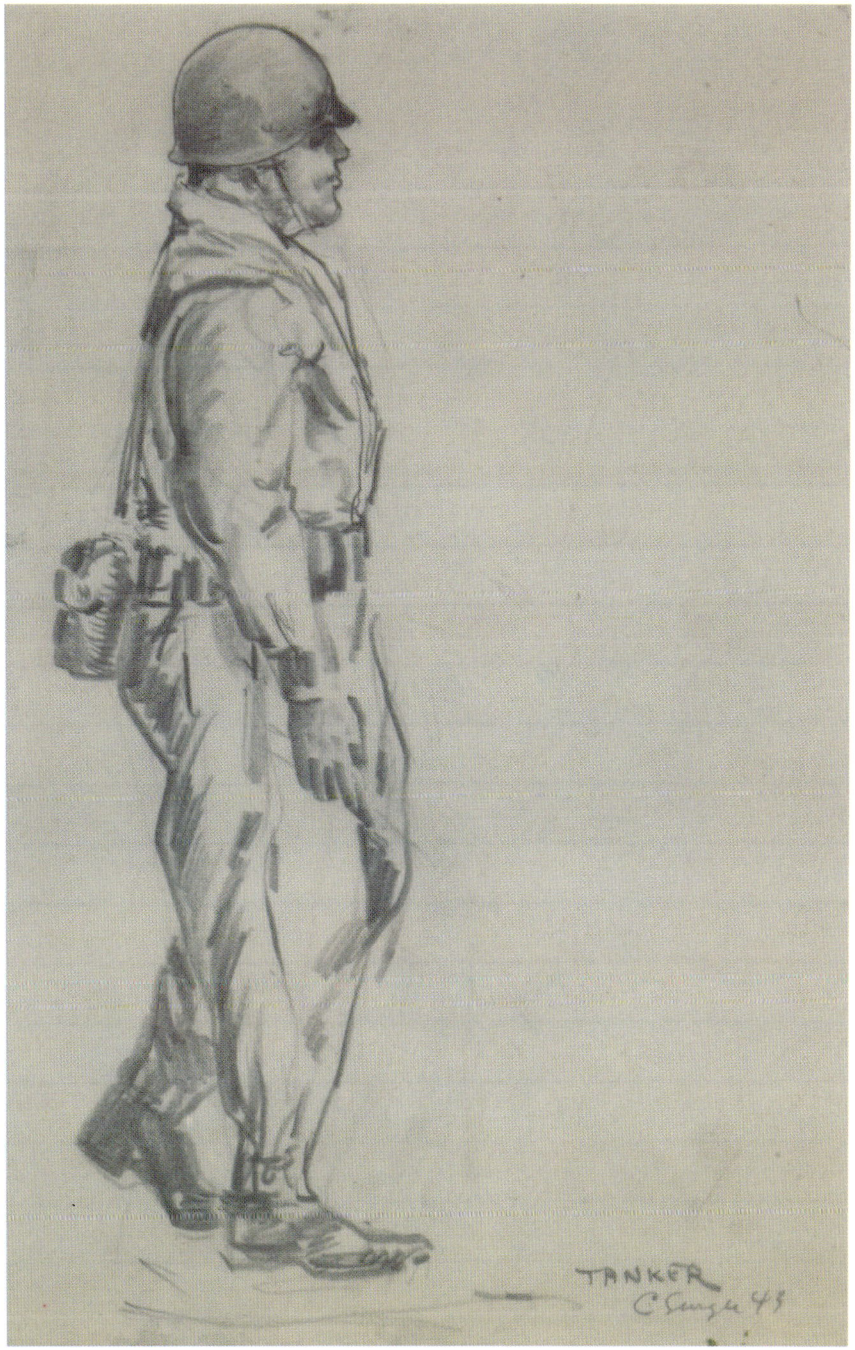

Fig. 86. *Tanker,* 1943. Graphite, 8 x 5. Courtesy of Thomas W. Darling

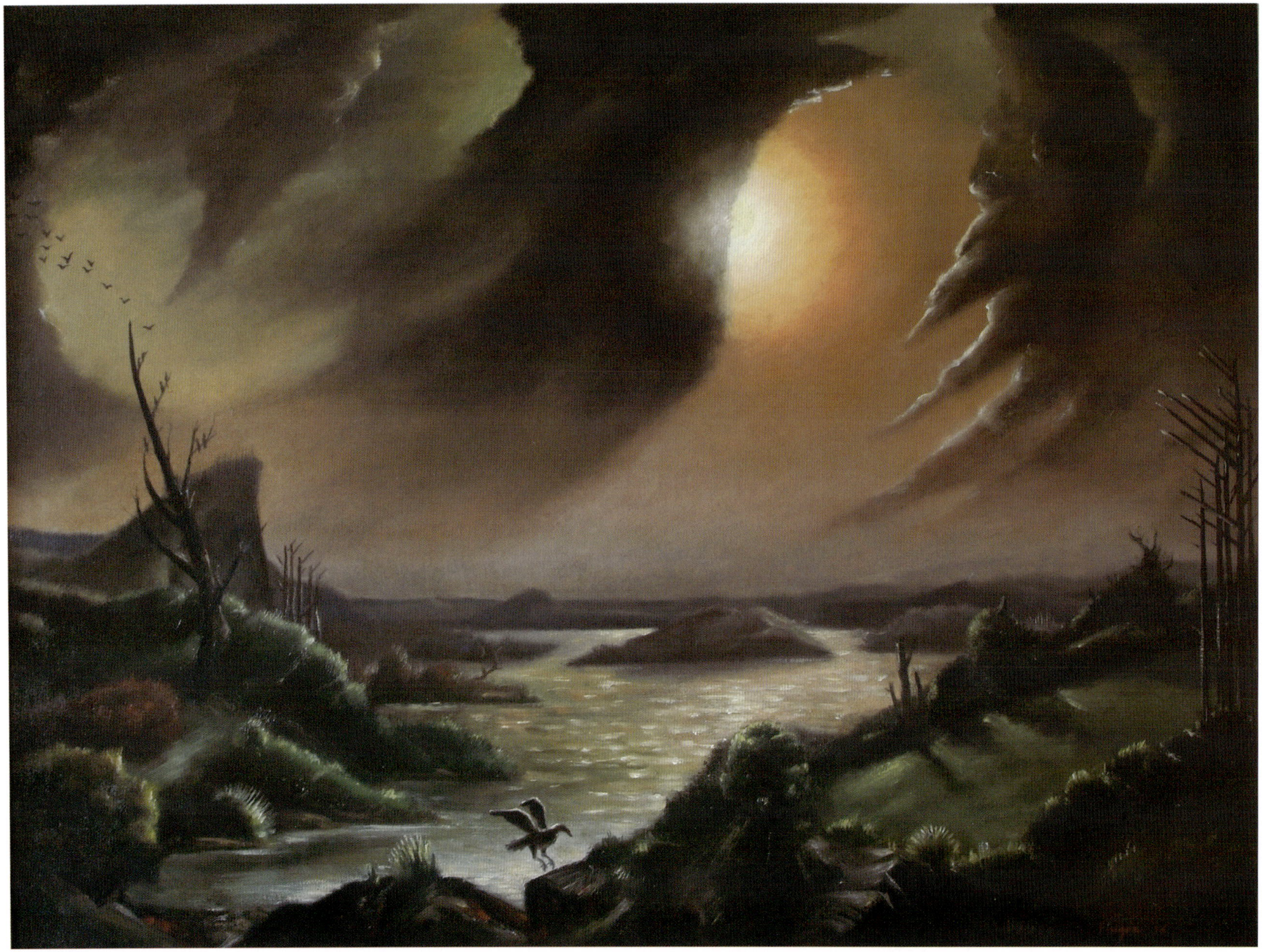

Fig. 87. *Aftermath,* 1946. Oil, 30 x 36. Courtesy of Thomas W. Darling

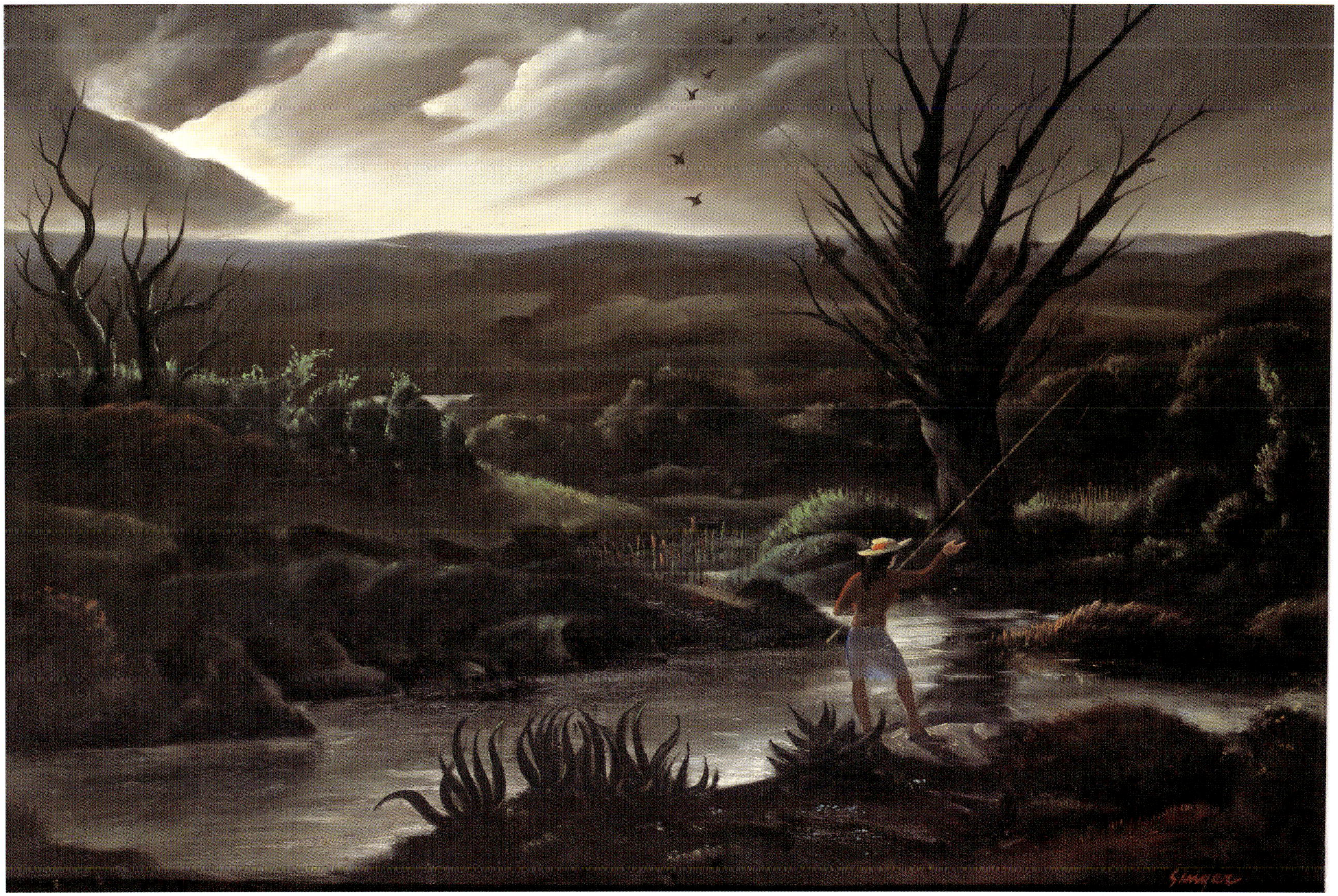

Fig. 88. *Dreary Day,* 1946. Oil, 24 x 36. Courtesy of Ed and Karen Ogul, Franklin, Michigan

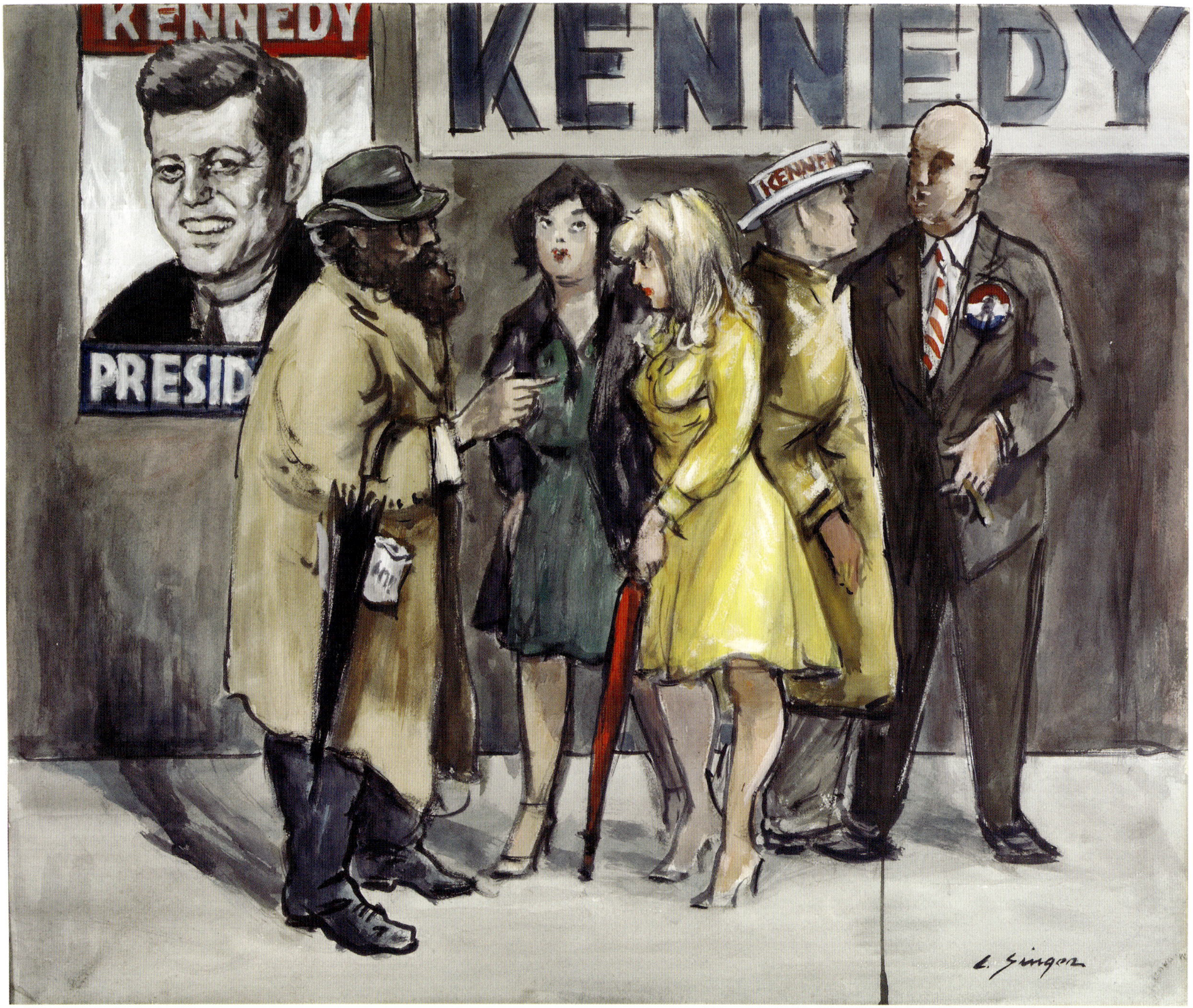

Fig. 89. *Democratic Headquarters on Broadway,* 1960. Casein, 18 x 24. Courtesy of a private collector

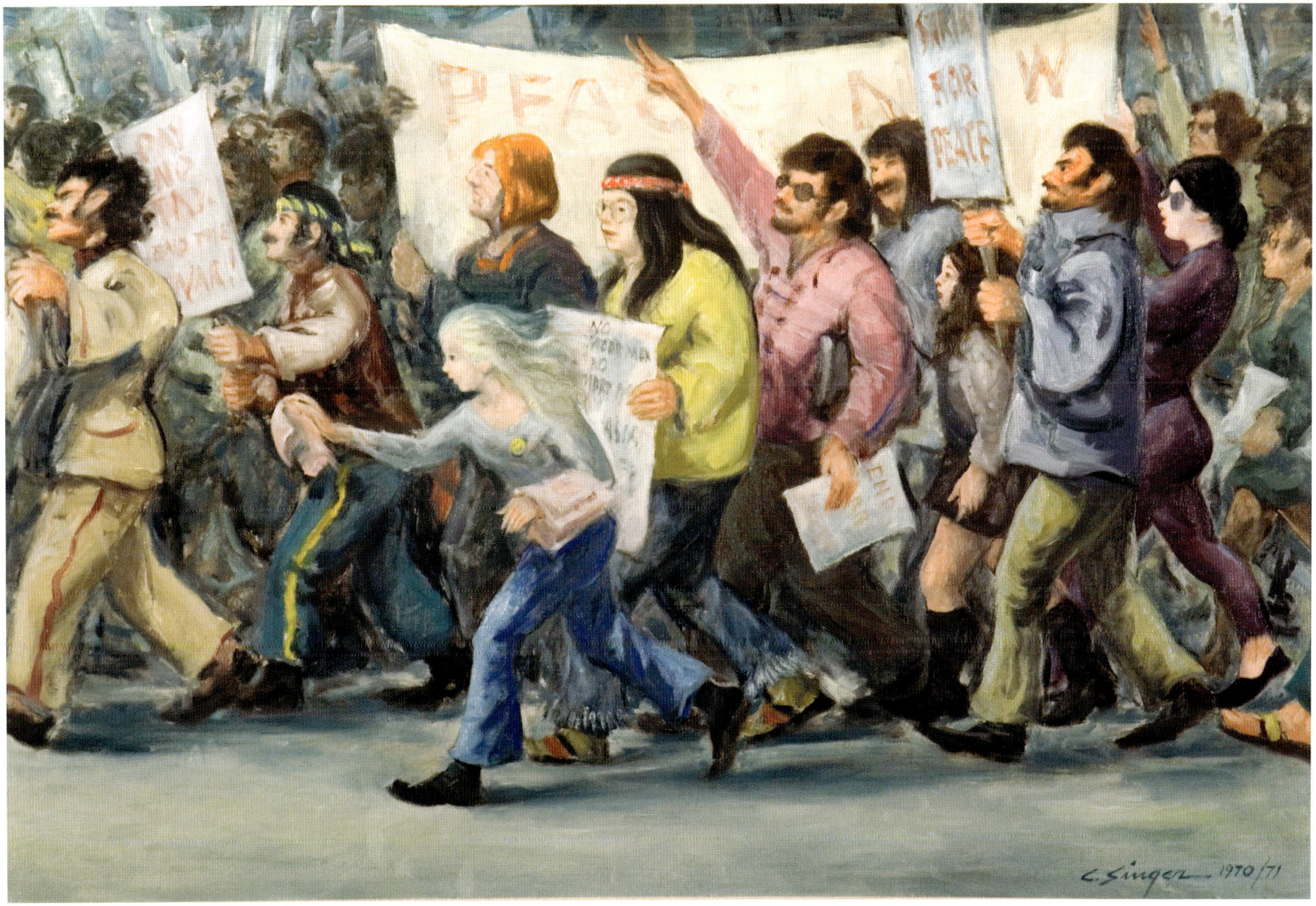

Fig. 90. *Demonstrators,* 1970–71. Oil, 23¼ x 35½. Courtesy of a private collector

In the Ring and on the Field

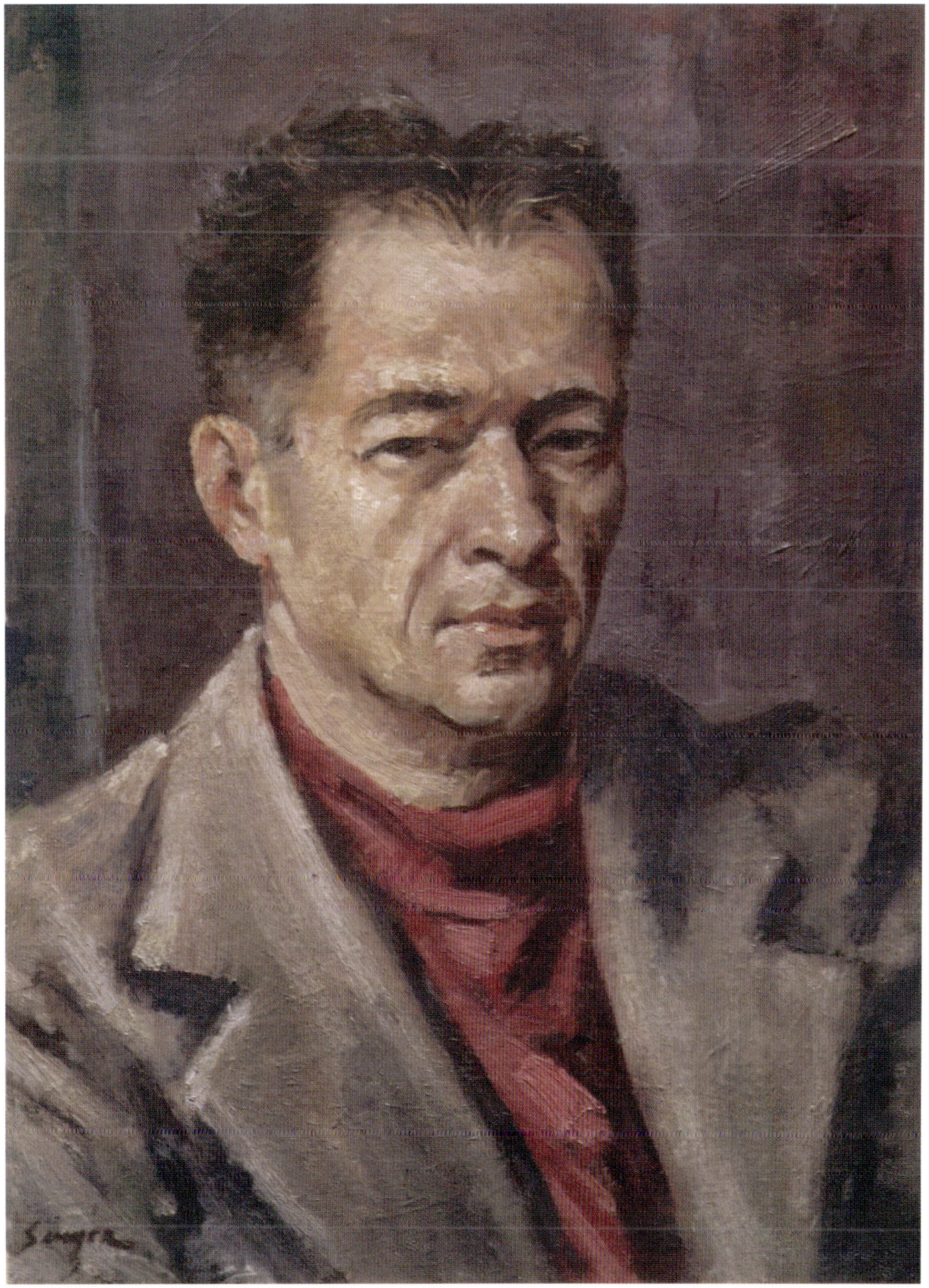

Fig. 91. *Self-Portrait,* no date. Oil, 16 x 12. Courtesy of Donald "Pete" Slates

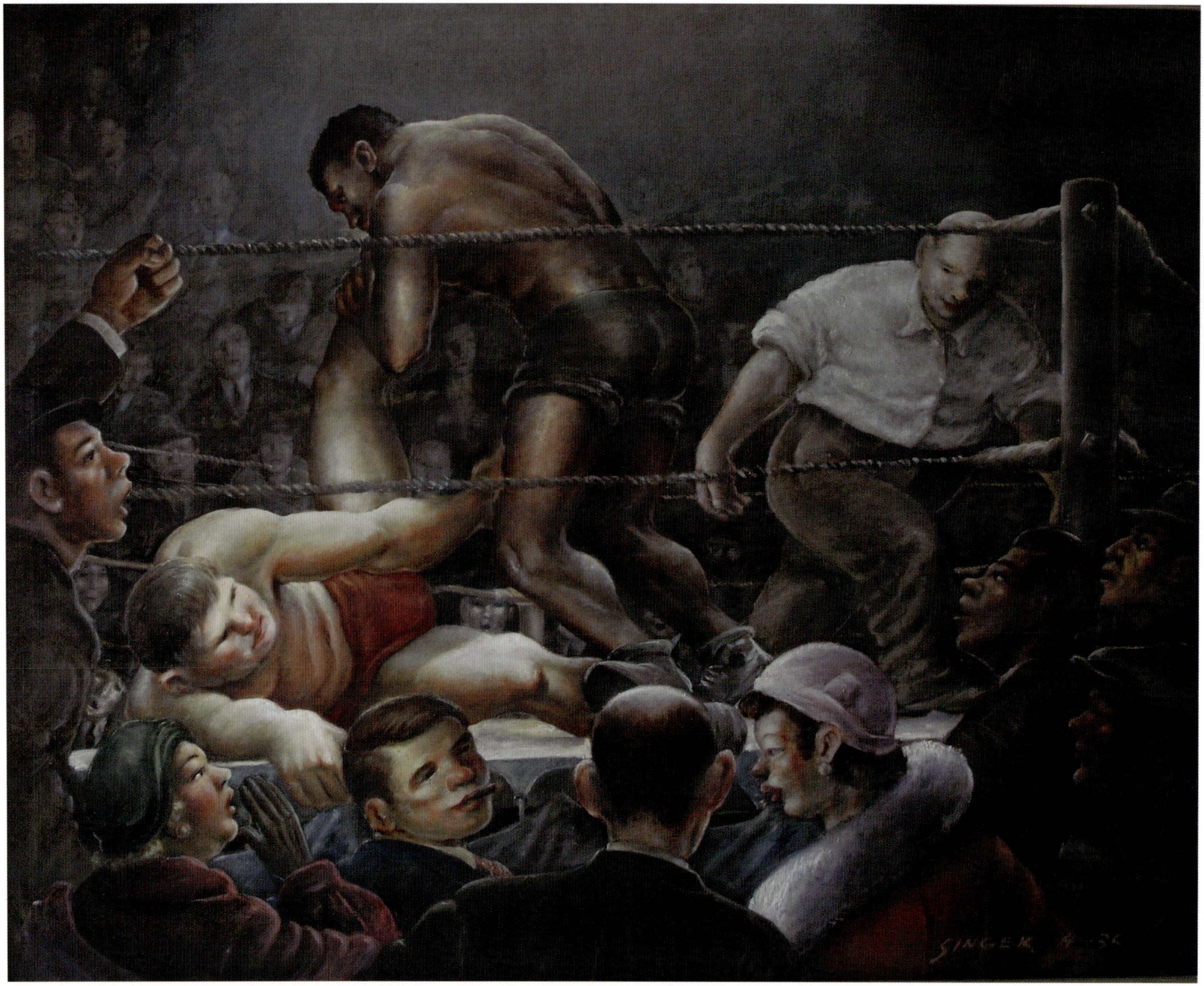

Fig. 92. *Wrestling Night,* 1935. Oil, 40 x 50. Courtesy of Thomas W. Darling

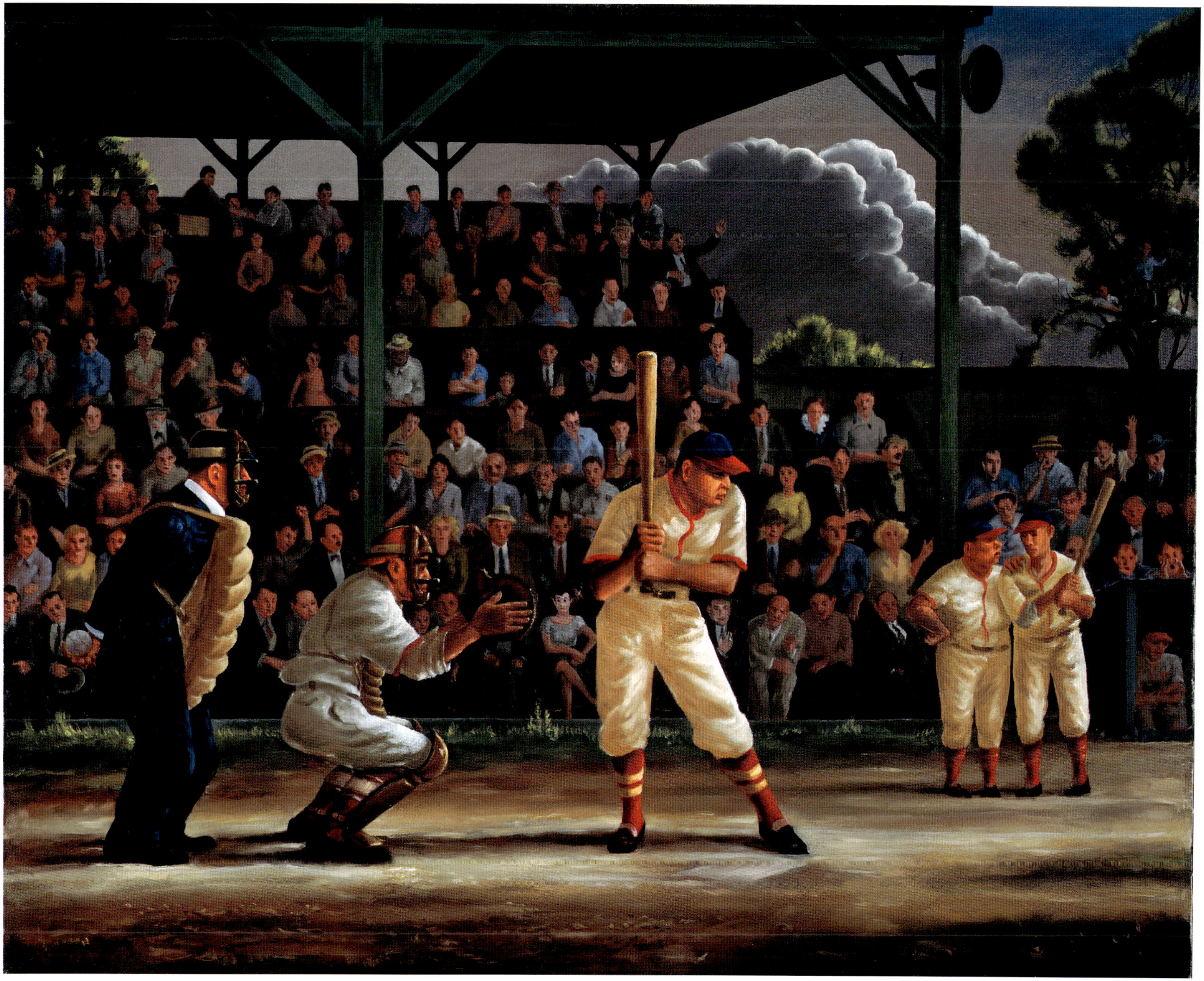

Fig. 93. *Minor League,* 1946. Oil, 40 x 50. The Butler Institute of American Art, gift of the Friends of American Art

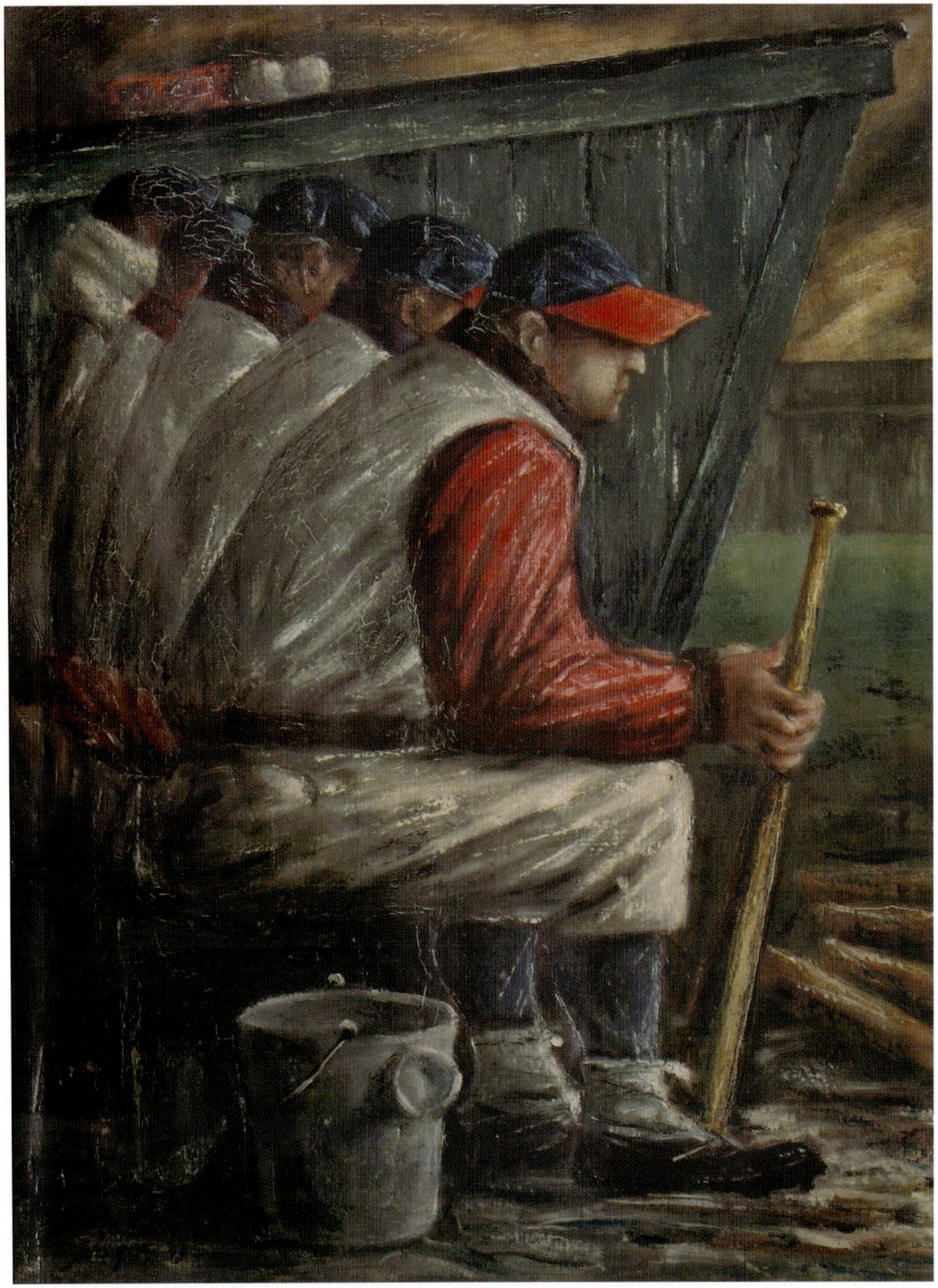

Fig. 94. *Beaten Ball Club,* 1949. Oil, 28 x 22. Courtesy of Donald "Pete" Slates

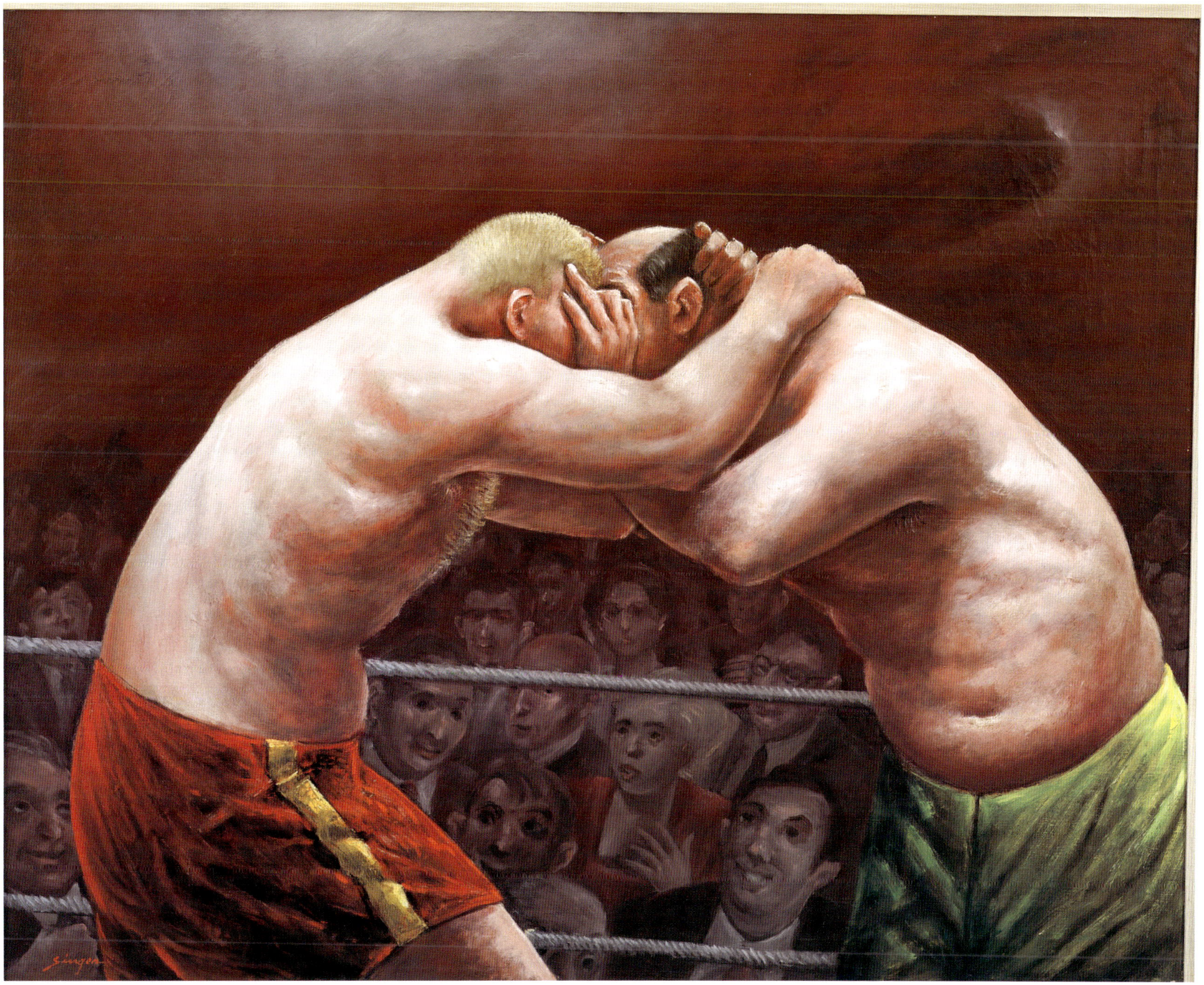

Fig. 95. *The Wrestlers,* 1952. Oil, 32 x 40. Courtesy of a private collector

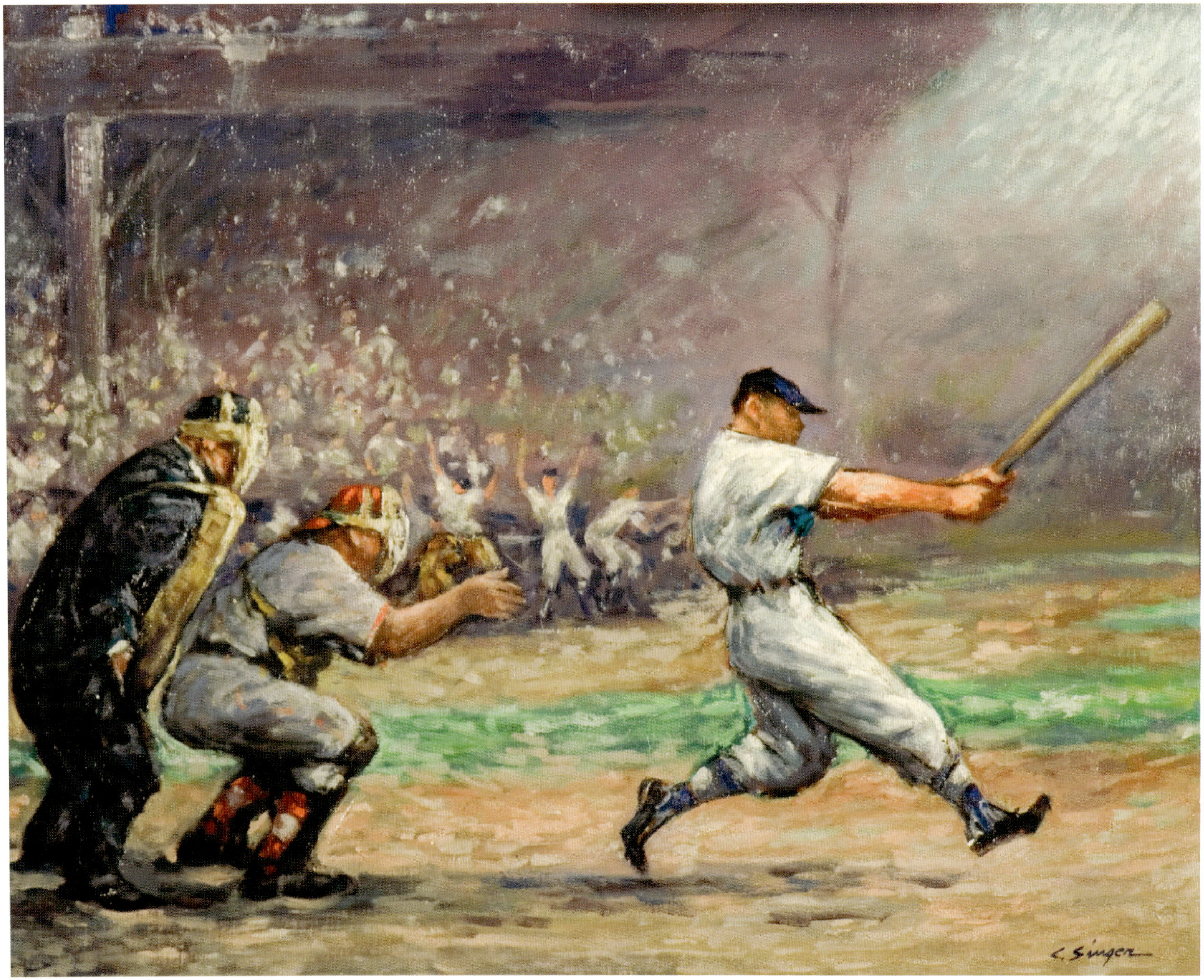

Fig. 96. *Mickey Mantle,* 1957. Oil, 22 x 28½. Courtesy of a private collector

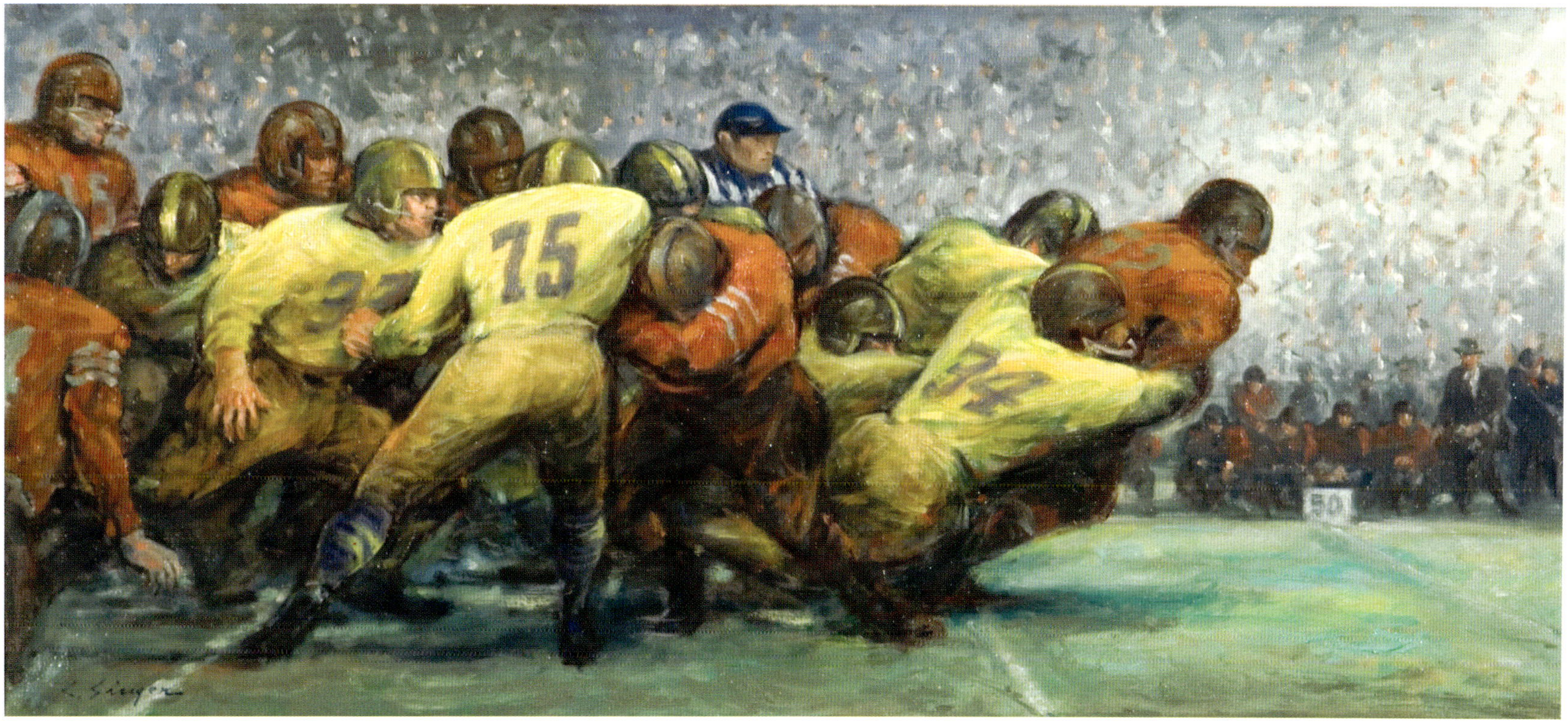

Fig. 97. *First Down,* 1960. Oil, 15 x 36. Courtesy of a private collector

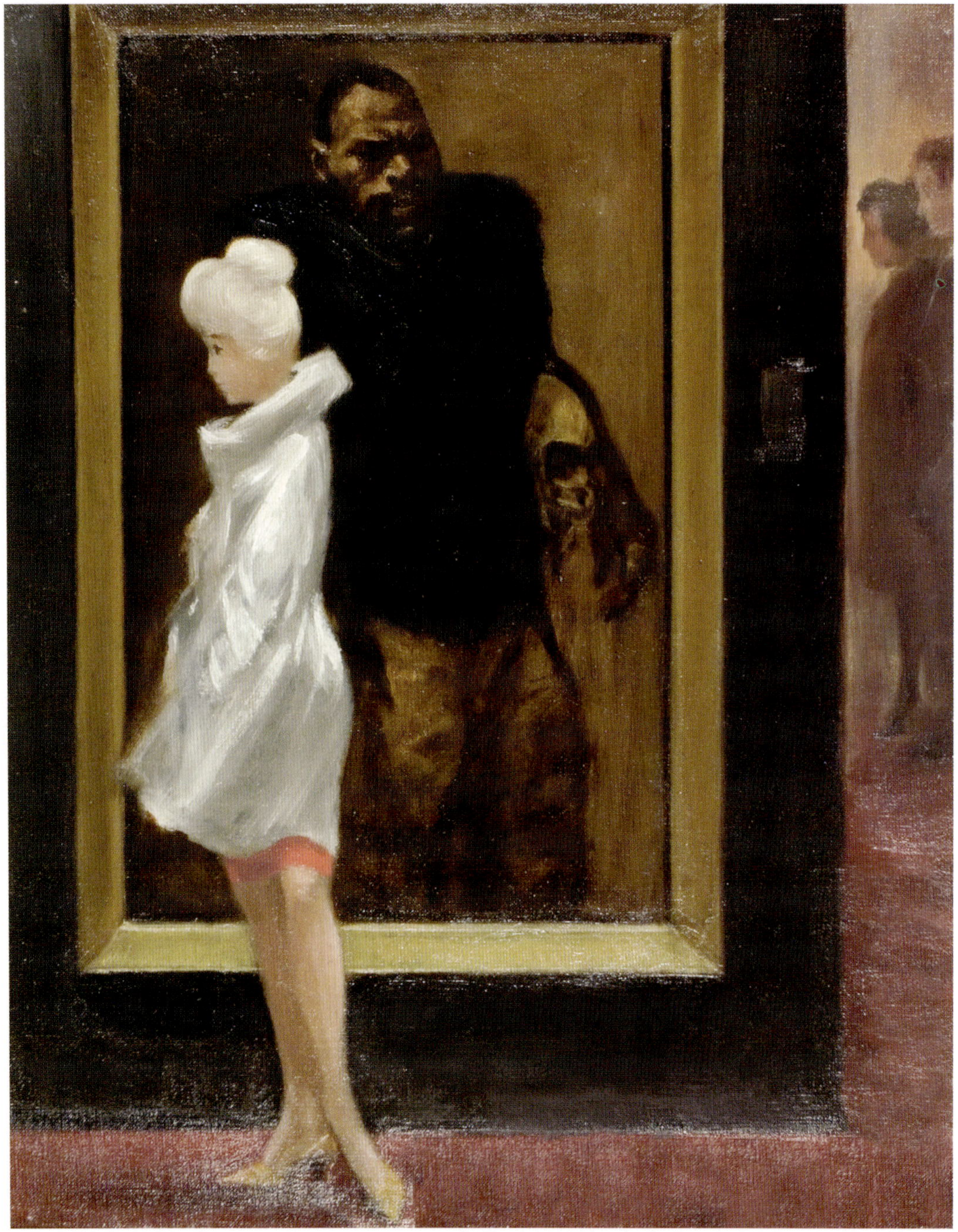

Fig. 98. *Blonde & Big Daddy Liscomb,* 1962. Oil, 20 x 16. Courtesy of Dr. Michael and Sue Lehmiller

People Watching

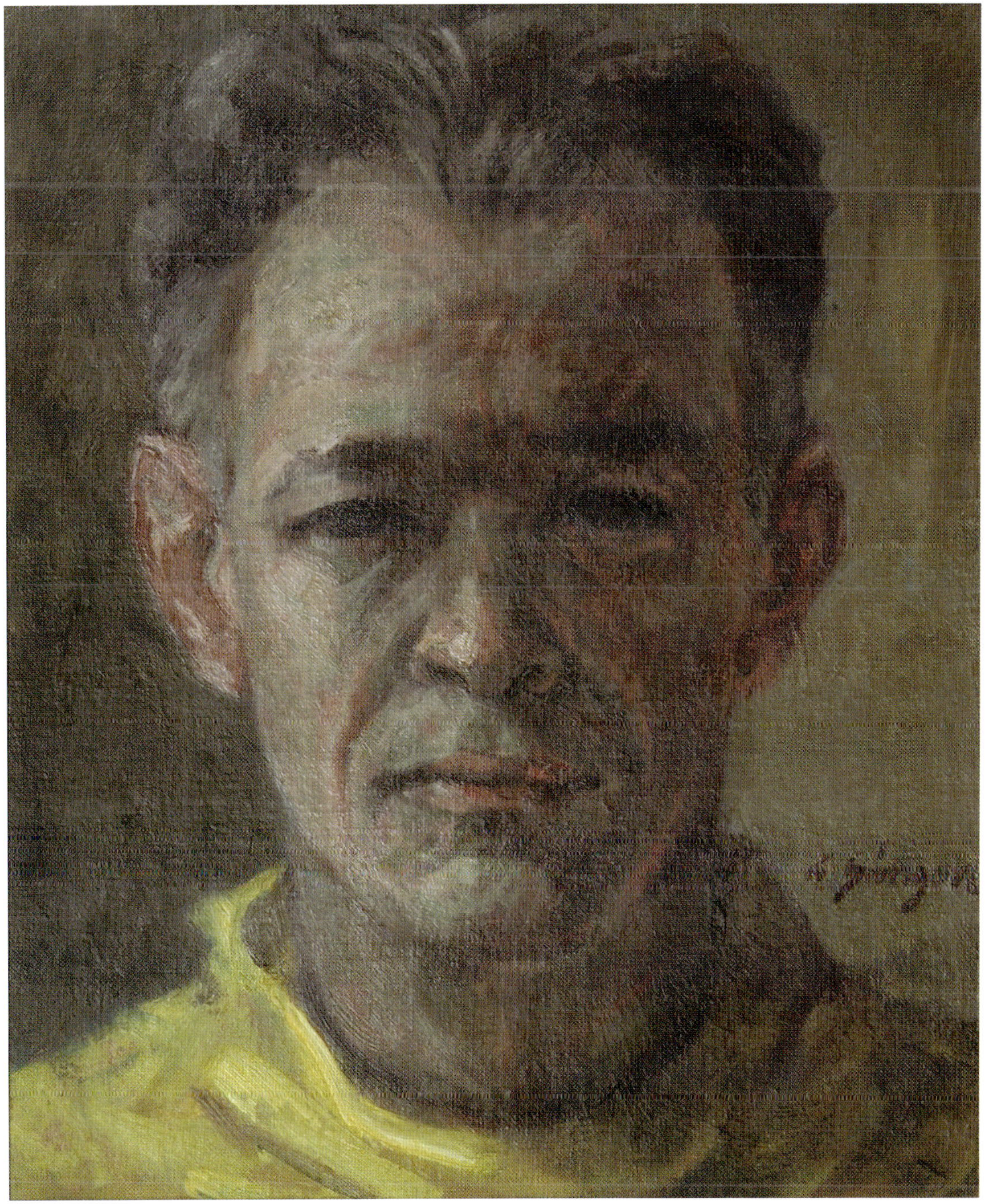

Fig. 99. *Self-Portrait,* 1986. Oil, 12 x 10. Courtesy of a private collector

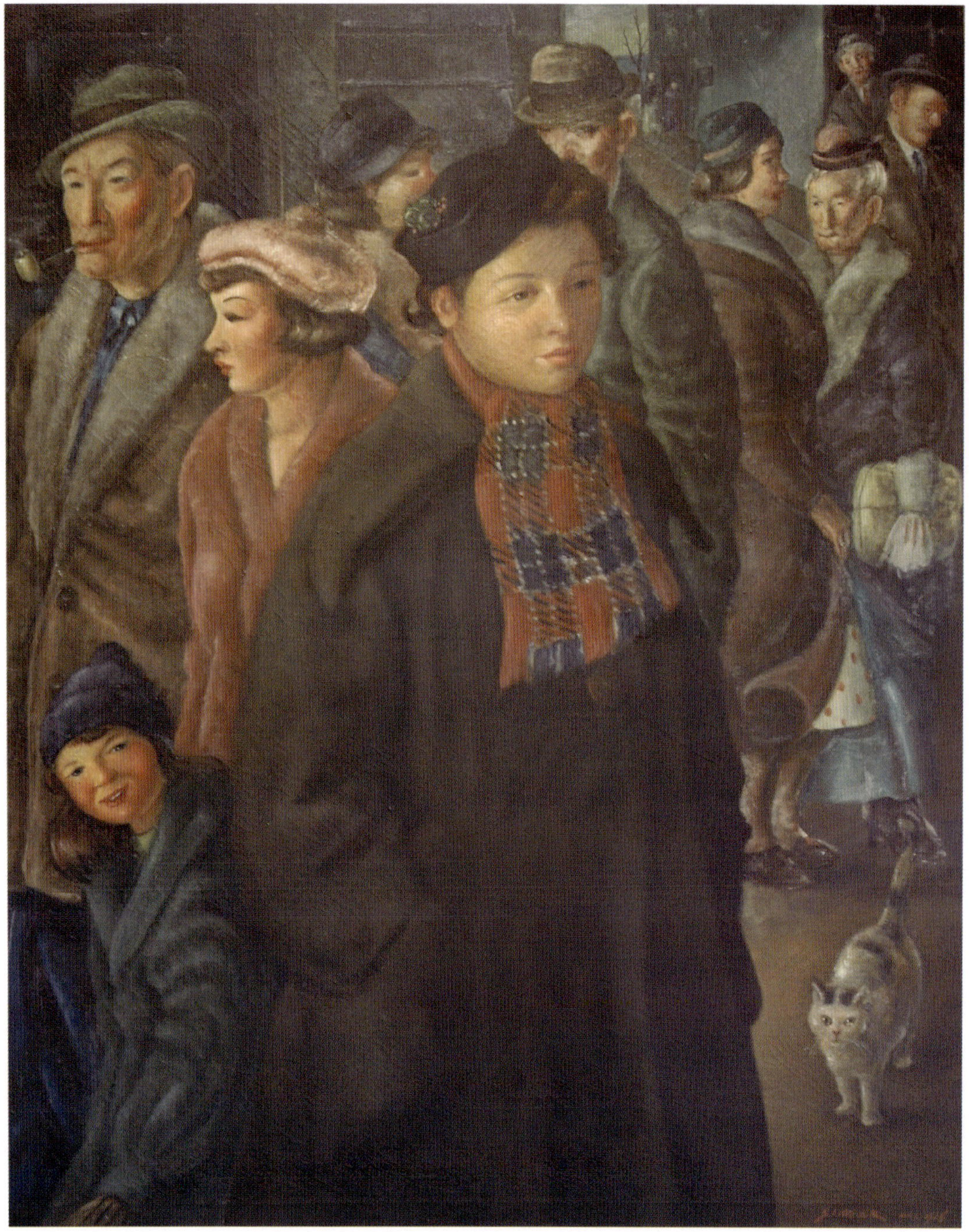

Fig. 100. *Street Portrait,* ca. 1930s. Oil, 49½ x 40. Courtesy of YWCA of Canton, Ohio

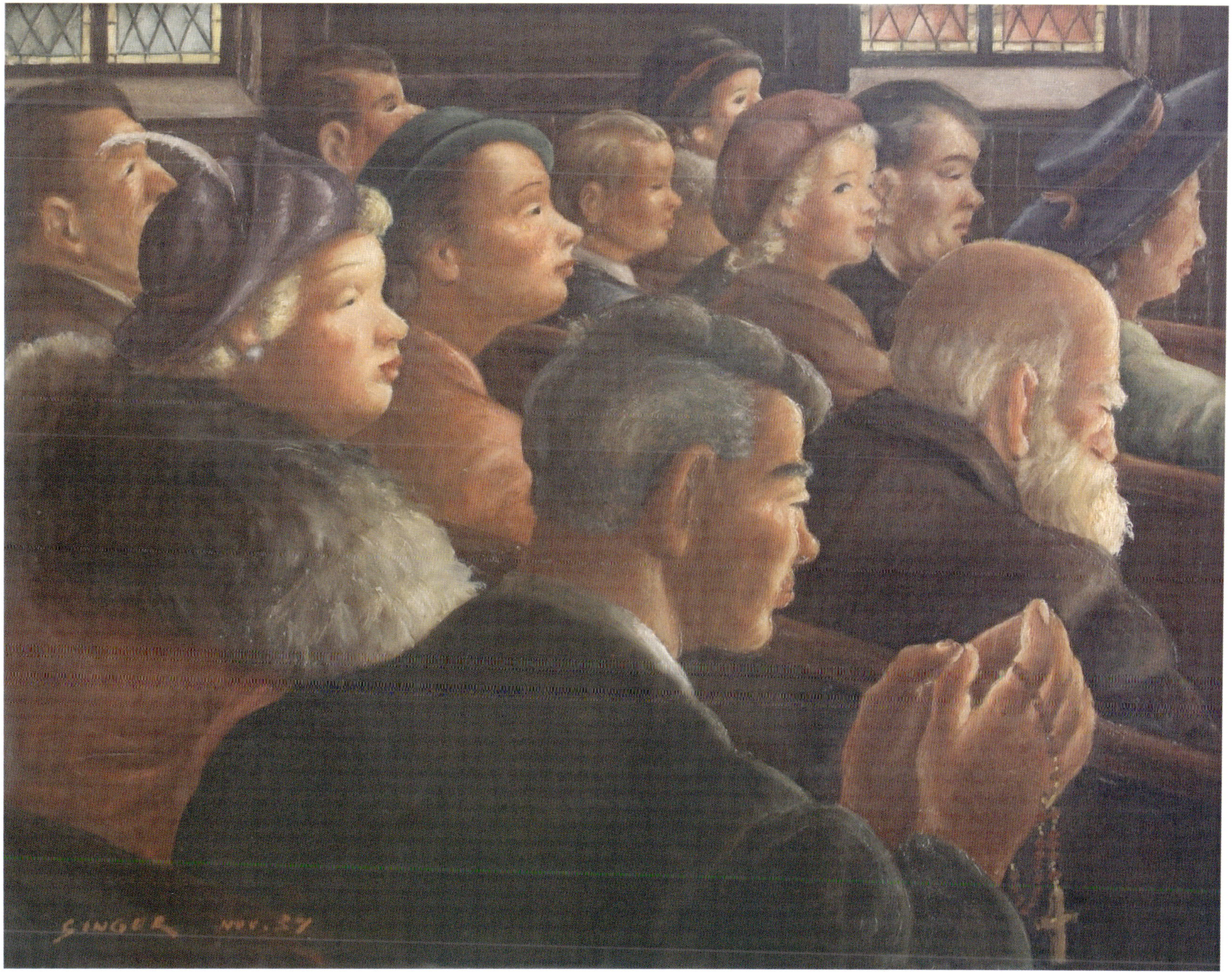

Fig. 101. *The Sermon,* 1937. Oil, 25 x 30. Courtesy of the Massillon Museum

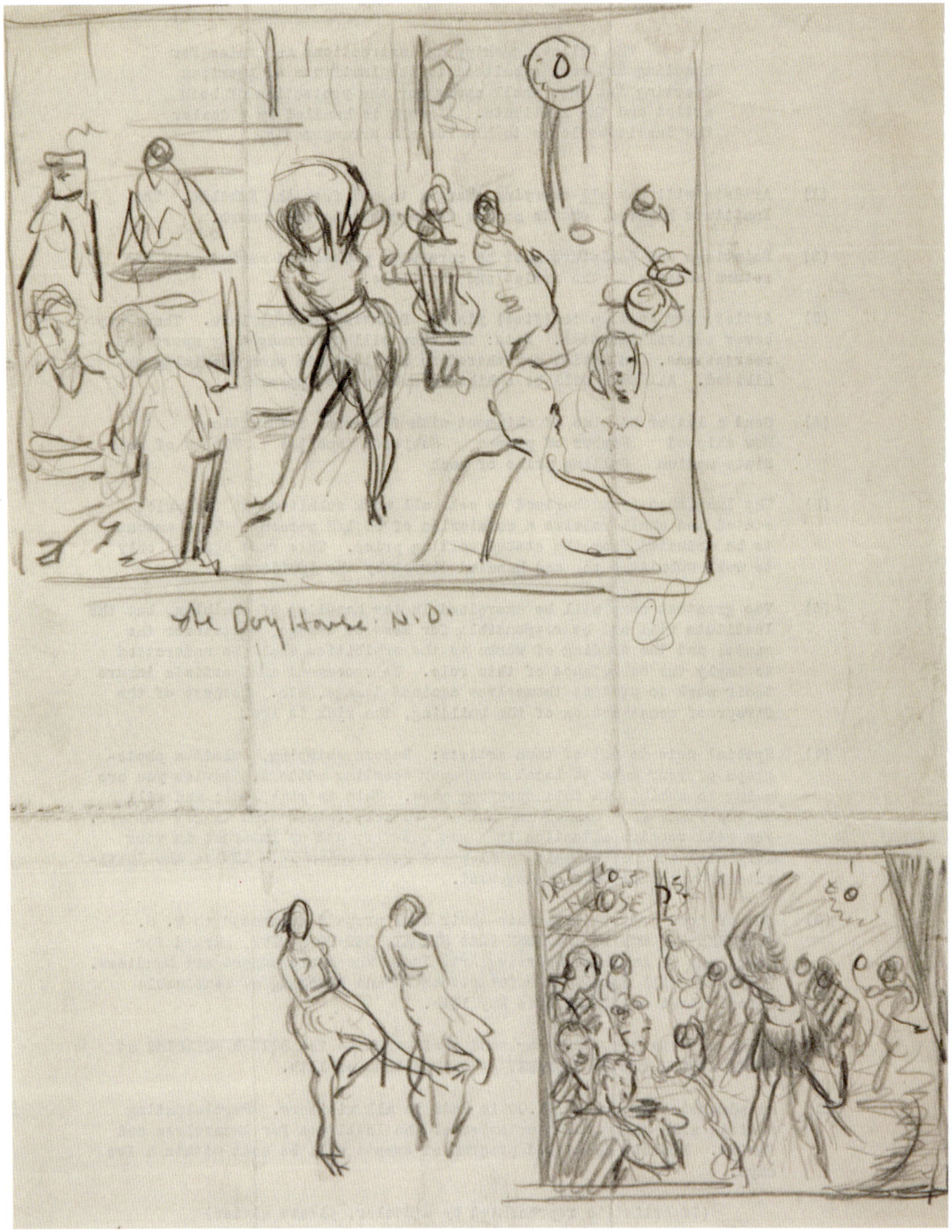

Fig. 102. *Sketch for Dog House*. Graphite, 10½ x 8¼. Courtesy of Lazar's Art Gallery & Creative Framing

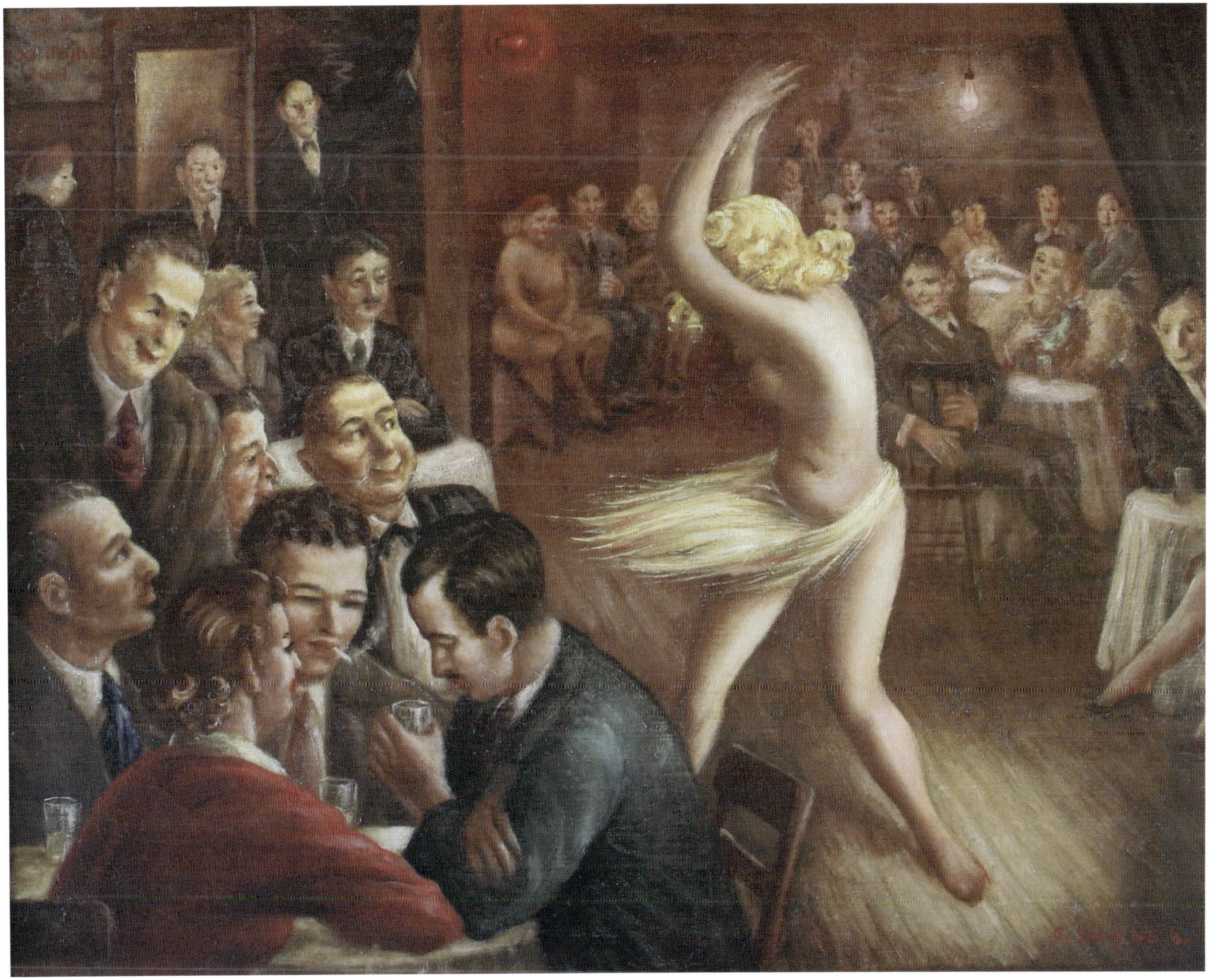

Fig. 103. *The Dog House, New Orleans,* 1940. Oil, 30⅛ x 38½. Courtesy of Thomas W. Darling

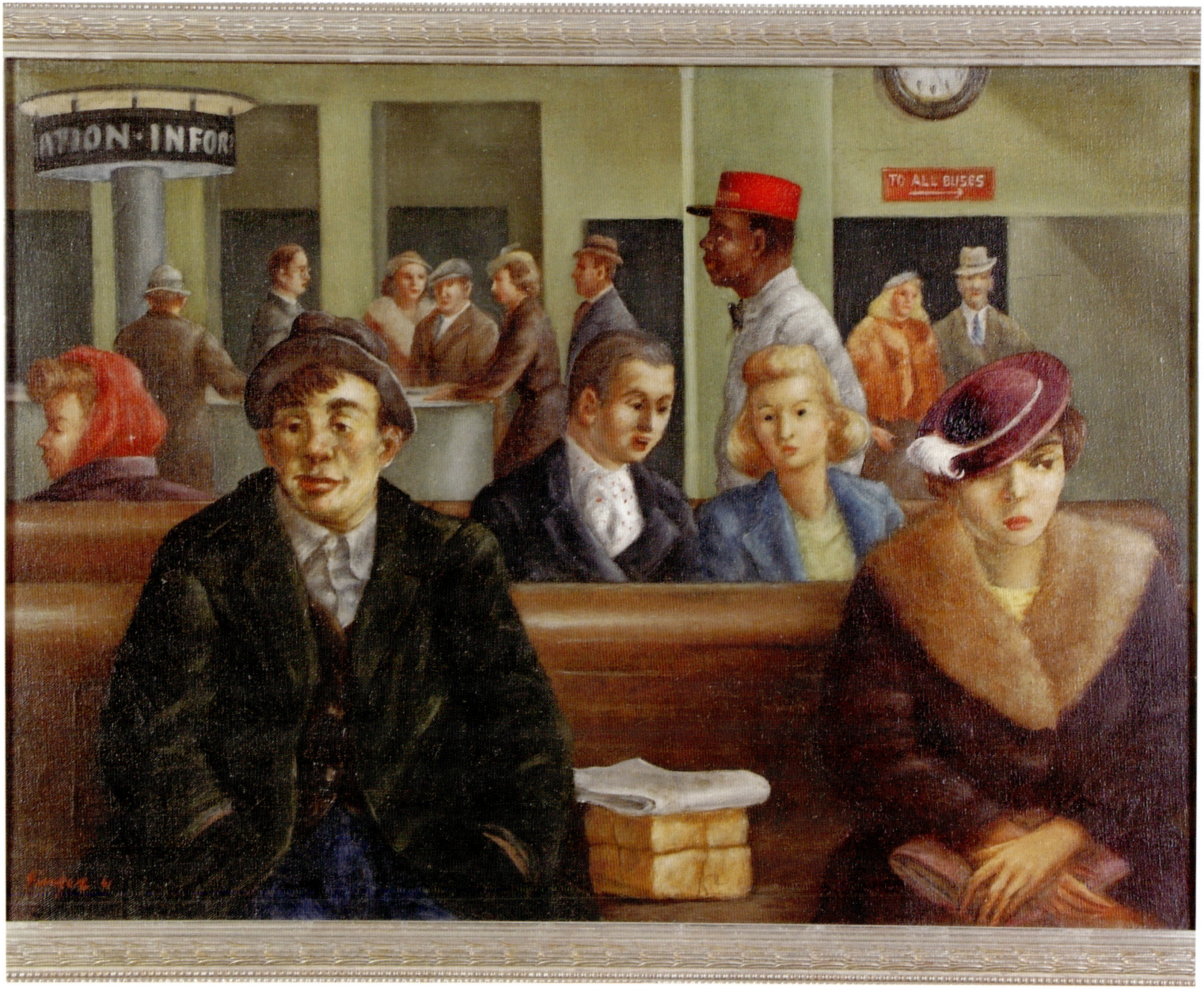

Fig. 104. *Bus Depot, Pittsburgh, PA,* ca. 1941. Oil, 18 x 26. Courtesy of Lee and Barbara Maimon

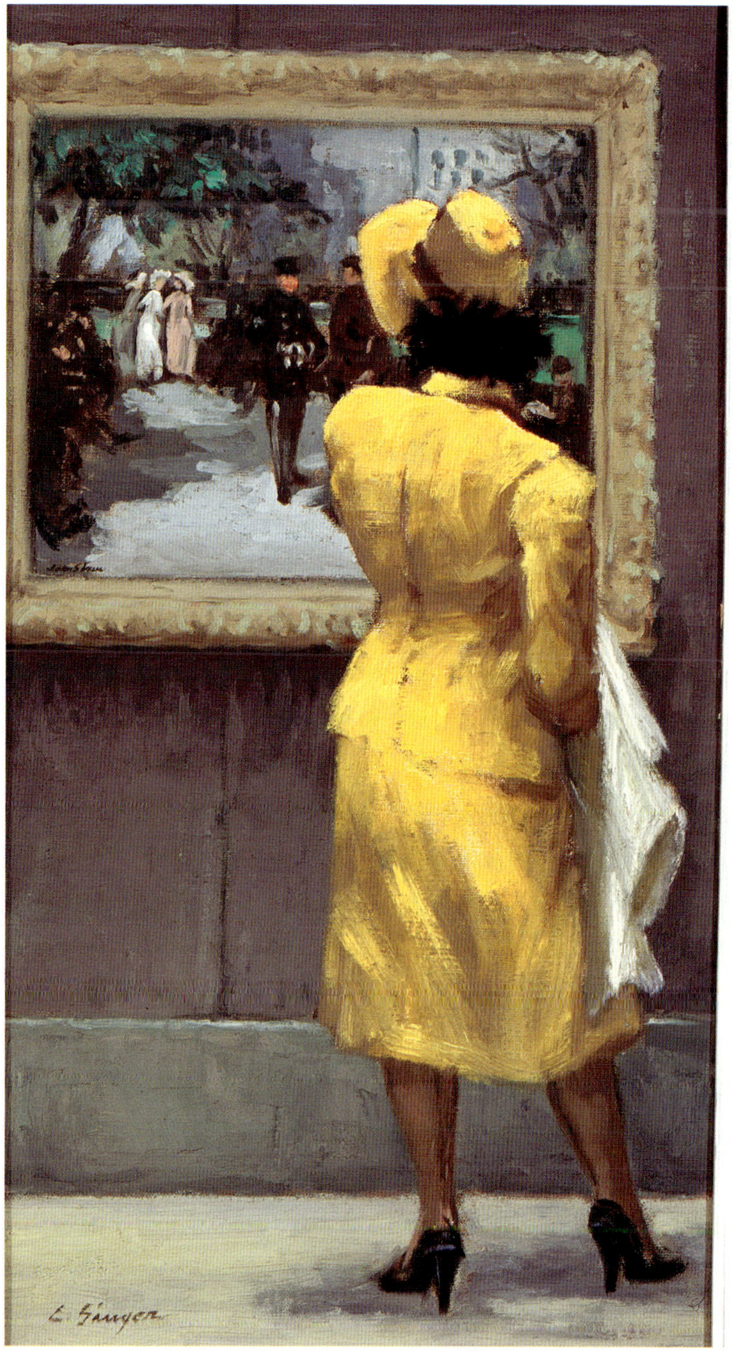

Fig. 105. *Yellow Dress, Looking at John Sloan Painting,* 1945. Oil, 22 x 12. Courtesy of a private collector

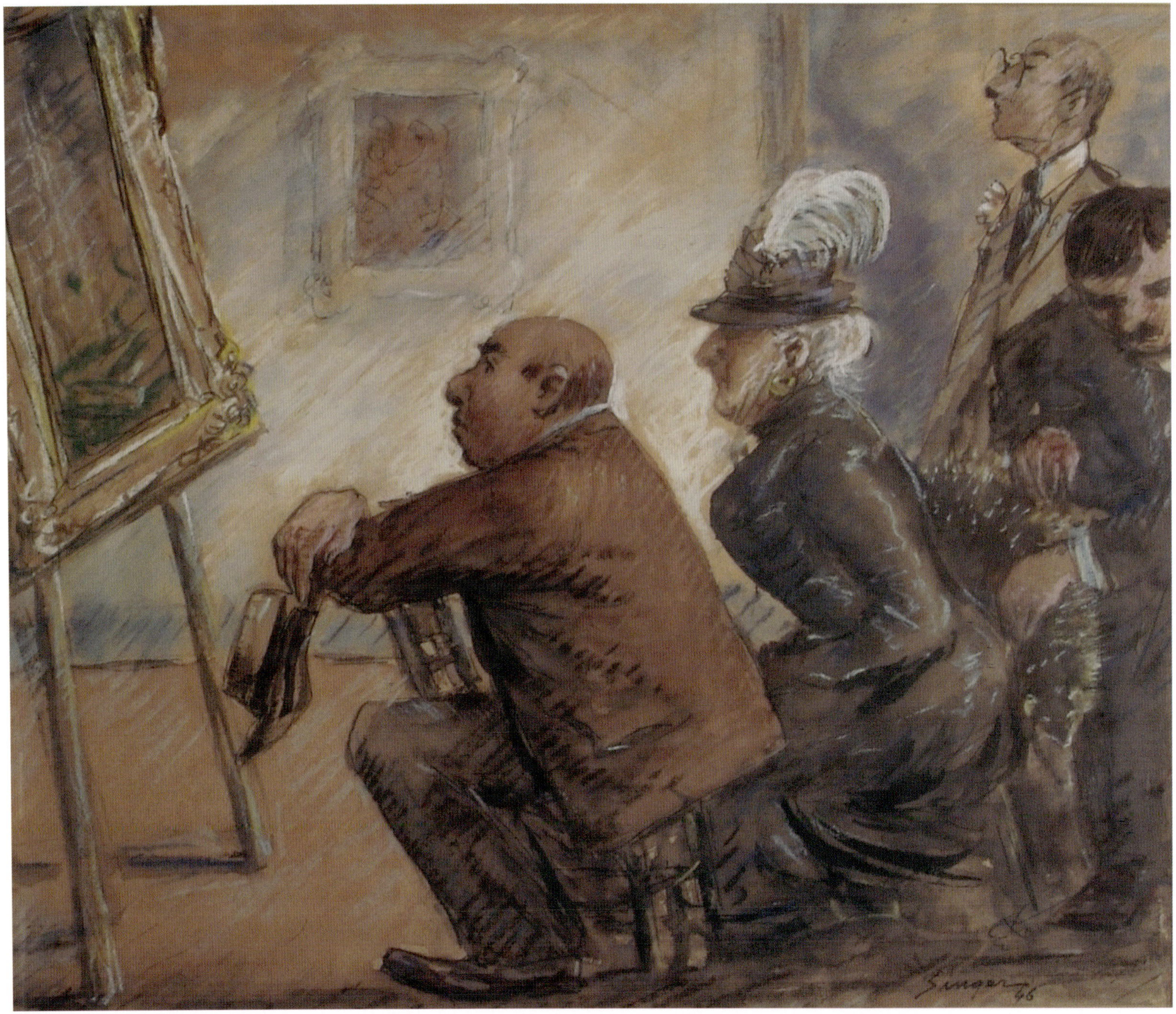

Fig. 106. *Art Gallery,* 1946. Gouache, 19 x 16. Courtesy of Mr. and Mrs. James M. Conley

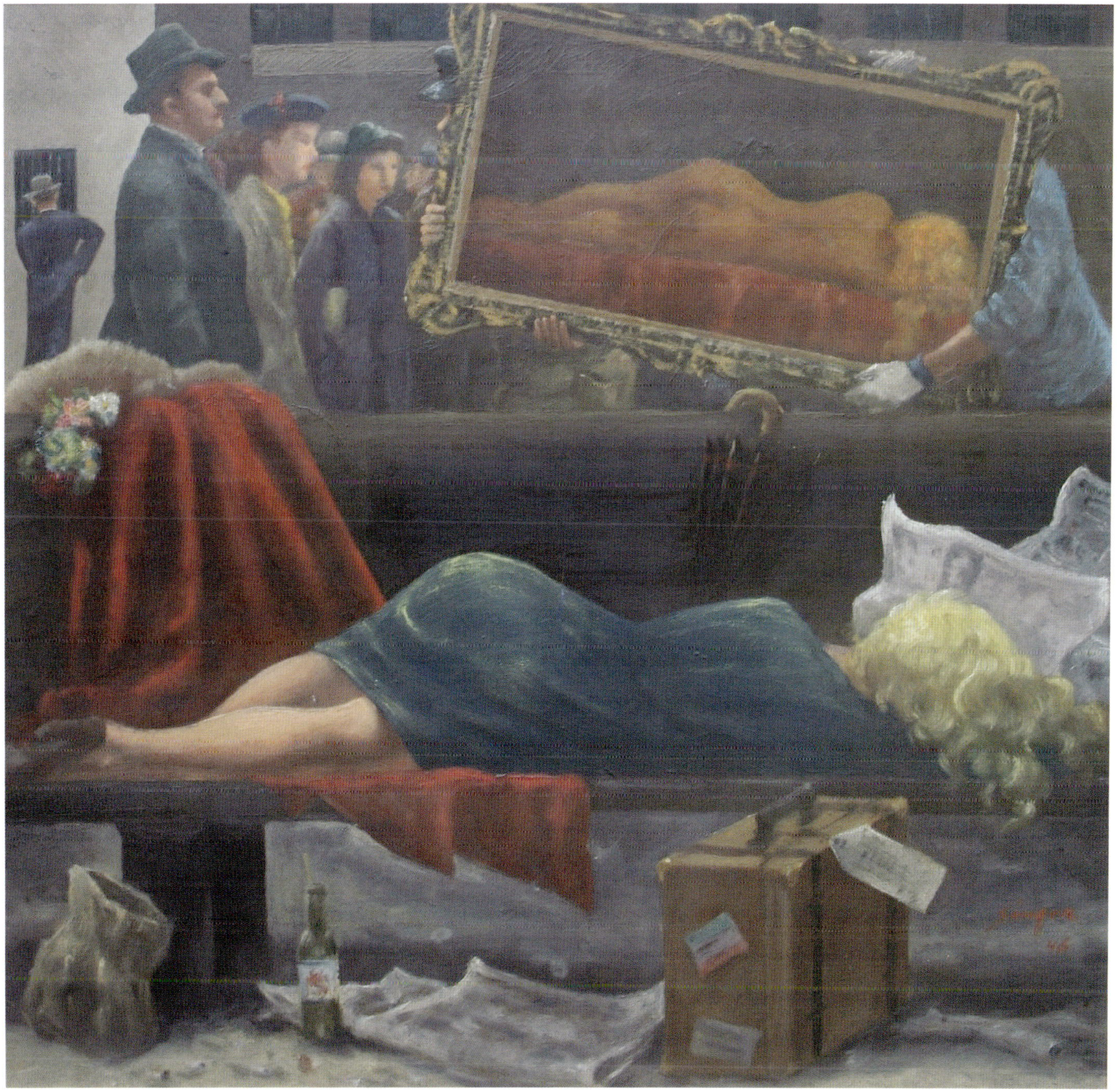

Fig. 107. *Nude at Union Station, Chicago,* 1946. Oil, 17½ x 51½. Courtesy of Mr. and Mrs. Larry Nile Basford

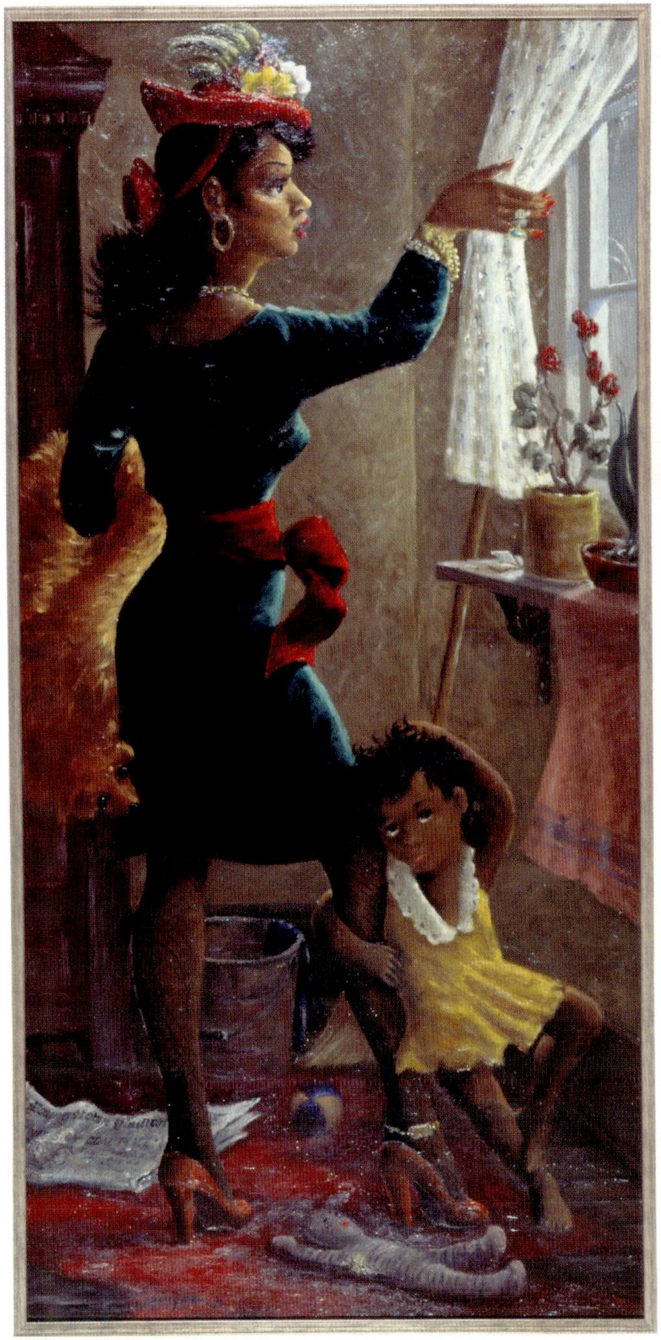

Fig. 108. *Ain't Gonna Rain,* 1946. Oil, 48 x 24. Courtesy of Theodore and Corinne Davidov

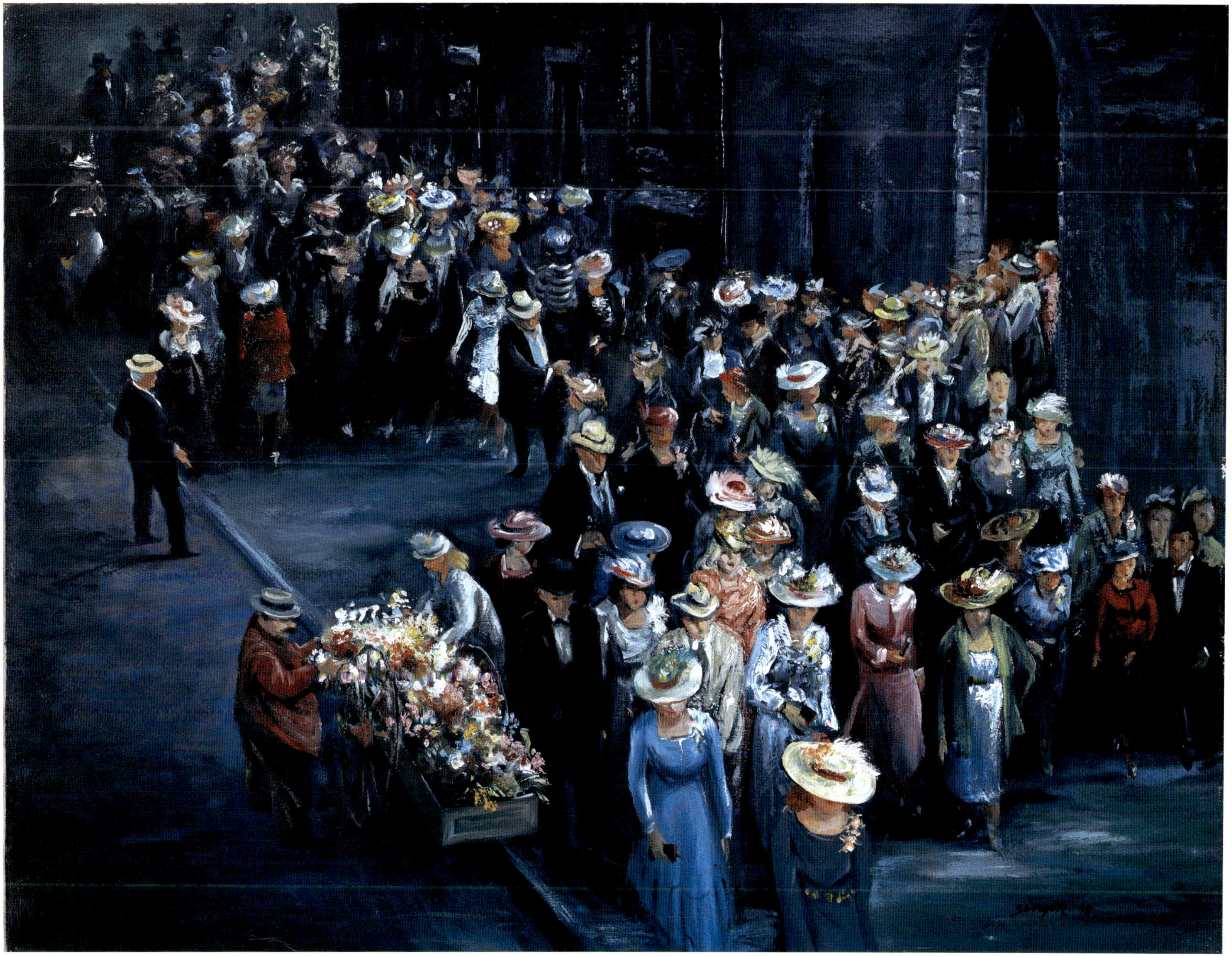

Fig. 109. *Easter Morning,* 1948. Oil, 32 x 42. Courtesy of Westmoreland Museum of American Art, Greensburg, Pennsylvania

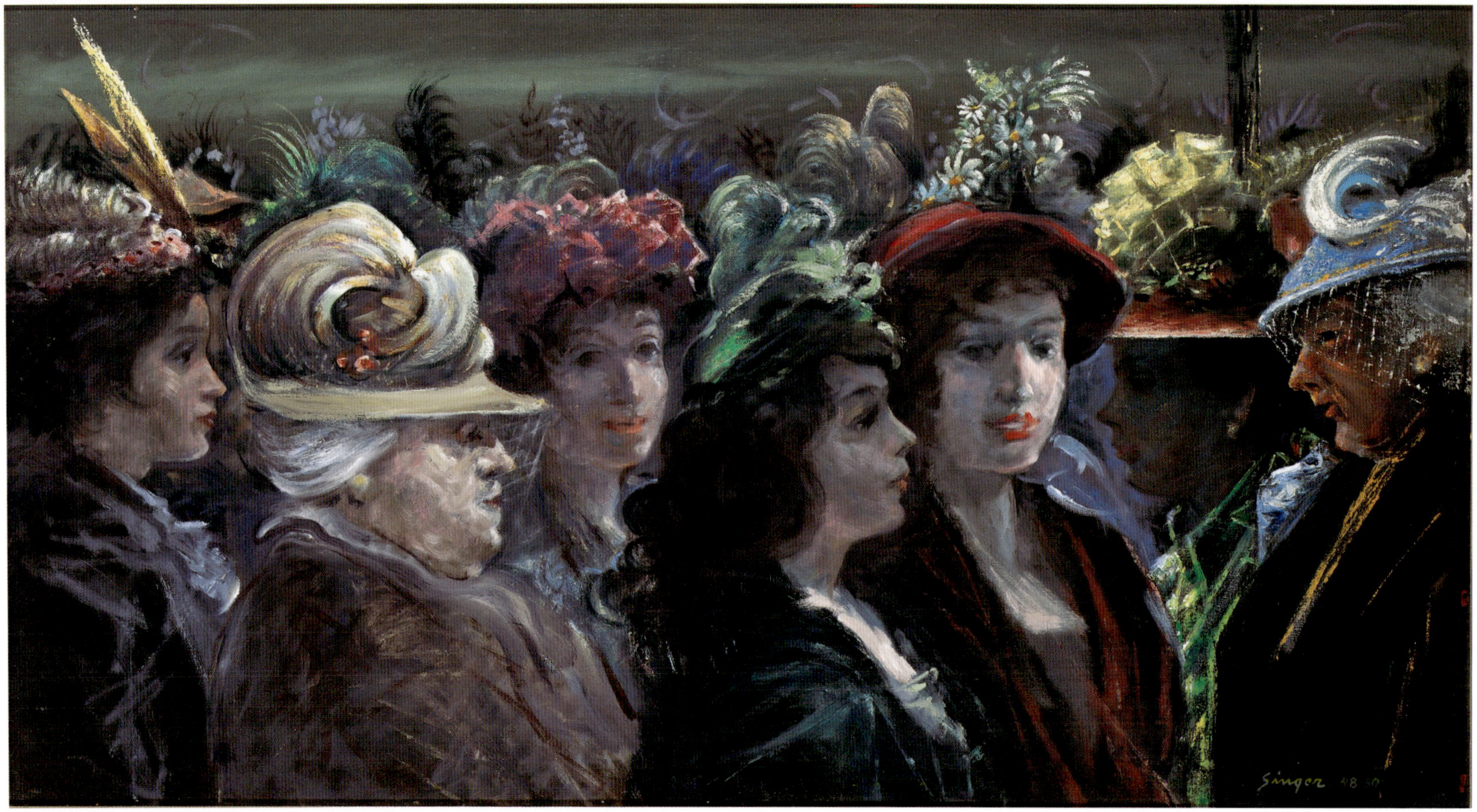

Fig. 110. *Garden Party,* 1948–50. Oil, 22¼ x 41½. Courtesy of Ed and Karen Ogul, Franklin, Michigan

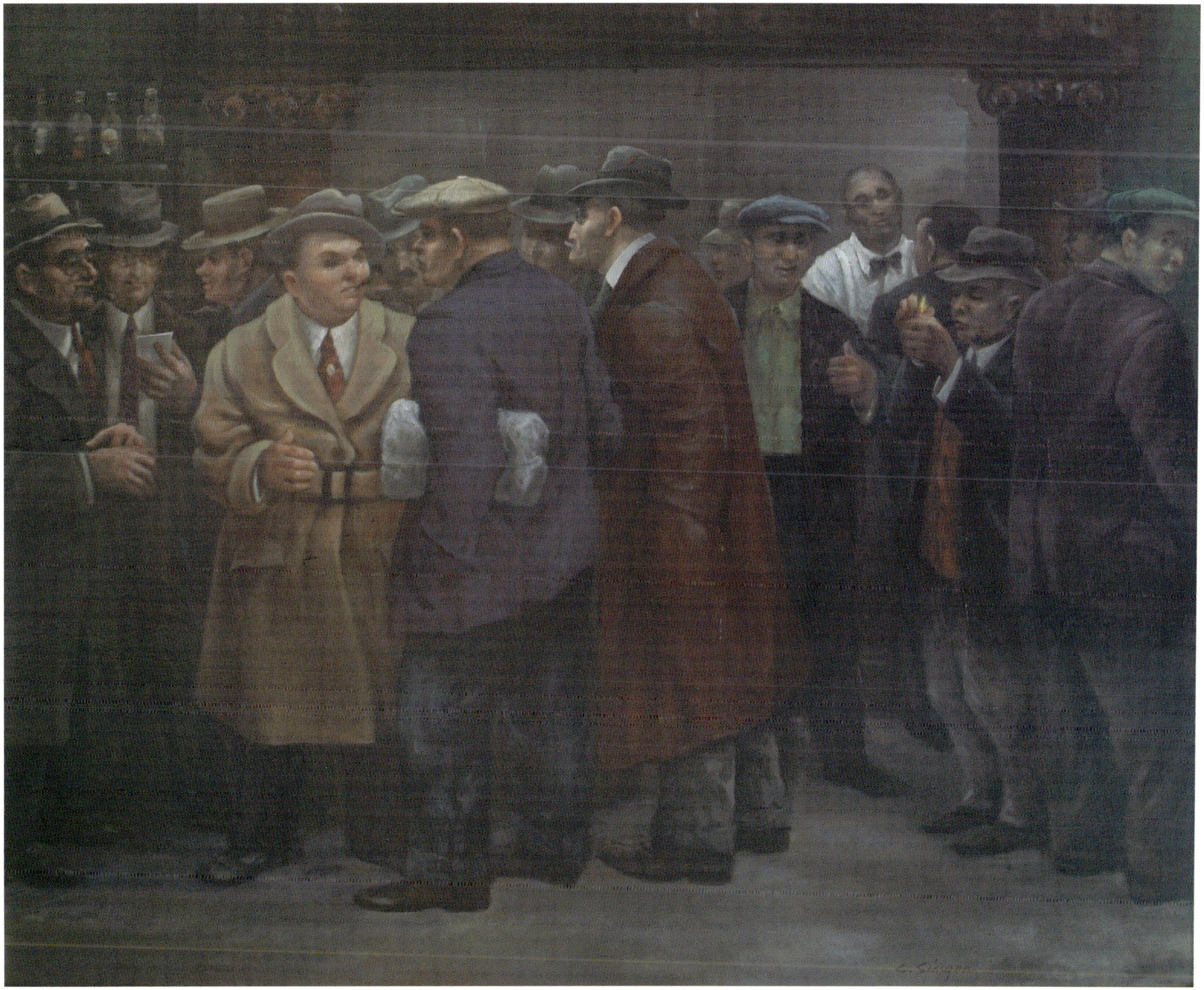

Fig. 111. *Men of Smoke,* 1952–57. Oil, 40 x 50. Courtesy of Thomas W. Darling

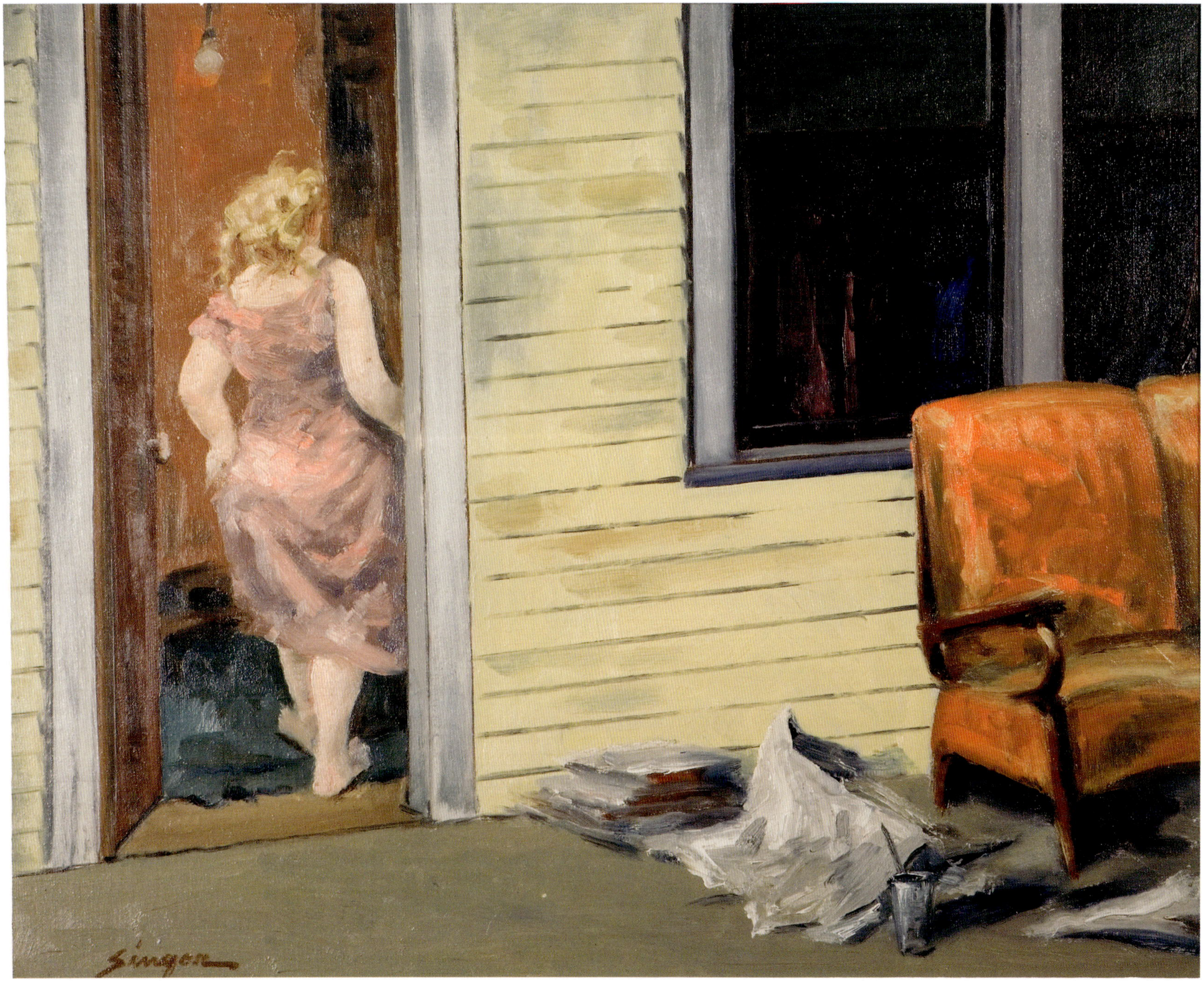

Fig. 112. *Hot Day,* 1953. Oil, 16 x 20. Courtesy of Brenda and Manning Cohen

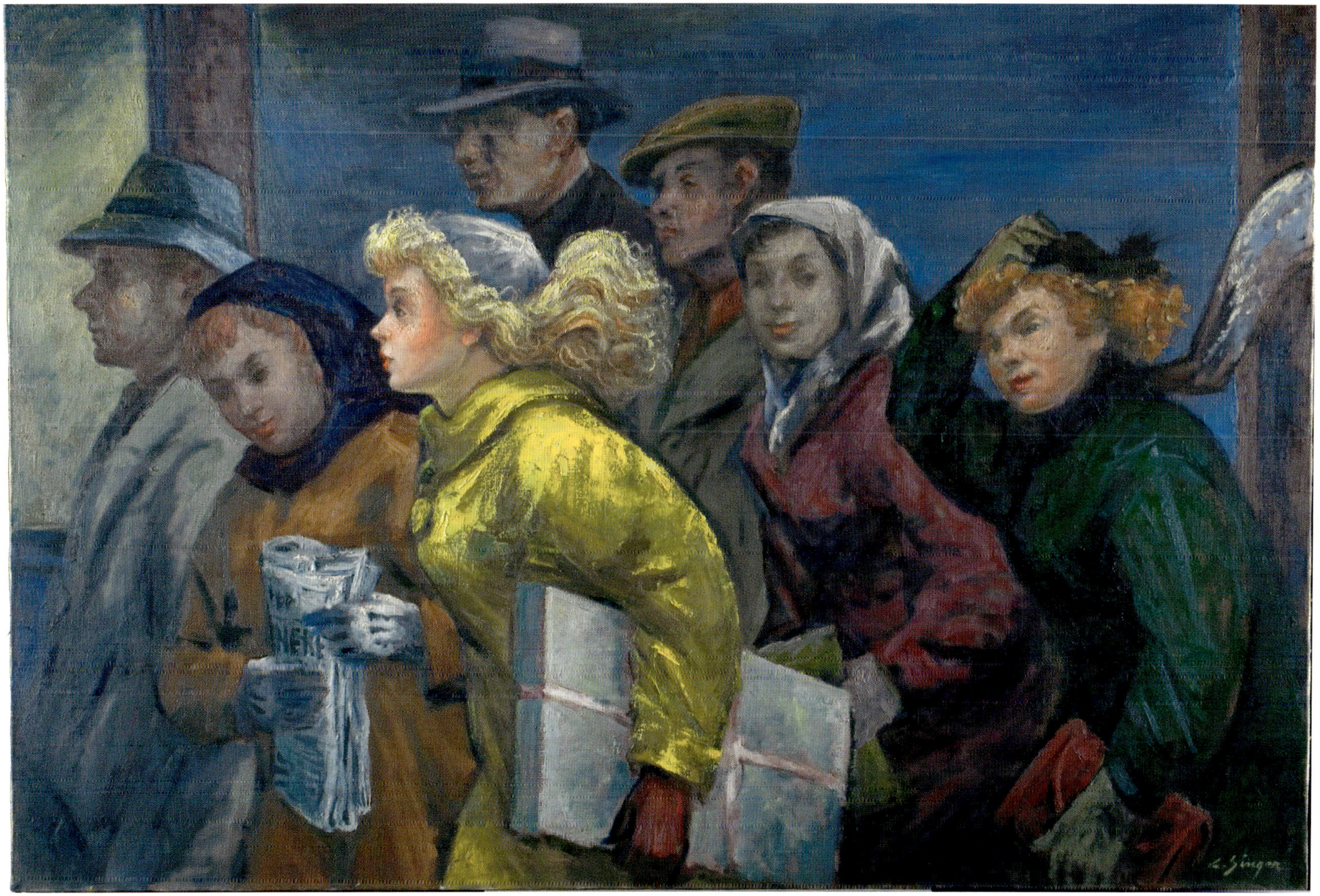

Fig. 113. *Pedestrians,* 1958–59. Oil, 28 x 42. Courtesy of the Chrysler Museum of Art, Norfolk, Virginia, gift of the artist

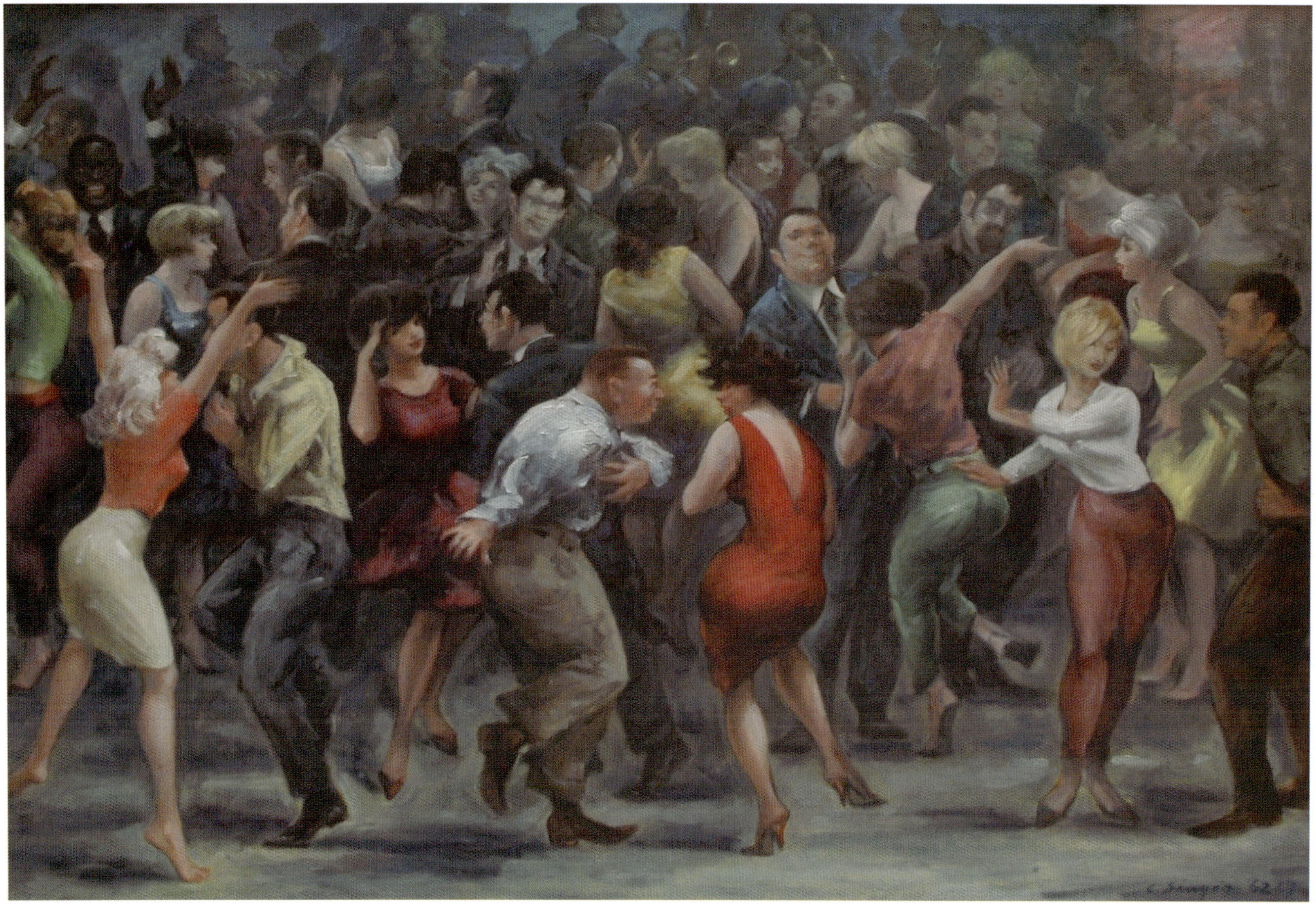

Fig. 114. *Twister,* 1962–69. Oil, 23 x 33½. Courtesy of Mr. and Mrs. James M. Conley

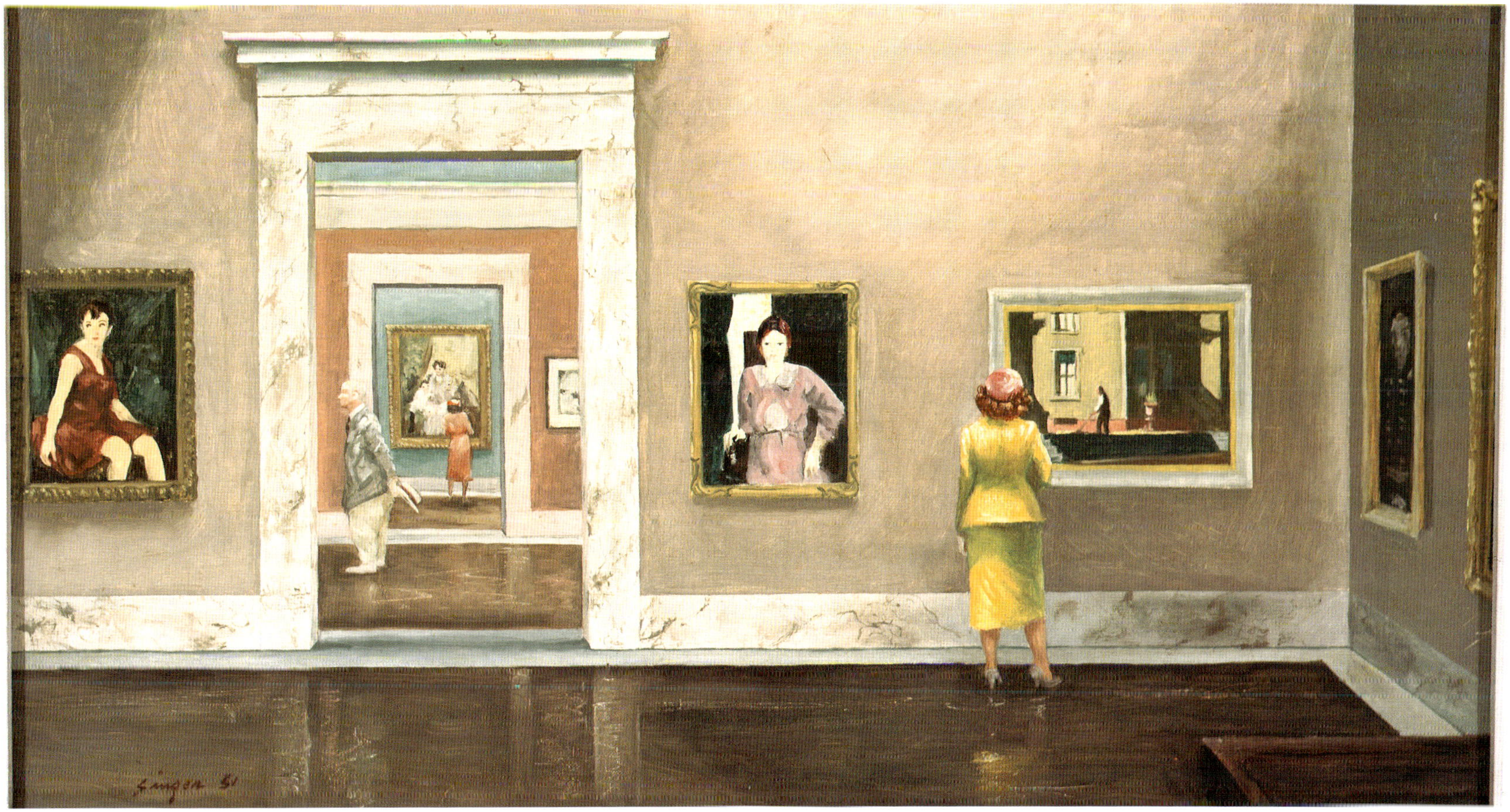

Fig. 115. *Selections from the Permanent Collection,* 1951. Oil, 13¾ x 25¾. The Butler Institute of American Art

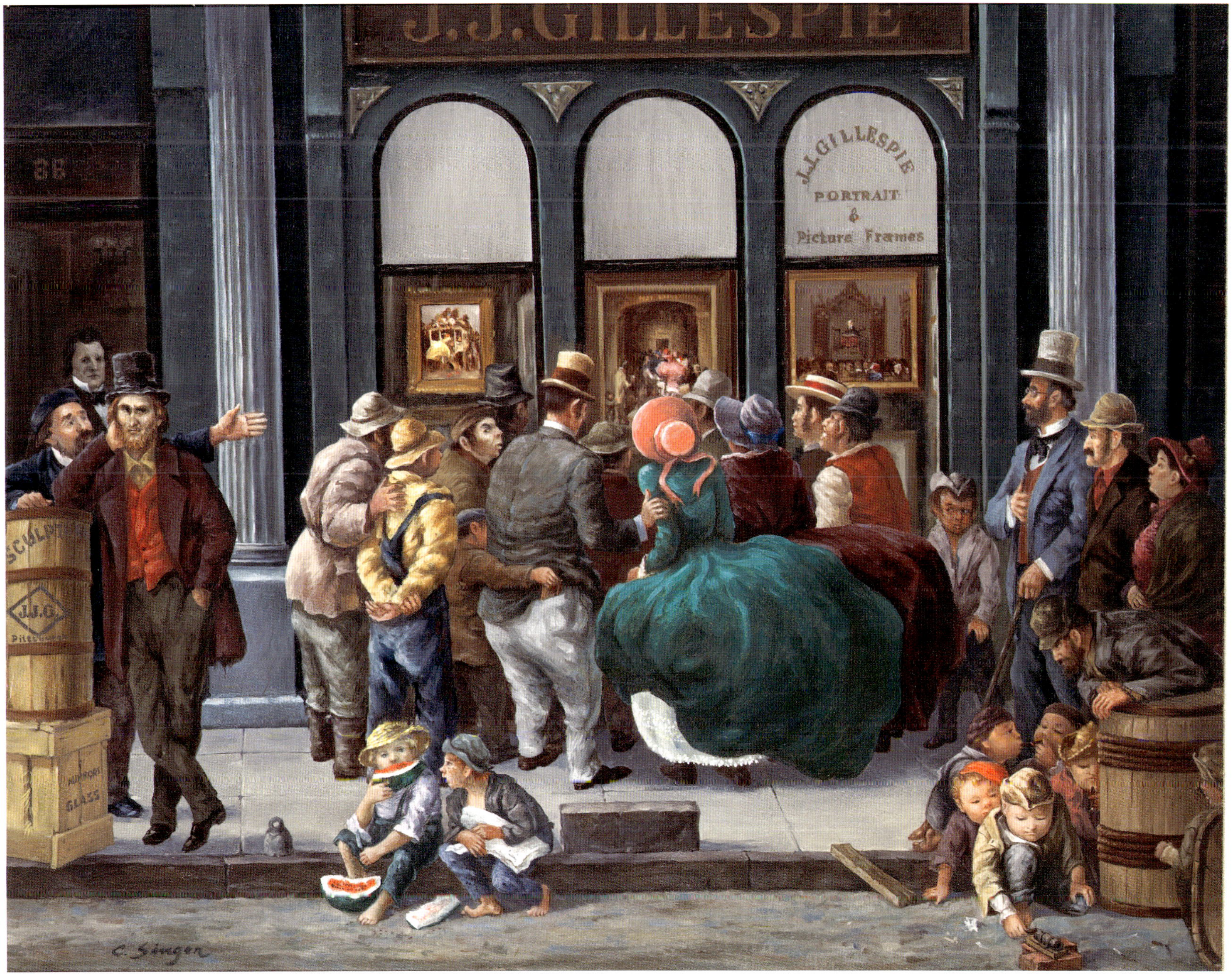

Fig. 116. *An Incident in the Life of David Blythe,* 1955. Oil, 21¾ x 27½. The Butler Institute of American Art

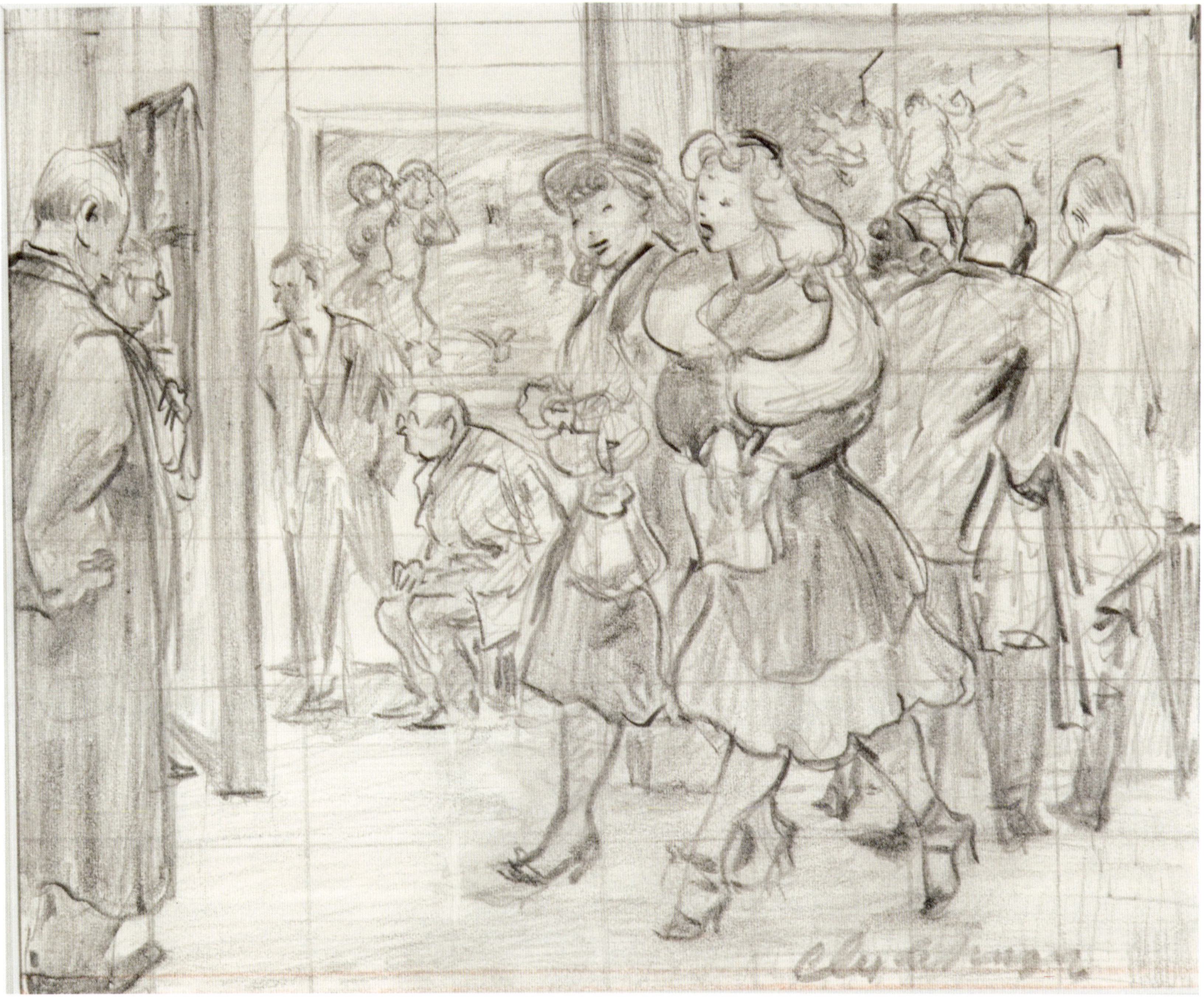

Fig. 117. *Sketch for Marsh at the Whitney*. Graphite, 6 x 7½. Courtesy of Lazar's Art Gallery & Creative Framing

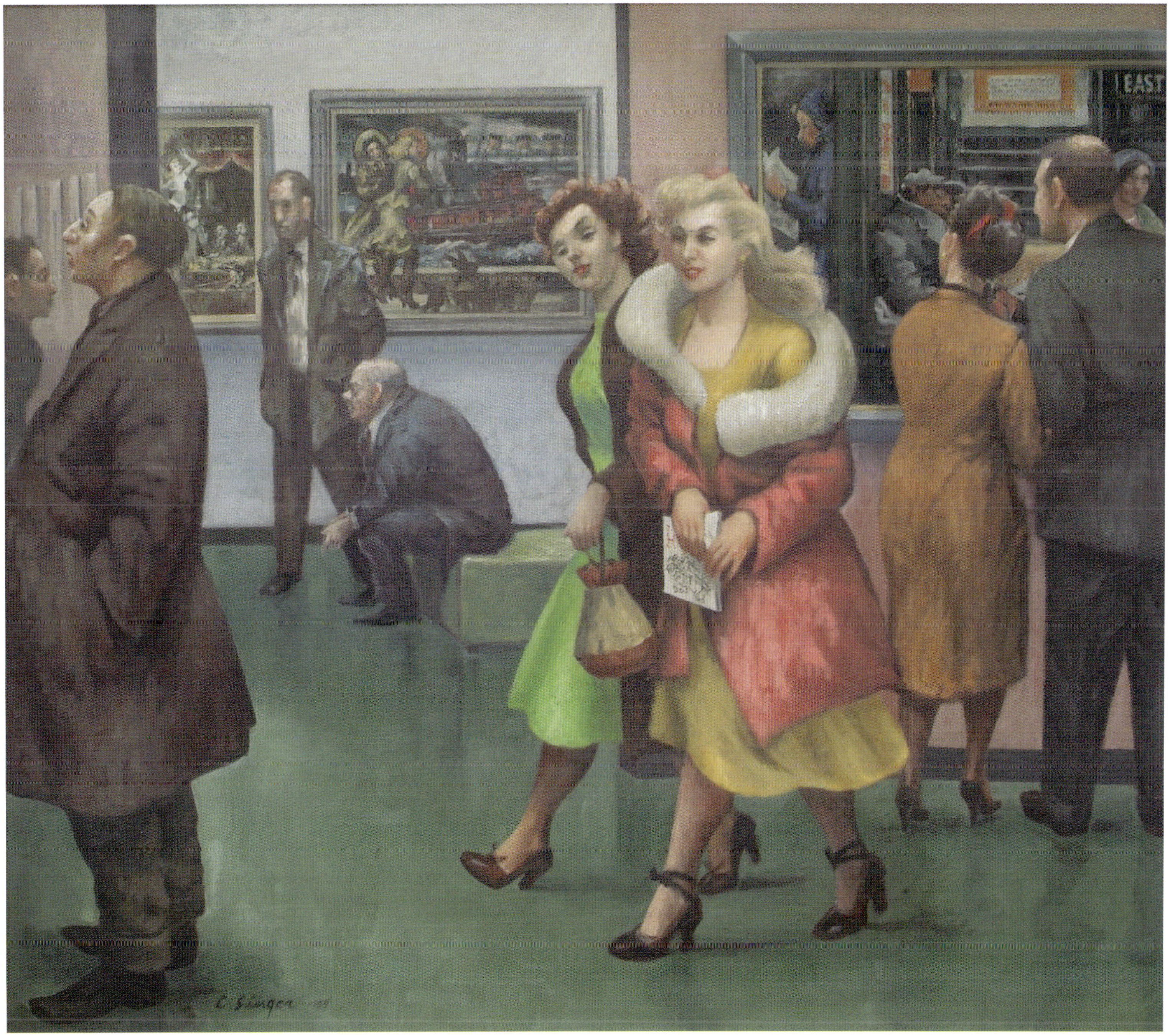

Fig. 118. *Marsh at the Whitney,* 1955. Oil, 32 x 38. Courtesy of a private collector

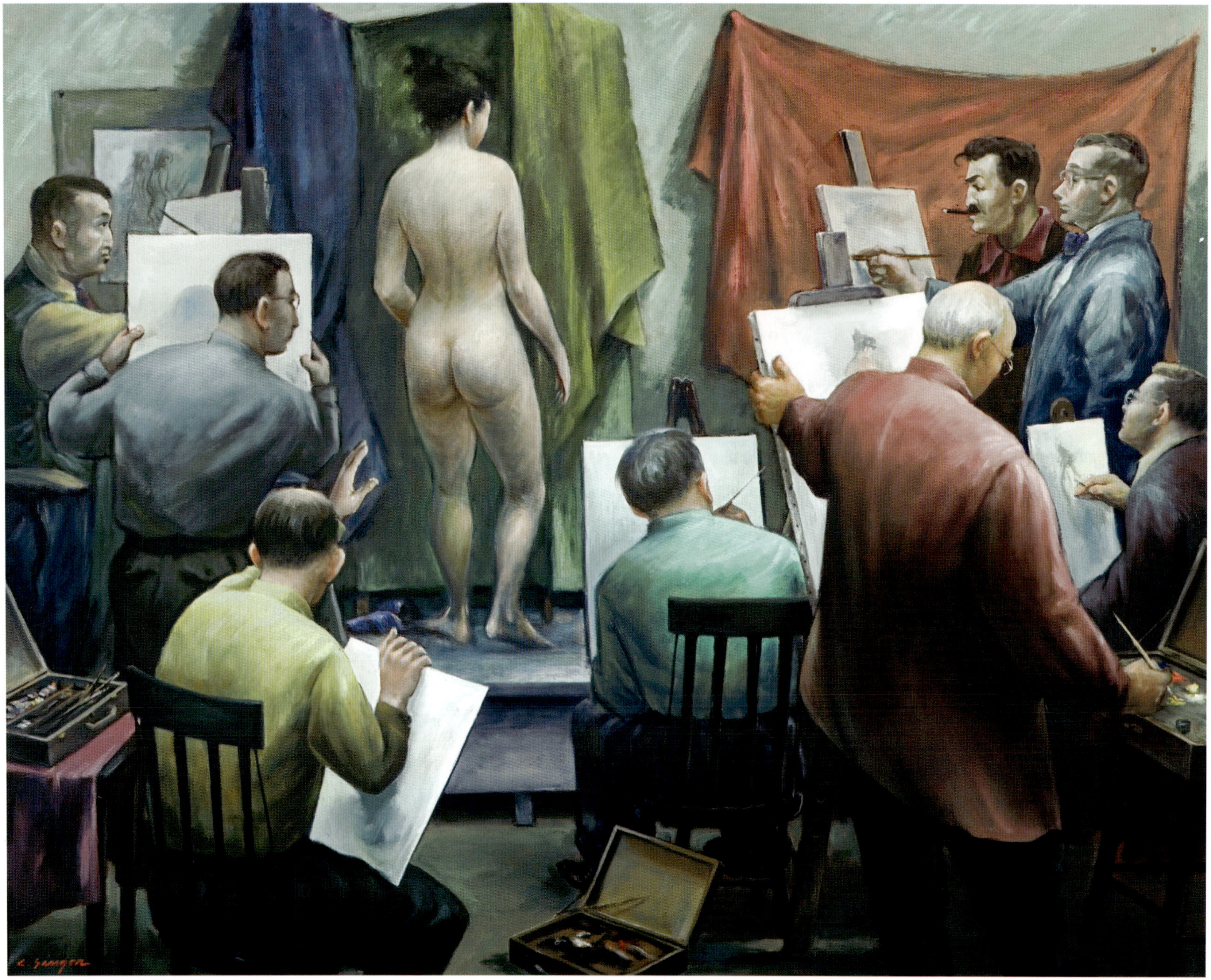

Fig. 119. *Men's Art Club,* 1957. Oil, 38 x 48. Courtesy of Gilcrease Museum, Tulsa, Oklahoma

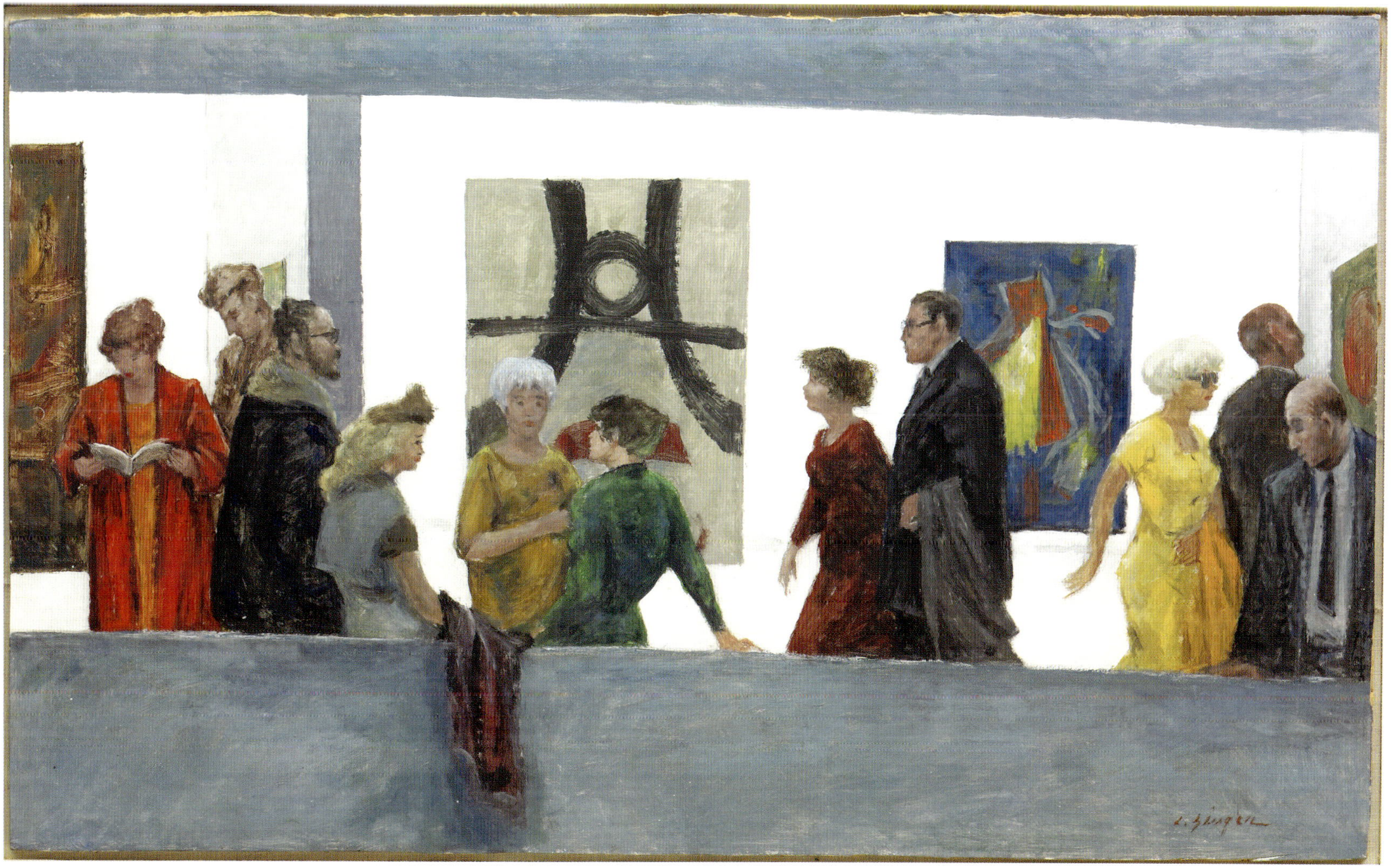

Fig. 120. *95% Guggenheim,* 1959. Casein, 24 x 39½. Courtesy of a private collector

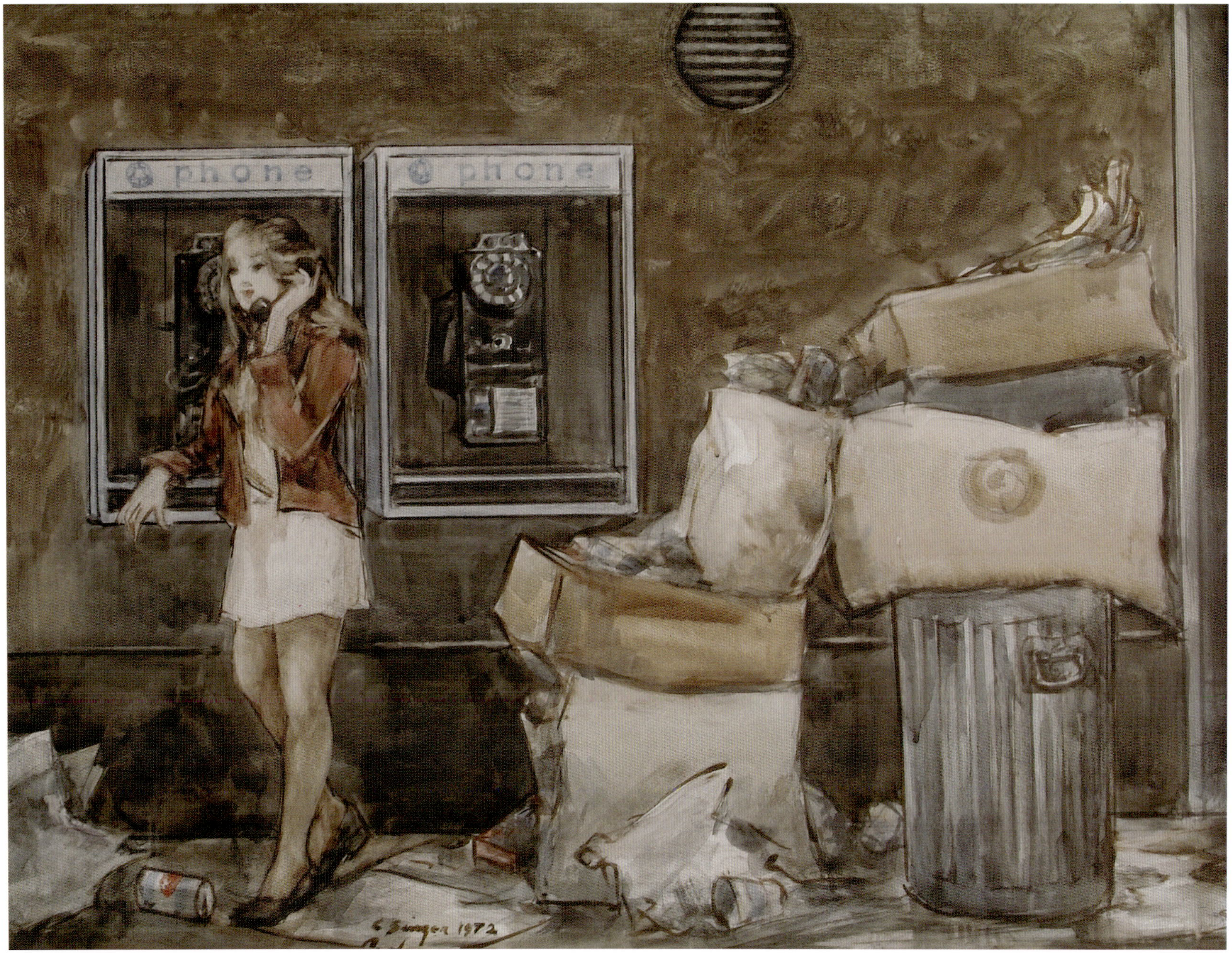

Fig. 121. *Girl on the Phone,* 1972. Watercolor/Casein, 17½ x 23. Courtesy of Mr. and Mrs. James M. Conley

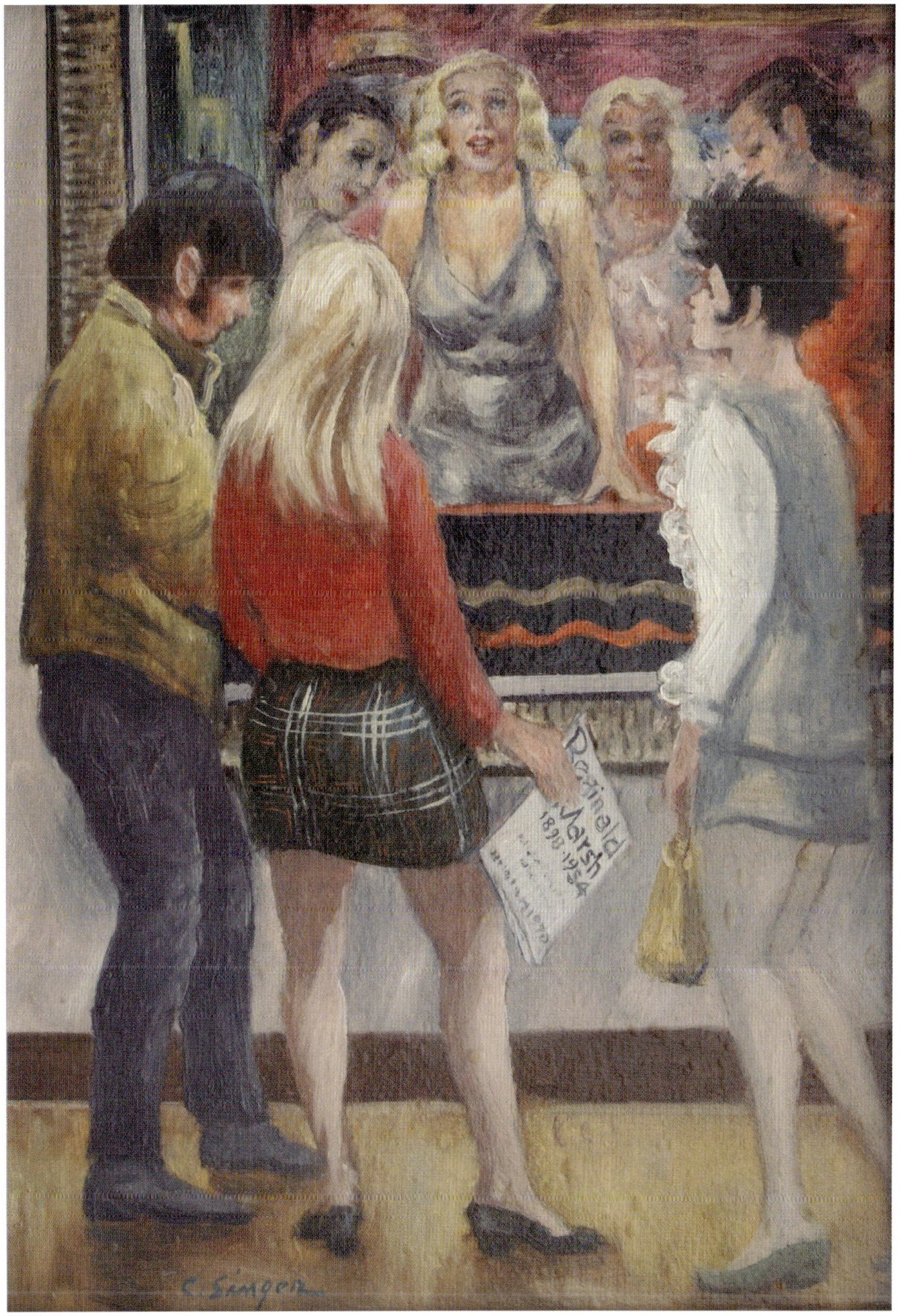

Fig. 122. *Reginald Marsh in Pittsburgh,* 1970. Oil, 18 x 14¼. Courtesy of Mr. and Mrs. Paul Herron

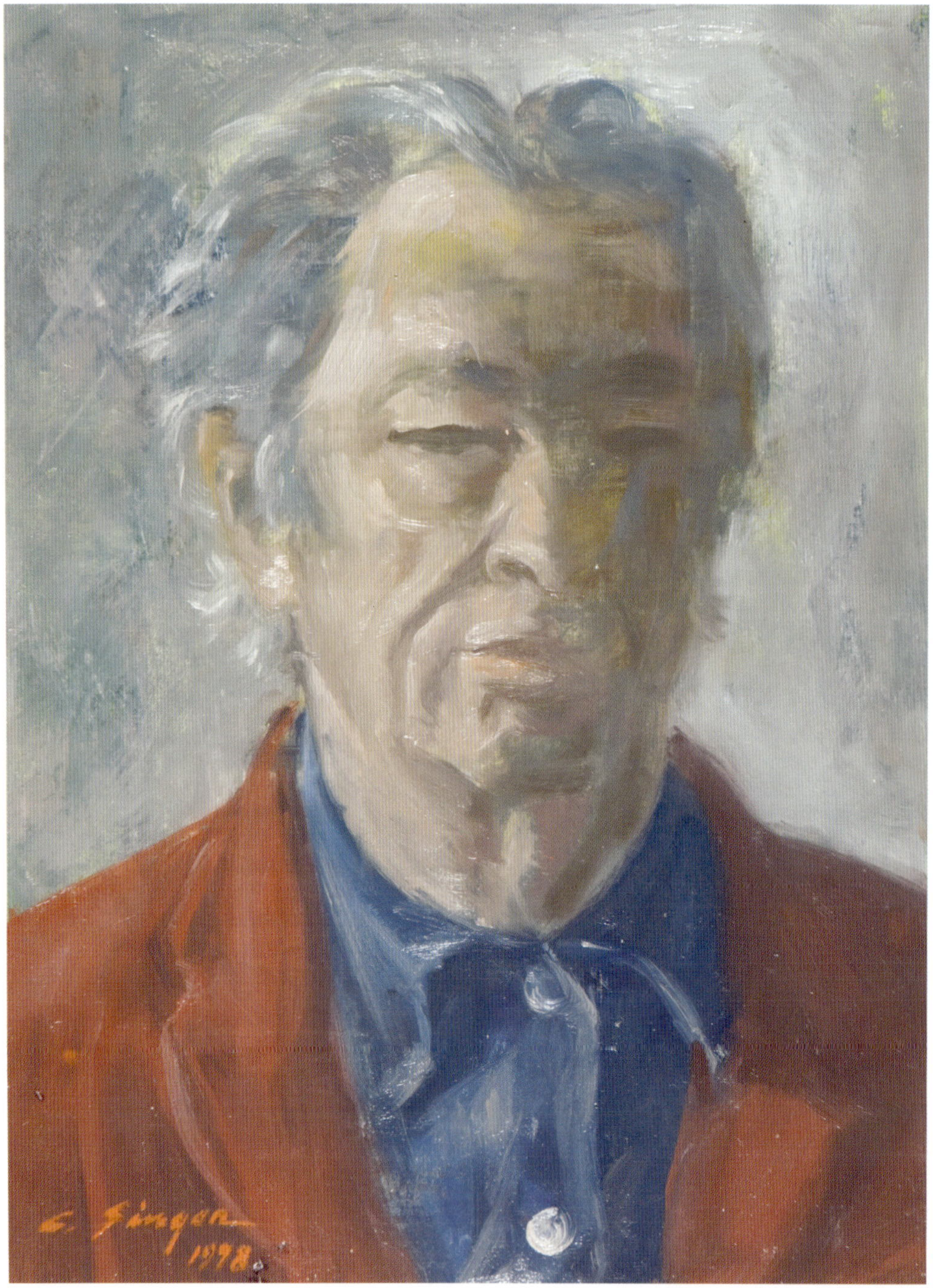

Fig. 123. *Self-Portrait,* January 5, 1998. Oil, 16 x 12. Courtesy of Lazar's Art Gallery & Creative Framing

Appendix: Singer Chronology

1908

Born October 20 in Malvern, Ohio, to Andrew and Margaret (Sorg) Singer. The youngest of four boys and with two younger sisters.

1931–32

Attended the Columbus Arts School (Columbus College of Art and Design), Ohio, on scholarship.

1933

Received scholarship to Art Students League in New York.

Adolescence and *The Medicine Man* reproduced in the *New York Herald-Tribune,* April 17.

First visited McSorley's Ale House, New York City, the saloon depicted in the work of his "heroes" John Sloan and George Bellows.

1934

Returned to Ohio.

Painted *Sandy Valley.*

First one-man show, The Little Civic Art Gallery (Canton Art Institute), Ohio. Exhibited 30 oils and watercolors, including *Winter—Malvern, Ohio.*

One-man show, Baldwin Museum (Massillon Museum), Ohio. Exhibit included *Winter—Malvern, Ohio.*

1935–36

Exhibited in 82 exhibitions in 56 cities within 18-month period.

1935

Norman Wait Harris Silver Medal and $500 for *Sandy Valley,* 46th Annual Exhibition of Contemporary American Painting, Art Institute of Chicago. Also exhibited *Democrat Rally.*

Through the Art Institute of Chicago, *Sandy Valley* toured to the Minneapolis Institute of Arts, University of Iowa, and William Rockhill Nelson Gallery of Art, Kansas City.

46th Annual American Painting and Sculpture Exhibition, Pennsylvania Academy of Fine Arts. Exhibited *Democrat Rally* and *Winter Along the Hudson.*

Exhibited at the Malvern Homecoming.

Honorable Mention for *Winter Along the Hudson,* 41st Annual Exhibition, Denver Art Museum, Colorado.

42nd Annual Exhibition of American Art, Cincinnati Art Museum. Exhibited *Democrat Rally* and *Sandy Valley.*

Philadelphia Art Alliance Circulating Picture Club, Pennsylvania. Exhibited two oil paintings.

Baldwin Museum. Exhibited oil paintings and watercolors, including *Sandy Valley* and *Malvern, Ohio.*

4th Annual, Portland Art Museum, Oregon. Exhibited *Landscape with Fishermen* and *Ohio Architecture.*

Juryless Exhibition, Cincinnati Art Museum. Exhibited *Wrestling Night.*
Isochromatic Exhibition, Newman Galleries, Philadelphia. Exhibited *Self-Portrait.*

1936

John Lambert Purchase Award and $100 for *Bill,* Pennsylvania Academy of Fine Art, Philadelphia, Annual Exhibit. Also exhibited *Flower Vendor.*

Isochromatic Exhibition, Grand Central Galleries, New York. Exhibited *Self-Portrait.* Exhibition toured to more than 100 galleries nationwide, including Denver Art Museum, Washington County Museum of Fine Arts in Maryland, Oregon State College, University of Oklahoma, Montgomery Museum of Fine Arts in Alabama, Newman Galleries in Philadelphia, West Virginia Federated Clubs, and Rhode Island School of Design.

26th Annual Columbus Art League Exhibition, Columbus Gallery of Fine Art. Exhibited *Springtime in the Valley, Winter in the Valley, Nocturne,* and *Ohio Architecture.*

Malvern Homecoming. Exhibit included *Charlie's Place, Sandy Valley, Democrat Rally,* and *Street People.*

42nd Annual Exhibition, Denver Art Museum. Exhibited *Wrestling Night.*

Annual Exhibition of Watercolors by American Artists, Art Institute of Chicago. Exhibited *Winter Along the Hudson.*

47th Annual Exhibition of American Paintings and Sculptures, Art Institute of Chicago. Exhibited *Jim* and *Flower Vendor.*

Carnegie International, Carnegie Museum of Art, Pittsburgh. Exhibited *Charlie's Place.*

The Centennial Exhibition of Paintings, Sculpture, and Graphic Arts, Dallas Museum of Art. Exhibited *Democrat Rally.*

Third Biennial Exhibition of Contemporary American Paintings, Whitney Museum of American Art, New York. Exhibited *The Show Off.*

26th Annual Exhibition, Connecticut Academy of Fine Arts, Avon. Exhibited *Sandy Valley.*

43rd Annual Exhibition of American Art, Cincinnati Art Museum. Exhibited *The Flower Vendor.*

111th Annual Exhibition of National Academy of Design, New York. Exhibited *Charlie's Place.*

Oakland Art Gallery (Oakland Museum of California Art Department), California. Exhibited *Landscape with Fishermen.*

Ohio State Fair. Exhibited *Springtime in the Valley.*

Juryless Exhibition, Cincinnati Art Museum. Exhibited *Street Portrait.*

Isochromatic Exhibition from Grumbacher Collection, The Little Civic Art Gallery, travels to Baldwin Museum, Akron Art Institute, and The Butler Art Institute (The Butler Institute of American Art). Exhibited *Self-Portrait* and *Head of W. Maki.*

Annual Exhibition of Contemporary American Paintings, John Herron Art Museum (Indianapolis Museum of Art). Exhibited *Democrat Rally.*

5th Annual, Portland Art Museum, Oregon. Exhibited *Nocturne: Charlie's Front* and *Italian Girl.*

17th Annual Exhibition of Painting and Sculpture, Los Angeles Museum (The Los Angeles County Museum of Art). Exhibited *Coming 'Round the Bend.*

Annual Show, New Haven Paint and Clay Club, Connecticut. Exhibited *Nocturne: Street Lightning.*

Touring exhibition to West Virginia, Oklahoma, New Jersey, Pennsylvania, Tennessee, Notre Dame University, and New York Industrial School Galleries. Exhibited several small oils.

Young Malvern Artist: Clyde Singer, Canton Art Institute (Canton Museum of Art). Also exhibited *Sandy Valley, Coming 'Round the Bend,* and *Wrestling Night.*

Texas Centennial Exhibition, Dallas Museum of Art. Exhibited by invitation *Democrat Rally* and *Winter Along the Hudson.*

1937

43rd Annual Exhibition, Denver Art Museum.

27th Annual Columbus Art League Exhibition, Columbus Gallery of Fine Art. Exhibited *Before the Deluge—A.D. 1936* and *Democrat Rally.*

2nd Annual New Year Show, The Butler Art Institute. Exhibited *Street Portrait, Grand Theatre Burlesque, Before the Deluge—A.D. 1936*

Malvern Homecoming. Exhibited *The Old Swimming Hole, Approach the Village, Grand Theatre Burlesque,* and *Wind on the Avenue.*

Annual Exhibition, Pennsylvania Academy of Fine Arts. Exhibited *Street People.*

Ohio State Fair. Exhibited *Jim. Jim* included on cover of the fair catalog.

Carnegie International, Carnegie Museum of Art. Exhibited *Wind on the Avenue.*

Canton Art Institute. Exhibited *Democrat Rally.*

47th Annual American Exhibition of Paintings, Dallas Museum of Art. Exhibited *Wind on the Avenue.*

Art of the Americas: Pre-Columbian and Contemporary, Dallas Museum of Art. Exhibited *Street People.*

48th Annual Exhibition of American Paintings and Sculptures, Art Institute of Chicago. Exhibited *Approach to the Village.*

First Prize for Figure Composition for *Street People,* 28th Annual Columbus Art League Exhibition, Columbus Gallery of Fine Art.

Columbus Art League New Year Show, Exhibited *Waitin' at the Corner* and *Democrat Rally.*

15th Biennial Exhibition of Contemporary American Oil Paintings, The Corcoran Gallery of Art, Washington, D.C. Exhibited *Approach to the Village.*

Touring Exhibition, 1937–38: Pennsylvania, Everhart Museum; New York, Binghamton Museum of Art, Albany Institute of History and Art, Utica Public Library, Cayuga Museum of History and Art, and Eastman School of Music. Exhibited *Democrat Rally* and *Wrestling Night.*

One-man show, Binghamton Society of Fine Arts, Binghamton Public Library, New York. Exhibited oils and watercolors.

24th Annual Exhibition of Selected Paintings by Contemporary American Artists, Toledo Museum of Art, Ohio. Exhibited *Charlie's Place.*

Greater Texas and Pan-American Exposition, Dallas.

Portland Art Museum 6th Annual, Oregon. Exhibited *Before the Deluge—A.D. 1936* and *Waitin' at the Corner.*

18th Annual Exhibition of American Art, Detroit Institute of Art. Exhibited *Henry's House.*

44th Annual Exhibition of American Art, Cincinnati Art Museum. Exhibited *Charlie's Place* and *Jim.*

1938

First Julius Hallgarten Prize and $175 for *Barn Dance,* Annual Exhibition, National Academy of Design.

Malvern Homecoming. Exhibited 30 paintings, including *Marion.*

First Place in Oil Painting–Landscape for *Approach to the Village* and First Place in Oil Painting–Figure Composition for *The Old Swimming Hole,* 29th Annual Exhibition of Paintings, Sculpture and Pottery, Columbus Art League, Columbus Gallery of Fine Arts. Also exhibited *Katz Meow.*

One-man show, Eastman Corridor Gallery (Memorial Art Gallery), University of Rochester, New York. Exhibit included *Coming 'Round the Bend, Wrestling Night,* and *White Cloud.*

Baldwin Fund Purchase Award for *The Sermon,* Exhibition of Paintings: Clyde Singer, Massillon Museum. Exhibit included *Sandy Valley, Wrestling Night, Charlie's Place,* and *Barn Dance.*

44th Annual Exhibition, Denver Art Museum. Exhibited *Winter in the Valley* and *Democrat Rally.*

Listed in *Who's Who of American Art.*

Montclair Art Museum, New Jersey. Exhibited *Barn Dance.*

Akron Society of Artists, Business Men's Art Club of Cleveland, Buckeye Art Club of Youngstown, Akron Art Institute. Exhibited *The Rush Hour.*

One-man show, Canton Woman's Club, Ohio.

First Prize and $200 for *The Rush Hour,* 3rd Annual New Year Show, The Butler Art Institute. Also exhibited *Old Swimming Hole, Waitin' at the Corner, The Sermon,* and *November Snow.*

Canton Art Institute. Exhibited *Street Portrait, Back Yard,* and *East River—New York.*

Portland Art Museum Seventh Annual, Oregon. Exhibited *The Grey Coat* and *Park Bench Bum—Madison Square.*

Carnegie International, Carnegie Museum of Art. Exhibited *Barn Dance.*

49th Annual Exhibition of American Paintings and Sculpture, Art Institute of Chicago. Exhibited *Wind on the Avenue.*

Institute of American Sporting Art, Midland Club Hotel, Chicago. Exhibited *Wrestling Night.*

45th Annual Exhibition of American Art, Cincinnati Art Museum. Exhibited *The Rush Hour.*

Annual Exhibition, Pennsylvania Academy of Fine Arts. Exhibited *Springtime in the Valley.*

One-man show, North Canton Public Library, Ohio.

1939

One-man show, Malvern Homecoming. Exhibited 30 oils and 20 watercolors.

Second Place for *The Evening Mail,* 8th Annual Exhibition of Painting and Sculpture, Portland Art Museum, Oregon. Also exhibited *Old Chicago.*

Magnuson Award for *Wind on the Avenue,* 30th Annual Columbus Art League Exhibition, Columbus Gallery of Fine Art. Also exhibited *The Rush Hour.*

Golden Gate International Exposition, San Francisco. Exhibited *Charlie's Place.*
Art of Tomorrow Exhibit, New York World's Fair. Exhibited *East River—New York.*
Carnegie International, Carnegie Museum of Art. Exhibited *Homecoming.*
4th Annual New Year Show, The Butler Art Institute. Exhibited *East River—New York, Park Bench Bum—Madison Square.* Exhibit traveled to Akron Art Institute, Kent State University, Miami University, and Massillon Museum.
16th Biennial Exhibition of Contemporary American Oil Paintings, The Corcoran Gallery of Art. Exhibited *Springtime in the Valley.*
33rd Annual Exhibition of Paintings by American Artists, City Art Museum of St. Louis (St. Louis Art Museum). Exhibited *Barn Dance.*
46th Annual Exhibition of American Art, Cincinnati Art Museum. Exhibited *Barn Dance.*
Annual Exhibition, Pennsylvania Academy of Fine Arts. Exhibited *Approach to the Village* and *The Rush Hour.*
49th Annual American Exhibition of American Paintings and Sculpture, circulated by the Art Institute of Chicago, Columbus Museum of Art. Exhibited *Wind on the Avenue.*

1939–40

Studied at the Research Studio in Maitland, Florida.

1940

Accepted position as assistant director and becomes artist-in-residence, The Butler Art Institute.
Began writing weekly art reviews for the *Youngstown Vindicator.*
Taught landscape and figure painting at Youngstown College.
Served as juror for the Westminster College First Western Pennsylvania Print Exhibition.
Contemporary American Artists, The John Herron Art Institute, Art Association of Indianapolis. Exhibited *Barn Dance.*
Malvern Homecoming. Exhibit includes *Skaters,* New Concord mural.
1940–41 Annual Exhibition of Contemporary American Painting, Whitney Museum of American Art. Exhibited *Shotgun Wedding.*
First Prize for *McSorley's On Sunday,* Youngstown Watercolor Annual, The Butler Art Institute. Exhibition featured the combined works of the Art Alliance, Buckeye Art Club, Mahoning Society of Painters, and Youngstown Watercolor Society.
Clyde Singer Paintings, First Comprehensive and Most Important One-Man Show, The Butler Art Institute. Exhibit includes *Sandy Valley, Evening Mail, Street People, Barn Dance, Approach to the Village,* and *Charlie's Place.*
Taught at the Ohio River School of Painting, Marietta. Instructor exhibit included *Wrestling Night.*
46th Annual Exhibition, Denver Art Museum.
The Friends of American Art, First National Exhibition, The Grand Rapids Art Gallery (Grand Rapids Art Museum), Michigan. Exhibited *County Fair.*
Exhibited at Ogunquit Art Center, Maine.
2nd Biennial Exhibition of Contemporary American Painting, Virginia Museum of Fine Arts, Richmond. Exhibited *The Rush Hour.*
Exhibited at the Oakland Art Gallery, California.
47th Annual Exhibition of American Art, Cincinnati Art Museum. Exhibited *Park Bench—Madison Square.*
5th Annual Ohio Artists and Craftsmen Exhibition, Massillon Museum.
C. Singer Paintings, Massillon Museum. Exhibit included *Shotgun Wedding.*
5th Annual New Year Show, The Butler Art Institute. Exhibited *Homecoming, Daytona Beach,* and *WPA in Florida.* Exhibit traveled to Riverside Museum and Rochester Art Memorial in New York and to the Cleveland Museum of Art and Massillon Museum.
One-man show, North Canton Public Library.

1941

48 States Competition. Installs *Skaters,* a mural for the United States Post Office in New Concord, Ohio, as a WPA Project awarded by the Public Buildings Branch of the U.S. Treasury Department.
Annual Exhibition, Pennsylvania Academy of Fine Arts. Exhibited *Barn Dance.*
32nd Annual Columbus Art League Exhibition, Columbus Gallery of Fine Arts. Exhibited *Eatonville Elite* and *The Popcorn Women.*
One-man show, Mount Union College, Ohio.
One-man show, Mount De Chantel Academy, West Virginia.
Ohio River School of Painting Exhibit of Teachers and Students, Canton Art Institute.
47th Annual Exhibition, Denver Art Museum.

6th Annual New Year Show, The Butler Art Institute. Exhibited *Down by the Ohio, Youngstown Shamrock, The Street Preacher, Southern Ohio, Beverly Fire House,* and *Belpre Flower Boxes.*

Married Bernice Elizabeth Shimp, November 3, St. Francis Catholic Church, Malvern.

Drafted into the U.S. Army (age 34) in December.

1942

First Prize for Best Oil Painting and $125 for *Stormy Weather,* 7th Annual New Year Show, The Butler Art Institute. Also exhibited *Street People* and *Steamboat on the Ohio.*

New Haven Paint and Clay Club, Connecticut.

May Show Juried Exhibition, Canton Art Institute.

One-man show, Massillon Museum.

3rd Biennial Exhibition of Contemporary American Paintings, Virginia Museum of Fine Arts. Exhibited *Fight for a Woman.*

48th Annual Exhibition, Denver Art Museum. Exhibited *Day's End.*

1943

8th Annual New Year Show, The Butler Art Institute. Exhibited *Democrat Rally, Wrestling Night,* and *The Flower Seller.*

Honorable Mention, Ohio Valley Show, Athens, Ohio.

Honorable Mention/Watercolors for *Tennessee Maneuvers,* Ohio Servicemen's Watercolor and Drawing Exhibition, The Butler Art Institute. Exhibited *Week-End Pass, Sailors in New Orleans,* and *Rain at Post No. 2.*

1944

One-man show, Massillon Museum.

Artists for Victory, Rockefeller Center, New York. Exhibited *Barn Dance.*

1945

Honorably discharged from U.S. Army.

10th Annual New Year Show, The Butler Art Institute. Exhibited *Day's End, Eatonville Fire* and *Nocturne: Franklin Park.*

1946

Returned to The Butler Art Institute and resumed his column for the *Youngstown Vindicator.*

Honorable Mention, Fall Show, Canton Art Institute.

Robinson Purchase Award, Columbus Art League.

Second Honorable Mention in Oils Division for *Let It Rain,* Spring Show, Mint Museum of Art, North Carolina. Also exhibited *River and Boat.*

Clyde Singer Retrospective Exhibition 1929–1946, The Little Art Gallery, North Canton Library. Exhibit included *Nocturne, Tire Shop, Waitin' at the Corner, Bernice, Ring Around the Moon,* and *Park Bench Bum.*

One-man show, Canton Woman's Club. Exhibit included *Nocturne: Charlie's Front, The Sermon, Before the Deluge—A.D. 1936,* and *East River—New York.*

One-man show, The Butler Art Institute.

Painting in the United States, Carnegie Museum of Art. Exhibited *Dreary Day.*

First Spring Annual Exposition, California Palace of the Legion of Honor, San Francisco. Exhibited *Park Bench Bum.*

11th Annual New Year Show, The Butler Art Institute. Exhibited *Fight for a Woman.*

1947

One-man show, Maitland Research Studio, Florida.

One-man show, Columbus Gallery of Fine Arts.

One-man show, Columbus University Club.

Painting in the United States, Carnegie Museum of Art. Exhibited *Aftermath.*

12th Annual New Year Show, The Butler Art Institute. Exhibited *Minor League, Aftermath* and *Everywhere the Night.*

1948

One-man show, Marietta College.

Second Award and $100 for *Big Business,* 13th Annual New Year Show, The Butler Art Institute. Also exhibited *Ain't Gonna Rain.*

Third Prize, Ohio State Fair.

Baldwin Purchase Award for *The Bridge Project,* Annual Exhibition, Massillon Museum.

Painting in the United States, Carnegie Museum of Art. Exhibited *Big Business.*

1949

Honorable Mention and $25 for *Eternal Idler,* 14th Annual New Year Show, The Butler Art Institute.

Third Prize, Ohio State Fair.

Purchase Award to CAI Permanent Collection and Award in Portrait or Figure Group for *Early Edition,* 2nd Annual Fall Show, Canton Art Institute.

Annual Exhibition, Pennsylvania Academy of Fine Arts. Exhibited *Sunday Morning.*

1950

Recent Paintings by Clyde Singer, 34th One-Man Show, Canton Art Institute. Exhibit included *Chicken Lover, Sunday Morning, Dreary Day,* and *Let It Rain.*

Honorable Mention and $25 for *April Showers,* 15th Annual New Year Show, The Butler Art Institute.

Annual Exhibition, Pennsylvania Academy of Fine Arts. Exhibited *Eternal Idler.*

Taught portrait drawing, painting, and landscape painting at the school of The Butler Art Institute (1950–51).

1951

Outstanding Painting Award for *Happy Holiday,* Ohio Artists and Craftsmen Exhibition, Massillon Museum.

Maramor Prize and Levin Purchase Award for *Sunday Morning,* 41st Annual Columbus Art League Exhibition, Columbus Gallery of Fine Arts. Also exhibited *High Explosives.*

One-man show, Maitland Research Studio, Florida.

C. Singer Paintings, Massillon Museum. Exhibit included *Easter Morning, Bernice in Profile, Sandy Valley,* and *Bus Stop.*

16th Annual New Year Show, The Butler Art Institute. Exhibited *Afternoon News.*

1952

One-man show, Salem Public Library, Ohio.

Art Benefit Party, held by J. Fred Seiberling of Seiberling Rubber Company.

17th Annual New Year Show, The Butler Art Institute. Exhibited *High Explosives* and *Selections from the Permanent Collection.*

1953

Annual Exhibition, National Academy of Design. Exhibited *Defeated Theatre.*

Buckeye Art Club First Award and $50 for *Defeated Theatre,* 18th Annual Midyear Show, The Butler Art Institute.

1954

Purchase Award for *Corner in Central Square,* Fall Show, Canton Art Institute.

19th Annual Midyear Show, The Butler Institute of American Art. Exhibited *Hotel Back Door* and *Mystic Light.*

First Prize for *The Whistle,* Area Artists Annual, The Butler Institute of American Art.

1955

Annual Exhibition, National Academy of Design. Exhibited *The Whistle.*

The First Hundred Years of Pittsburgh History, Western Pennsylvania Historical Society, Pittsburgh. Exhibited *An Incident in the Life of David Blythe.*

First Prize for Oils, Ohio State Fair. Exhibited *The Whistle.*

20th Annual Midyear Show, The Butler Institute of American Art. Exhibited *City Bridge.*

1956

Buckeye Prize for *Marsh at the Whitney,* 21st Annual Midyear Show, The Butler Institute of American Art.

One-man show, The Butler Institute of American Art.

1957

Allied Artists of America, New York. Exhibited *The Whistle.*

Served as juror for the 13th Irene Leache Exhibit of Contemporary Virginia and North Carolina Oil and Watercolor Painting.

22nd Annual Midyear Show, The Butler Institute of American Art. Exhibited *Club Night.*

1958

First Prize and Purchase Award for *Men's Art Club,* 1958 Art Annual, Thomas Gilcrease Institute of American History and Art, Tulsa, Oklahoma.

Annual Exhibition, National Academy of Design. Exhibited *Dreary Day.*

One-man show, Thiel College, Pennsylvania.

Exhibited at Chautauqua Art Center, New York.

Third Prize for Oils, Ohio State Fair.

23rd Annual Midyear Show, The Butler Institute of American Art. Exhibited *Early Easter.*

1959

24th Annual Midyear Show, The Butler Institute of American Art. Exhibited *Federal Street—East.*

1960

Buckeye Art Club Award for *St. Cloud Hotel Lobby,* 25th Annual Midyear Show, The Butler Institute of American Art. Also exhibited *95% Guggenheim.*

One-man show, Mount Union College.

C. Singer Paintings, Massillon Museum.

1961

26th Annual Midyear Show, The Butler Institute of American Art. Exhibited *Two Girls.*

1962

The Youngstown Group: A Three Man Show, The Brill Gallery, Cleveland. Exhibited *Red Front, Sunday in Mill Creek Park, Christmas Shopper, The First Ride, City Blizzard,* and *Bus Rider.*

27th Annual Midyear Show, The Butler Institute of American Art. Exhibited *Street Corner.*

1963

28th Annual Midyear Show, The Butler Institute of American Art. Exhibited *Rent Due.*

1964

Honorable Mention, 17th Annual Fall show, Canton Art Institute.

29th Annual Midyear Show, The Butler Institute of American Art. Exhibited *Penn Station.*

1965

First Prize for Watercolor, Fine Arts Exhibit, Ohio State Fair.

Paintings by Clyde Singer Exhibition, Canton Art Institute. Exhibit includes *McSorley's Back Room, Washington Square Night,* and *Parade 1953.*

Clyde Singer: 25 Year Retrospective, The Butler Institute of American Art. Exhibited 34 paintings, including *Stormy Weather, Dreary Day,* and *Aftermath.*

Purchase Award for *An Incident in the Life of David G. Blythe,* 30th Annual Midyear Show, The Butler Institute of American Art. Also exhibited *Girls and Gulls.*

Served as juror for Columbus Art League Sculpture and Drawing Exhibit.

1966

Purchase Award for *Memorial Day,* 31st Midyear Show, The Butler Institute of American Art.

One-man show, Circle Gallery, Cleveland. Exhibit includes *Tallulah* and *Rainy Day Shopper.*

Clyde Singer's Fiftieth One-Man Show Since 1934, Art Institute of Zanesville, Ohio. Exhibit included *Self-Portrait #8, On 14th Street, Chicken Lover, Conference Corner,* and *McSorley's.*

Honorable Mention, 19th Annual Fall Show, Canton Art Institute.

1967

Second Prize for Oils, Ohio State Fair.

Purchase Award for *Barber Pole on 14th,* 20th Annual Fall Show, Canton Art Institute.

32nd Annual Midyear Show, The Butler Institute of American Art. Exhibited *57th & 7th.*

1968

First Prize for Watercolor, Ohio State Fair.

33rd Annual Midyear Show, The Butler Institute of American Art. Exhibited *Six P.M.*

1969

34th Annual Midyear Show, The Butler Institute of American Art. Exhibited *Standees–McSorley's* and *No Left Turn.*

One-man show, Modarelli Gallery, Youngstown. Exhibit included *The Lincoln: Rent Due.*

1970

First Annual All Ohio Fall Show, Canton Art Institute. Exhibited *Standees–McSorley's.*

35th Annual Midyear Show, The Butler Institute of American Art. Exhibited *P.J. Clarke's Corner.*

1971

Clyde Singer Exhibition, Massillon Museum. Exhibited 40 paintings, including *Barber Shop, The Village,* and *Standees–McSorley's.*

Clyde Singer: 35 Years in Retrospective 1936–1970, The Butler Institute of American Art. Exhibit included *Stormy Weather, Defeated Theatre, An Incident in the Life of David G. Blythe,* and *Memorial Day.*

1972

Clyde Singer: A Retrospective Exhibition of his work from 1932–1972, Westmoreland County Museum of Art, Pennsylvania. Exhibited 84 works, including *Wrestling Night, Democrat Rally, Sandy Valley,* and *Wrestlers.*

Pegasus Award, Ohioana Library Association, Columbus, for "his talent in art and for preserving contemporary scenes in his notable paintings."

1973

First Honorable Mention for Painting for *McSorley's Facade,* All Ohio Show, Canton Art Institute.

37th Annual Midyear Show, The Butler Institute of American Art. Exhibited *McSorley's Facade.*

1974

38th Annual Midyear Show, The Butler Institute of American Art. Exhibited *McSorley's Invaded.*

1975

A Retrospective: Clyde Singer . . . 35 Years, The Butler Institute of American Art.

39th Annual Midyear Show, The Butler Institute of American Art. Exhibited *After Theatre.*

1976

Featured in filmstrip entitled *Major Ohio Painters,* Capital University, Columbus. Included *Barn Dance, Minor League,* and *Business Block.*

Clyde Singer: A Retrospective Exhibit 1932–1976, Westminster College of Art Gallery, New Wilmington, Pennsylvania. Exhibit included *Medicine Man, Sandy Valley,* and *Flower Vendor.*

40th Annual Midyear Show, The Butler Institute of American Art. Exhibited *Matinee.*

1977

One-man show, Canton Art Institute. Exhibit included *Barn Dance, On the Green,* and *Central Park.*

41st Annual Midyear Show, The Butler Institute of American Art. Exhibited *Gallery of Women.*

1978

42nd Annual Midyear Show, The Butler Institute of American Art. Exhibited *In Lincoln Center.*

1980

44th Annual Midyear Show, The Butler Institute of American Art. Exhibited *McSorley's—Quiet Moment.*

1981

An Unfulfilled Dream: The Neglected Generation of American Scene Painters, The Wichita Art Museum. Exhibited *Sandy Valley* and *Democrat Rally.*

45th Annual Midyear Show, The Butler Institute of American Art. Exhibited *Waiting in the Rain.*

1982

Two Perspectives: The Art of Clyde Singer and Dorothy Dennison, Keny Galleries, Columbus.

46th Annual Midyear Show, The Butler Institute of American Art. Exhibited *Rain Downtown.*

1986

50th National Midyear Show, The Butler Institute of American Art. Exhibited *Fast Food.*

1987

Clyde Singer's New York, Painting from the Collection of Joseph Erdelac, The Butler Institute of American Art. Exhibited 60 paintings from 1934 to present.

1989

Clyde Singer's New York, Canton Art Institute.

1990

Clyde Singer's New York (From The Butler Institute of American Art), The University Museum, Indiana University of Pennsylvania.

1992

56th National Midyear Exhibition, Invited Artist, The Butler Institute of American Art. Exhibited *Waitin' at the Corner.*

1993

Governor's Award for the Arts in Ohio, Individual Artist Category, Ohio Arts Council.

A Separate Reality: Paintings, Assemblages and Constructions by Nine Youngstown Area Artists, Riffe Gallery, Columbus. Exhibited *McSorley's—No Women Permitted* and *At The Whitney.*

1994

Lifetime Achievement in the Arts, The Evening of Music Committee Honors, An Evening of Music with Congressman James A. Traficant Jr., Youngstown Symphony Center.

1997

Retires from The Butler Institute of American Art after 55 years.

1998

Recognition of Clyde Singer's work, First Christian Church, Malvern.

1999

Dies on January 5, in Boardman, Ohio, at age 90.

The Clyde Singer chronology has been researched and verified through museum records, artist and personal records, catalogs, newspaper accounts, and magazine articles. It is as complete as the documentation materials available will allow

Index to Paintings